The Don McLean Story

Killing Us Softly With His Songs

By

Alan Howard

Copyright

Acknowledgments

Thanks to Don McLean for putting the post-war, twentieth century experience to words and music and singing it all with a voice that transports us to a better place. I want to thank him for sharing his story.

Thanks to Fred Hellerman, Erik Darling, Pete Murphy, Pete Childs, Rob Stoner, Ed Freeman, Jerry Corbitt, Ed Begley Jr., Bob Dearborn, Joel Dorn, John Peters, Larry Butler, Gordon Stoker, Fred Snel, Chris Horsnell, John Platania, Tony Migliore, Ralph Childs, Jerry Kroon, Patrisha McLean, Dick Boak, Pat Severs, Garth Brooks, Ron Buck, Bob Gregg, Alan Young, and Bill Nisbet for allowing me to include their thoughts on Don McLean and his music.

Thanks to Ann Morris at the Owl and Turtle Bookshop in Camden, Maine, for editing the manuscript.

And thanks to all the Don McLean fans who read and respond to my web sites: don-mclean.com and americanpie.com.

Alan Howard
Brinkworth, England
January, 2007

Contents

Did You Know...?

- Don McLean's "American Pie" was selected as one of the five greatest songs of the 20th century in a poll by the National Endowment for the Arts and the Recording Industry Association of America. The other four songs were "This Land is Your Land," "Somewhere Over the Rainbow," "Respect," and "White Christmas."
- "American Pie" was inducted into the Grammy Hall of Fame in 2003.
- Don McLean was inducted into the Songwriters' Hall of Fame in 2004.
- Don McLean has over 40 gold and platinum records, world-wide.
- The following Don McLean songs have each been played over three million times on American radio: "American Pie," "And I Love You So," "Vincent," and "Castles in the Air."
- General Jay Garner presented Don McLean with the Medal of Honor to thank him for his music.
- Don McLean attended the Founder's Dinner at the Clinton White House on New Year's Eve, 1999. He then performed at the "Concert for the Millennium," produced by Quincy Jones. The dinner and the concert honored people who had influenced the 20th century.
- Don McLean's first real job was as a paperboy for the *Standard Star* in New Rochelle from 1957 to 1959.
- In 1961, when Don was 16, he turned down an opportunity to appear on the Ted Mack Amateur Hour.
- Don McLean won the folk-singing contest at the 1964 World's Fair in New York.
- In 1968 the New York State Council for the Arts hired Don McLean as the only Hudson River Troubadour to sing in every town along the Hudson River.
- In 1968 Don McLean earned a BA degree from Iona College with a major in finance and a minor in philosophy.
- In 2001 McLean received an honorary doctorate from Iona College.
- Don McLean always sings "American Pie" in concert, despite press accounts to the contrary.
- An urban legend claims that "American Pie" was the name of Buddy Holly's plane. It is not true. Buddy Holly did not own a plane.
- The song "Tapestry" inspired the creation of the environmental action group "Greenpeace."

- Don McLean's song "Babylon" is the theme song for the German Green Party.
- A bronze plaque containing the poem "So Long Hopalong Cassidy," from the original *American Pie* album, hangs in the hospital where William Boyd, the star of Hopalong Cassidy, died in 1972.
- Johnny Cash wrote "I Wish I Could Yodel" after hearing Don sing "Lovesick Blues" in Cash's home.
- Don's performance of "Empty Chairs," at the Troubadour Nightclub in Los Angeles in 1972, was heard by singer Lori Liebermann. She was asked, "How did you like Don McLean?" And she answered, "He killed me softly." This inspired her producers, Norman Gimble and Charles Fox to write the song, "Killing Me Softly" for Lori.
- The Van Gogh Museum in Amsterdam plays McLean's "Vincent" regularly. A copy of the sheet music is buried along with Van Gogh's paint brushes in a time capsule at the museum.
- Because of McLean's song "The Legend of Andrew McCrew," radio station WGN in Chicago raised money for a headstone for the mummified hobo featured in the song.
- Don McLean's "And I Love You So" is the last song on *Elvis in Concert*, the last album Elvis Presley recorded.
- Don McLean's hit record "Crying" features Elvis' band and back-up singers, the Jordanaires.
- Don McLean wrote the score for the 1976 movie "Fraternity Row." In 1981 he sang the title song in the children's movie "Flight of Dragons."
- The song "Jerusalem" was composed for that city at the request of its mayor.
- George Michael sang McLean's anti-war song "The Grave" in protest of America's invasion of Iraq, in March of 2003.
- Artists as diverse as: Madonna, Fred Astaire, Chet Atkins, Weird Al Yankovic, Elvis Presley, Josh Groban, Perry Como, and Coolio have performed McLean's songs.
- According to the movie "Tupac, the Resurrection," Tupac Shakur was influenced by Don McLean, and his favorite song was "Vincent."
- Madonna introduced low-rider jeans in her video, *American Pie*. She first sang the song in summer camp.
- Mike Mills of REM says the album *Don McLean* is one of his all-time favorites.

- Don McLean's favorite artist is Elvis Presley. His favorite song is White Christmas. His favorite year is 1957. His favorite car is a black and yellow 1957 Ford Fairlane 500.
- Don's favorite bluegrass group is Flatt and Scruggs. His favorite folk group is the Weavers. His favorite politician is Franklin D. Roosevelt. His favorite authors are Balzac, F. Scott Fitzgerald, Emerson, and Will James. His favorite actor is Clark Gable. His favorite actress is Marilyn Monroe. His favorite play is *Death of a Salesman* by Arthur Miller. His favorite artist is Edward Hopper. His favorite sports are baseball and Olympic swimming. His favorite athlete is Muhammad Ali. He likes: Edith Piaf, Frank Sinatra, Josh White, Fred Astaire, Bing Crosby, Judy Garland, Mahalia Jackson, Bessie Smith, Buddy Holly and Mabel Mercer.
- Don McLean is a skilled western horseman. He owns and trained three Appaloosa horses.
- Don McLean has 50 pairs of custom-made western boots, and he wears only Levi 501 button-fly jeans.
- Don McLean has more than 40 Martin guitars. They are the only brand of guitar he uses.
- In the year 2000 the Martin Guitar Company created a limited edition signature Don McLean guitar, the D-40DM.
- Don McLean drew the second largest audience in British history, next to the Rolling Stones, at his 1975 concert in Hyde Park.
- Don McLean was the first American artist to perform at the Sydney Opera House.
- Don McLean holds the attendance record for the Capitol Theater in Australia, with 18 consecutive performances in 1981. He broke the record of Joni Mitchell.
- Don McLean was the guest artist at the Boston Pops Fourth of July celebration in 2000, the first of the century.
- Garth Brooks introduced Don McLean as "my idol" to over 1,000,000 New Yorkers at a 1997 concert in Central Park. And the musicians sang "American Pie" together.
- Don McLean was the first songwriter to have No. 1 singles in two separate centuries.
- Don McLean has completed 14 world tours and performed more than 3,500 concert appearances.
- Don McLean has visited every major city in America and many foreign countries.

- David New, a British fan, has a picture of Don McLean tattooed in color across his entire back. He was the first fan to do this in 1978.
- Don McLean does not read music.
- Don McLean does not have a computer, e-mail, or a pager.
- Don McLean has five registered trademarks: "American Pie," "Starry, Starry Night," "The Day the Music Died," "Bye, Bye, Miss American Pie" and "Don McLean."
- The Don McLean Foundation sends students, who cannot otherwise afford it, to college and contributes to homeless shelters and food banks in the state of Maine.

Introduction

At this stage in my life, I can say that I am responsible for everything good, and everything bad, that I ever did. Certainly, I had a lot of help, but I did it.
Don McLean

When Garth Brooks introduced Don McLean at the ceremony inducting McLean into the Songwriters' Hall of Fame in 2004, McLean said:

"When I was going off to college I went to Villanova University, and while I was at Villanova I met Jim Croce. He was two years older than I was, and he kind of adopted me. Then, on November 22, 1963, Kennedy was assassinated while I was on that campus. I made my mind up that I wanted to leave school for good, and I left school, and I went on the road. Exactly 40 years from that day, I got the notice, on November 22, 2003, that I was going to be here tonight and inducted into this Hall of Fame. As I stood in the little post office looking at that notice, you can imagine what came over me. I thought, 'What a long, long road it has been.' We've seen America change, some for the better, some for the worse. I am an American artist, everybody here is an American artist, and this old song here probably changed the world a little bit."

And then McLean sang, "A long, long time ago…" And the entire, star-studded audience sang along to "American Pie."

A long road indeed… Don McLean was being recognized by his peers with the highest honor a songwriter can receive. This magical evening, broadcast repeatedly, paid tribute to the songs, the performances, and the stories that are the legend of Don McLean.

Through the many ups and downs of his long career, McLean's songs keep bringing him back, decade after decade. Through scores of musical and cultural sea changes his songs have endured.

Chapter 1: Everyone's Caught on a Carousel Pony...Growing Up in New Rochelle

Don McLean was born at 4 a.m. on October 2nd, 1945, the only son of Elizabeth and Donald McLean of New Rochelle, New York. Until the age of seventeen Don lived at 15 Mulberry Lane in New Rochelle, in a neighborhood known as Larchmont Woods, just outside of New York City. New Rochelle was a popular retreat for noted actors, artists, and authors who commuted to the suburb from Manhattan.

Today, as one travels through Larchmont and New Rochelle, along streets lined with expensive houses, past large schools and apartments with no undeveloped land in sight, it is difficult to visualize the New Rochelle of fifty years ago. Even as Don was growing up, forests were being nibbled away by development, as large estates were subdivided by real estate developers. "I think the gradual loss of the forest affected me. I loved the woods, and I think that I always wanted to be in the forest, in the wilderness, any place but in the city."

Don and his friends often played in the new houses going up all over Larchmont. There were obvious dangers. Sometimes blasting caps were present at the building sites, and they would explode if thrown. Naturally, this provided boys with endless excitement. But, as exciting as it was to cavort in an unfinished home, the new construction went hand in hand with the destruction of the wilderness. Every new house meant a chunk of woods was gone.

The McLean's enjoyed an American suburban lifestyle. Their home was perched on the crest of a hill, overlooking Larchmont Woods. In wintertime, kids rode sleds from the McLean house all the way down to the bottom of Mulberry Lane, where it ended at Forest Avenue. In one direction the incline was particularly steep, and neighborhood children and adults went sledding until dark all weekend.

Donald and Elizabeth had a large group of friends with whom they socialized. This eclectic mix of people included the announcer for the Tommy Dorsey television show, a cancer researcher, a man who produced television commercials, and various other professional types. When the party was at the McLean's, Don would sometimes sing for the group. He says, "I like what Mick Jagger said, 'I started performing for family, only the shows got bigger.'"

Family life was important to the McLean's, with frequent visits from relatives. 15 Mulberry Lane often overflowed with aunts and uncles. Don's Uncle Malcolm and Auntie Anita and their three children lived just one block away. Don's only sister, Bette Ann, was 15 years older than Don. When she was sixteen, Bette Ann went to live with her grandparents, and when she was 21 she moved to California. She was always leaving and always coming home.

Don's parents came from very different backgrounds. It caused quite a stir when Elizabeth Bucci, an Italian Catholic, married Donald McLean, a Protestant of Scottish ancestry. Italian girls just did not marry Protestant men.

The McLean clan traces its roots to the Isle of Iona in the Scottish Hebrides, an area that has been home to many Scottish poets. McLean ancestors were revolutionary war heroes with children who had names like George Washington McLean. One ancestor was a president of the Daughters of the American Revolution. Both Don's grandfather and father were named Donald McLean, which often lead to confusion since Don was also christened Donald McLean.

Don's great grandfather was a New York physician named Malcolm McLean. Don's grandfather, Donald I, also went to medical school. Don did not know his grandfather at all. He could have been a medical doctor, but he chose to spend his life as a farmer. He was suspected of bigamy, and in the 1970s, Don met many cousins he never knew he had.

Throughout his childhood, Don was very close to his grandmother, Olive McLean. Her maiden name was Carnwright, and her family was from Upstate New York. When Don's grandparents were divorced, his grandfather wrote many letters to Don's great grandfather complaining bitterly about his ex-wife and suggesting that she be given nothing by the McLean's. With barely enough food to eat, Olive got a job as a bookkeeper for the Leheigh Valley Railroad, and she did the best she could with her three sons, Malcolm, Donald, and John. The boys had been born in New York City in the early 1900s, at the end of the Victorian era, when teeming tenements existed next to "Millionaire's Mile."

Olive sent her oldest son, Malcolm, to live with his McLean grandparents. He attended the well-to-do Horace Mann School and always carried himself with an air of pretension, even though he left school after the 8th grade. Don's mother summed him up by saying, "He's a little guy who thinks he's a big shot." McLean claims that "such remarks by my mother reflected the tension between her and Malcolm McLean's family. Those tensions ruined my relationship with my cousins. In later years relations have been restored, as we realized we were victims of our parents' discord."

Don's father, on the other hand, was sent to live with various relatives. He moved frequently and was treated indifferently, still managing to receive an eighth grade education. More than anything in the world he wanted Don to be educated, to have a college degree. Don's Uncle, John, was sent to a foster home.

Donald I

In 1971 Don's Uncle Malcolm sent the following letter to his half brother, Randolph. It reveals much about their father, Donald I.

23 December 1971

Dear Randy,

Yes, your children are related to Don McLean — he is their half cousin, as he is your half-brother Donald's only son. He is quite an unusual guy. He graduated from Iona College and was accepted at Columbia School of Business, but decided to pursue a career in music, in which he is entirely self-taught. He is married and lives in Cold Spring, NY. He has no children.

Now for a little outline of our father's career:

He was born in New York City on 26 November 1879, the youngest of three children (Alfred Jewett McLean and Helen McLean Lasher Curtis were the others) of Dr Malcolm McLean, a prominent New York obstetrician, gynaecologist, and surgeon, and Mary Permelia Jewett.

His life seems to have been a series of disappointments to himself and to others; frustrations and failure, all, I believe, stemming from his willful disregard for conventions and the ordinary responsibilities of life. Instances of this are many, but to quote one in which I was personally involved, I asked him in 1919 or '20 (when I was 17 or 18 and he was working as a poultry man for Stephen Bizah, where your mother was also employed, I believe) if he was keeping up his G.I. insurance ($10,000, which every married soldier had to take out during World War I), and he told me that he had dropped it — that insurance is a "loser's game — you have to die to win." This is definitely not an attitude that I'd like to pass on to my children or a position that I would take relative to any responsibility towards them.

As a teenager, he went to Worcester Academy (Worcester, Mass.) for a while but was expelled for misbehavior. (I've heard that it was for drinking, although in later life I never knew him to drink.) Then, after finishing high school (where, I do not know), he went to Cornell as a pre-med student. He left or was kicked out after some more high-jinks.

His father then got him a job with Mr. George W. Merck's drug company. Mr. Merck was a friend of Grandfather's. (The company, Merck & Co., is one of the oldest drug firms and is listed on the N.Y. Stock Exchange.) Father, then about 20, didn't like working — or the drug business — or both, and he was hipped up to work on the farm of Mr. Alfred Cornelius, between Rock City and Bull's Head, N.Y. McLean's have muscle, and it was hoped that the isolation and hard work might straighten the young man out. It did, to a degree. At any rate, he married my mother, Olive Carnwright, in the early part of 1902, when he was 22 and she was 19. (Mother was the daughter of Capt. John Field Carnwright, owner, with his half-brother, of a Hudson River barge company. She is now just short of 89 years old).

Being a married man, he quit Mr. Cornelius and tried his hand at raising chickens, and, when that didn't work out, took a job with a Shaker colony up near where you live. I guess that didn't work out either, because soon his grandfather, Dr. George Wood Jewett, bought the Cornelius farm for Dad to work. (Gramp Jewett did not put the farm in Father's name, but it was to have been his — all 90 acres of it — if he made good.) He tried, I am sure, and the family invested in machines and a silo for him that were the envy of the area. But eventually he gave up and moved us all into Red Hook to live in the big Carnwright place, while he took a job at the W. H. Baker's Chocolate Factory as a cocoa bean roaster. I was then 7 or 8 and hadn't been to school yet, Father refusing to send me to the one room school near Bull's Head — and Don was 5 and John 1. After several jobs in Red Hook, he pulled up stakes and left us to go to New York City to work for General Film Company, where Uncle Al had an executive position. Things got pretty grim in Red Hook for lack of money, but somehow we weathered it for six months, or maybe longer, until Father was made the manager of a large, luxurious movie house in the Bronx, owned by the owner of General Film. He and Mother took an apartment on Fox Street and tried again to make a go of living together. It was a great failure. The movie theater job didn't last too long, and, when he lost it or gave it up, our parents broke up again, and we lost all meaningful contact with our father. Mother took a job in New York as a store cashier (the first job she'd ever had) and kept John with her in a furnished room, where the landlady baby-sat for John during the day. Don and I were shipped up to Brewster to live with Aunt Helen and her husband, Rev. James Lewis Lasher. (We liked it there — the school was nice, and, although she had two small sons of her own, Aunt Helen was kind and generous.) At this time I guess I was 10 or 11, and Don 8 or 9, and John about 5. So, you see, my recollections of our father are through the eyes of a pretty young boy.

During the next two or three years, Don and I spent the school year with Aunt Helen or with Uncle Al in Hackensack, sometimes together and sometimes separated. Summers were spent with our grandparents in Quogue.

John, Donald II, and Olive in rags on the farm

After Fox Street, my contacts with Father were few and far between. 1916 must have been a low spot in his fortunes, for he came to Quogue for the whole summer and worked on Grandfather's place as a gardener and handy man. It was a good summer for me, since I got to work with him and to know him better during that summer, when I was almost 14, than at any other time in our lives.

War was declared on April 6, 1917, (Good Friday, the day I was confirmed in the Episcopal Church) and Father enlisted within a matter of days. Still foot-loose at 37, with a broken marriage, and no money or prospects, I guess the army — and the war — were a welcome escape. I saw him twice in uniform — once soon after enlistment, before he was shipped to Texas for training, and then again before he was sent overseas.

As you know, he was a sergeant in Battery C, 21st Field Artillery, 5th (Red Diamond) Division. He was gassed a couple of times (which probably shortened his life) and spent 21 months in hospitals. Finally he was sent to Fox Hills Hospital on Staten Island, where he signed a waiver of responsibility (as he would!) to gain a discharge before the doctors wanted to let him go.

I saw him briefly after his discharge, when he came to Grandfather's sanitarium at 29 East 126th Street, where I was living, to let Grandfather examine his wound.

Then I saw him again quite frequently during the summer of 1919 or '20 when he was a poultryman for Stephen Birch. I was living with Uncle Al in nearby Manwah, N.J., and commuting to my first job as an office boy at Stephen Birch's Kennecott Copper Co. My final contact with my father was in 1920. I was selling appliances for the utility company and making "unbelievable" money. I took a vacation to Saratoga to see the races. I had written to Father occasionally, but don't believe I ever got an answer. So on this trip I decided to go over to Shaftsbury to see him. (The real reason for the trip was probably to see him and to show off my brand new car, a 1929 Nash roadster with a two-tone, tan and cedar, paint job and real leather seats. The seats were so low that I had to look through the large steering wheel when I drove it.) I do not remember how I got in touch with him, but I remember he insisted that I meet him in Bennington. I was shocked when I saw him. He looked small and skinny and gray. I am of about the same size and weight, but my recollections of him were of a stronger looking man with an athletic bearing.

We rode around and talked, self-consciously, I suppose, for two hours or so. My strongest remembrance of this meeting is of his questioning me as to why I had come to Bennington, and, when I told him that it was to see him, he said, "That was a damned fool thing to do." Obviously he wanted to be left alone. Nothing that he said that day indicated that he had married again and that I had half-brothers and a half-sister. From his viewpoint, no doubt, that was none of my business. After that short ride and talk, we parted in Bennington, and I never saw or heard from him again.

Of his character, standards, and ambitions I can tell you very little. As I see it, he was strong-willed and intolerant of opposition or restraint. He made few friends and none who were "close" to him. Although brought up in a church-going family (Grandfather was Senior Warden of St. Andrew's in N.Y.C.), I never knew of Father ever going to church. And, for all intents and purposes, he gave up his family, making no effort to see or contact any of us, including his parents or his brother and sister. He did not, I believe, attend the funeral of his father, who died in 1924, or his mother in 1923.

Later, when the furnishings of his father's sanitarium were being divided, he rejected Alfred's suggestion that he takes his share, saying that he would not "become one of the vultures." This was a strange and self-defeating attitude, for some of the things were very good.

Still, over the years when Grandfather's estate was being settled, Wallace Donald McLean, who was the executor, complained to me that Father was constantly pressing for advances against his share — a share, by the way, that he did not share with any of his "first" family. (None of us received a single penny from Grandfather's or Grandmother's estates.)

Of his abilities, you may know that he was a pretty good carpenter and handy man and a so-so farmer, but did you know that he had a fair ability as an artist? I don't believe that I ever saw more than one or two of his sketches, but they seemed very good to me as a youngster, and Mother says that they were outstanding. He also used to show off his fantastic memory by quoting verbatim whole pages of a book or magazine which he had just read — or by reciting Scott's "The Lady of the Lake" or "Marmion" in their entirety.

Malcolm

McLean reacted to that letter with the following insights about his father's family: "One can understand why my father was attracted to a large, Italian family, coming as he did from a background of emotional poverty. Lurking in the recesses of my father's psyche seems to have been the fear that I might somehow inherit the wayward, shiftless ways of his father, Donald I. The letter from my Uncle Malcolm to his half brother, Randolph, shows that my great grandfather, Malcolm, pulled out all the stops that a Victorian gentleman could, to save a son who he thought had gone mad, but maybe Donald I was just ahead of his time."

Don's mother's side of the family, the Buccis, came from Abruzzi, an unspoiled, mountainous region of Southern Italy, dominated by the Central Apennines. Abruzzi was the source of some of the most lyrical Italian folk melodies. The Buccis left Italy and settled in Port Chester, N.Y., at the end of the 19th century. Port Chester was gradually changing from a port and trading center to a manufacturing center. The establishment of major railroads contributed to its industrial growth. Large numbers of Italian immigrants had moved to Port Chester, and the Bucci family joined a colorful, thriving Italian community there. McLean said it reminded him of the movie *Marty*, which was filmed in Port Chester. "If you've ever seen that film, then you have a good idea of what my aunts, uncles, and cousins were like and of what Port Chester was like."

Despite the major change in lifestyle, the Buccis were determined to make the most of the opportunities America offered. They accepted that, as newcomers, they would face discrimination and they would need to work twice as hard. This, combined with their gentle nature, quickly made them well-respected members of the community. "My mother would not stand for being looked down on because she was Italian," McLean says. "She didn't like Mafia stereotypes, and slang words for Italians infuriated her."

Don's grandfather, Antonio Bucci, was one of the original Port Chester policemen at the start of the 20th century. Well over six feet tall, and with a formidable presence, he commanded respect. McLean remembers, "He didn't have to hit you; he just had to tell you to do something, and you did it." After Antonio retired, there was an annual dinner for the surviving original policemen. He outlived all the other men on the force, and, at the end, the dinner was just for him. Antonio Bucci lived to be 95 years old, active and independent throughout his life. He smoked Italian cigars, walked six miles a day, tended his vegetable garden and played with his scores of grandchildren well into the 1970s. McLean says, "I still can see blazing sun beaming down on my grandfather's face as he held up his prize tomatoes. He was addicted to the *New York Times* crossword puzzle. And his many discussions about the meaning of English words made me focus on English. To this day I have many dictionaries, and I love to learn new words, as well as the derivation of phrases we use but don't really know what they mean."

The Bucci's lived in a house built with dollars and dimes that Don's grandmother, Angelina, took from her husband's pockets after he came home from playing cards on Saturday nights, or so the story went. She managed to save thousands of dollars over many years, and eventually they bought a sizeable property for their rapidly expanding family. However, it was never quite big enough to accommodate all 10 children. It was not uncommon for some of the children to live with other family members for periods of time. This did not hinder their progress much, for all five of Don's uncles and one of his aunts attended Ivy League colleges. They became lawyers, accountants, pharmacists and doctors. Don's uncle, Frank Bucci, was the pharmacist at Woodstock in the 1960s. No doubt the Hard Rock Café would love to frame some of the prescriptions he filled. But, for the Buccis, the concept of dropping out did not exist. They were working too hard at dropping in.

The Catholic religion meant a great deal to the Bucci family. They never missed Sunday mass, and some went to church everyday. The Catholic religion was a great source of strength, the center of life for them. Like many Italians, Don's mother was not fearful of death, but as McLean says, "She tended to hold on longer than usual." She could relate to the joke about the Italian gentleman, sitting on a stoop, who said to his friend, "It's really sad about my mother, how she mourns and cries over my father." His friend says, "He's been dead twenty five years!" The Italian says, "He's not even cold yet."

Throughout the 1950s, Don and his parents went to Grandfather Bucci's house every Sunday for dinner. To Don that experience stood out as distinctly different from everything else all week: the food was different, the smells, the energy and even the language. One Sunday, in the early 1950s, Don was shocked to hear his mother having a conversation in Italian. He had no idea that his mother spoke Italian, and he said to his father, "Dad, Mom's making fun of Grandma. Grandma speaks a funny way, and Mom speaks back to her in a funny way. Why is she making fun of her?" McLean says, "This caused gales of laughter, but it shows that I was really a half-breed, not aware of my own background."

The house where Don grew up had a small front yard with huge oak trees, pachysandra beds, and flowers that Don's father planted. The lawn was separated from the sidewalk by pricker bushes, which often needed pruning. The front door opened into the living room. To the right was a little sunroom. To the left was the dining room. Behind the dining room was a small kitchen. At the back of the living room, stairs rose to the second floor. The stairs had a three-step landing that was Don's favorite place to sit with his Victrola, singing along with records or sometimes singing for his parents and friends. The second floor had three bedrooms, the smallest of which, no bigger than a closet, was Don's.

All the children in the neighborhood went to Mrs Belknap's nursery school in Larchmont (circa 1949). Much of the school yard was covered with deep sand. Raised platforms with boards ran along the edges of the sand, and the kids ran on the platforms and jumped off into the sand. A jungle gym stood in the corner of the yard. All the children loved this school. In fact, the school was so popular that kids would go there and play anytime. Mrs Belknap didn't care whether it was school time or not. McLean said, "Nobody ever shooed us out. We played everywhere, in everybody's yard, in the woods, and on the street."

Don attended the Henry Barnard Grammar School, where his favorite teacher was Marie Quigley. Miss Quigley was like "Mary Poppins"— fair, but firm, very firm. She reminded Don of a Catholic nun. Nevertheless, she had a special place in her heart for Don. When Don was in the 7th grade, she invited him to her wedding. Her husband died suddenly of encephalitis and left her with two toddlers. She remarried and moved to Florida, and Don still heard from her. Occasionally she would attend one of his concerts and reminisce about Larchmont. She always said, "One day, Donny will be famous, or infamous." In 2001 when McLean received an honorary doctorate from Iona College, Marie Quigley was there.

Unlike today, when kids spend most of their time inside, watching TV, playing computer games, or surfing the Internet, Don and his friends rarely played indoors. If a child was found in the house on the weekend, his parents would ask if there was something wrong. And if nothing was wrong, they would tell him to go outside and do something. "We were always doing something," McLean says. "We grew up playing outdoors. We were like a band of wild Indians. All we had to do was show up for dinner." One kid had parents who were so easy going that they let him build a "structure" that went up the side of their house, all three floors. His father was a construction worker.

Don spent much of his childhood in the woods and forests that covered large parts of Larchmont and New Rochelle. One of his friends had a house that backed up to the woods and a big clearing, used as a baseball diamond. They called it Bromley's Field. Kids played there all the time, although they were never certain what animal might come out of the woods in the middle of a baseball game, or what strange bird might be scared up by a home run. And kids were always hunting for the ball in the tall grass. McLean says, "I still remember the smell of the marsh and the frog noises from when we played baseball in the spring. The woods seemed to hold untold mysteries and treasures, and maybe even ghosts. You don't need vast holdings — a small patch of woods can have a profound effect on a child."

Don, aged 16, on the wooded path to Bromley's baseball field, New Rochelle, NY.

Although Don enjoyed school and the outdoors, he had chronic asthma. Both his parents' families were heavy smokers. His asthma often made him weak and breathless. His condition turned into pneumonia on several occasions. "I remember sinking down and down as I got sicker," McLean says. "I would sweat profusely and gasp for air. I know how it feels to fight for your life with only your willpower. I became very willful." His illness caused Don to fall behind in school, and, for a while, he struggled to keep up. The asthma persisted until Don was a teenager. His mother was fretful and became protective. She cared for assorted relatives over the years, and she always cared for Don when he was sick. When Don's grandmother, Olive McLean, moved to New Rochelle she also looked after Don.

During times of isolation caused by his illnesses, Don began to get hooked on music. He created his own world in which the radio and the record player were his best friends. "Your Hit Parade," "The Arthur Godfrey Show," and "The Make Believe Ballroom" were his favorite programs. He listened to 78 rpm records over and over again. As a five year old, Don was already aware of the music of Dinah Shore, Bing Crosby, Gracie Field, and even Enrico Caruso; and he loved to sing their songs. Don believes this isolation influenced his later music. He says, "During my formative years, I spent a lot of time at home, ill with pneumonia or asthma, so I spent a lot of time with my record player and records and with TV and radio. And I think I developed a lot of fantasies which found their way into the songs that I wrote later. In that sense my roots come from the things that became the roots for any rootless, suburban person: records, radio, television, and movies."

When Olive looked after Don, she would play the piano and sing with him. She taught him to harmonize with another voice. Whenever he sang a song, which was often, his grandmother would say, "Start that again, Donny, and I'll harmonize with you." She spent lots of time with her grandchildren, and Don loved to watch her mend clothes, darn socks and write letters. She taught Don to make script letters the way she did as a bookkeeper, and she filled his mind with stories of country life on the Hudson. Years later, when Don decided to purchase land in Upstate New York instead of New York City, his grandmother said he was being called back to the place of her birth. His uncle John said, "You love land, Donny. That's the Carnwright in you."

Years later Don learned that his great uncle, Alfred McLean, an executive with the General Film Company who got his brother (Donald I) a job running a movie theater in the Bronx, was a talented tenor and directed several church choirs and the Apollo Quartet in New York City at the turn of the century. The Apollo Quartet specialized in Negro spirituals which were very popular at that time.

Don's mother played the piano and encouraged Don to sing along to songs such as "Beautiful Dreamer" by Stephen Foster. But whenever anyone tried to give her credit for his musical accomplishments or his success, she always said, "He raised himself." To some extent that was true and it was very much like her to tell the truth in that way. Don always knew that music was the right path for him, and he was willing to let it take him wherever it would. He felt he was not as good at anything else. He never had as much fun doing anything else.

Bucci Family, circa 1920
Elizabeth Bucci McLean, fourth from left

When he was five or six years old, Don told his mother that he was going to be a famous singer and he was going to buy her a mink coat when he got rich. Mink coats were quite the thing in those days, desired by many, possessed by few. In 1973, Don made good on that promise and bought his mother a mink coat for her birthday. From time to time when he played Carnegie Hall, McLean would send a limo to his mother's house to pick her up in her mink coat and bring her to the show.

The Mink Coat

(Elizabeth McLean with Don backstage at Carnegie Hall in 1982)

Perhaps because he didn't have much of a home life as a child, Don's father absolutely loved 15 Mulberry Lane. He made many improvements on it. He would never talk about any projects he was planning to do, but Don would often return home to find a fireplace torn apart, or a doorway patched over, or bookshelves and cabinets in varying states of construction. Don spent lots of time in the basement where his father's workbench and tools were. He tried fixing things and making things, and he carved his initials in the crude hand railing of the cellar stairs many times. The basement also held a dusty, broken-down piano. A door led to the garage which held his father's navy blue 1950 Ford Custom.

Donald II, Don and Elizabeth at 15 Mulbery Lane, circa 1952.

Don's father worked for Consolidated Edison, and he never told Don much about anything. He never told Don what he did at work, or about the people he worked with. There were no heart-to-heart conversations where the deeper mysteries of life were discussed. McLean said, "The wife of the painter Edward Hopper said, 'Talking to Eddy is like dropping a dime in a well but not hearing it splash.' That's what talking to my father was like."

But Don's father shared with him in other ways. He taught Don how to use a knife and a hatchet and how to build a campfire. And he read to Don each evening. He read all of the works of Mark Twain, and he read from the *Rubaiyat of Omar Khayyam*.

"The Moving Finger writes; and, having writ,
Moves on; nor all thy Piety nor Wit
Shall lure it back to cancel half a Line,
Nor all thy Tears wash out a Word of it."

And it was during those shared moments that his father made Don aware of the passing nature of life.

Don's first experience playing a musical instrument happened when he was 10 years old. A man named George Andrews lived behind the McLean Family. He was a thin, bald, anxious, chain-smoker who worked for a public relations firm in New York. Tension ran in the family, and his son ended up being institutionalized after having a nervous breakdown. George played the baritone ukulele and sang songs like "I Don't Care If the Sun Don't Shine" and other jazzy prohibition tunes. He taught Don a few chords and allowed him to play his ukulele from time to time. After much persuading, Don's parents agreed to buy him a ukulele for Christmas.

A year later, Don discovered that his friend, Brad Bivens, owned a guitar. After baseball, they would go back to Brad's house and Don would practice the chords he had learned on the ukulele. Brad was the son of the TV announcer Bill Bivens and owned many great record albums. Those artists remain some of Don's favorites today: Carlos Montoya, Josh White, Django Reinhart, Johnny Smith, Chet Atkins, Duane Eddy and The Ventures.

On one visit, Brad's father got drunk and started playing the blues harmonica. He then took out his 16mm film projector and played a kinescope of Elvis Presley's first television appearance on The Tommy Dorsey Show. He was one of the few people in the world who had a copy of that film. The film captivated Don. It made him dream of performing on stage. Presley has always been McLean's favorite artist.

By the time Don started Albert Leonard Junior High School, his interest in music was well established. Many of his school friends had moved to the area from New York City, because their parents wished to escape city life. The kids, however, were comfortable with the city and returned often on the train. One friend went regularly to see Alan Freed's Rock and Roll Show at the Brooklyn Fox Theater. He brought home the programs for shows by Buddy Holly, the Big Bopper, the Five Satins and the Moon Glows. Don noticed that his friends were wilder after those shows, more energized, and he wanted to know what that was about. He decided, from then on, that rock 'n' roll was it.

Another friend at junior high owned a tape recorder, which was rare in those days. Therefore, it was a big deal when he let Don use the tape recorder to record his first song. Don sang "Love Me Tender," and he was shocked when he played it back and discovered that he sounded nothing like Elvis. "It sounded so God-awful. I realized that a tape recorder is the last word on what you sound like, not what you think you sound like. You have to learn to really hear yourself, and not just imagine what you sound like."

Don's favorite music store was the House of Music in New Rochelle. It occupied a building with a glass storefront on Main Street, across from the Loews Theater. You walked through the door in the center and stood in the middle of an enormous room which had a tin ceiling and light fixtures that hung from chains. The building must have dated from the late 1800s. On the right hand side was the record department with long rows of wooden bins holding vinyl albums. The left side of the store was for serious musicians who could read music. Here you could buy sheet music and place orders for instruments.

The store was run by Mrs. Cohen and her assistant, Henry. Henry became Don's friend. Don often took the bus into New Rochelle and hung out with Henry. Henry was in his early 30s, married and a graduate of Iona College in New Rochelle. He let Don go through all the records while he talked about the new releases, when they were coming out, and all about the different singers and musicians. Henry was Don's first contact with the music business.

In 2001, the City of New Rochelle held "Don McLean Day." As McLean was signing autographs, a man put out his hand and said, "Hi, Don. It's Henry." He never stopping rooting for Don, and Don never forgot what Henry taught him. Today, there are many publications and web sites that tell about every detail of the music business, and fans have become extraordinarily knowledgeable. This was not the case in the 1950s.

Don with daughter Jackie and son Wyatt at 15 Mulberry Lane

From 1957 to 1959, Don worked as a paperboy for *The Standard Star*, the local newspaper. He delivered the paper every day and collected money from the customers on Wednesdays. On Saturday, a German lady named Mrs. Steinmetz came to the house to go over the books and take away the money, leaving enough for a Hershey bar, if Don was lucky. More often than not, he had to borrow money from his mother, because he'd forgotten to collect from some customers. When he was sick, his mother helped with his route. Being a paperboy was the only "job" Don ever had. "The key to that lousy job was sucking up to the subscribers, so they would tip me. I was in love with the romance of being a paperboy, not with the money. Occasionally, I would throw a paper through a glass door or window, or up on the roof, or in the bushes. We would get angry phone calls at the house at dinnertime when my father was there, asking where the paper was."

Don saved as much money as he could from his earnings, because he wanted to buy a baritone ukulele like the one George Andrews let him play. Don's father said that if he was going to play an instrument he should play a real instrument. McLean says, "This was my father's nature. He didn't see the ukulele as a real instrument; he saw it as a novelty. He said, 'If you want to do something, do it all the way.' That was what he taught me, and, fortunately, I listened to him."

With this in mind, Don set out to the House of Music to purchase his first guitar, a Harmony F-hole with a sunburst finish. It was not a great guitar, and it was not the one he wanted. But it was the only one he could afford. And to his 14-year-old eyes it looked almost like the guitar Niki Sullivan played in the Crickets. Later, Don wanted a Martin guitar. He had not seen one in New Rochelle, but one day when he got off the bus to visit Henry, there, in the window of the House of Music, was a Martin guitar. Mrs. Cohen said, "That's the finest guitar there is." It was a Martin 00-18.

Don satisfied himself with his Harmony F-hole, electrified with a pickup. It enabled him to perform rock 'n' roll music, and he and his friend Brad Bivens formed a group. They played at dances all around New Rochelle. They played all the popular music of the time, from Buddy Holly to the Ventures to Santo and Johnny. Don played in many guitar bands during junior high and high school, and his sister paid for Don to have singing lessons with an opera coach, in New Rochelle, named Mrs. Wagner.

Donald II, John, Olive and Malcolm at 15 Mulberry Lane, circa 1952

Don developed strength and stamina on the Orienta Beach Club Swimming Team, coached by Jack Ryan. Ryan had coached the West Point Swimming Team and produced many state champions. One member of the Orienta Beach Club Swimming Team, Barbara Nulmeyer, narrowly missed representing the United States on the Olympic Swim Team. McLean said, "Watching Barbara swim was like watching poetry in motion."

Coach Ryan made Don swim hundreds of lengths in the ocean, week in and week out. The swimming, combined with the singing lessons, improved Don's breath control and caused his asthma to disappear, except for allergies and small attacks — especially in August.

Don walked for hours and sang popular songs. Frank Sinatra, Nat King Cole, and Elvis songs helped him to further develop his breath control. Years later, his breath control allowed him to sing long, continuous phrases without taking a breath in songs like "Crying," "And I Love You So," and "Vincent." When McLean bought a home in Garrison, New York, he had a swimming pool installed for the express purpose of swimming laps to maintain his breath control.

At the same time, Don was beginning to develop an interest in folk music. His introduction to folk music came from an unlikely source, his Uncle Malcolm. Malcolm McLean belonged to the Rotary Club in Garden City where he had moved after leaving New Rochelle. A YMCA executive named Frank Warner visited Rotary Clubs and other organizations and played folk songs that he had collected on his travels. Warner was famous for discovering the song "Tom Dooley" from a traditional singer named Frank Prophet, who called the song "Tom Dula." Warner's song collecting and his unique singing style, reminiscent of the mountain people from whom many of the songs came, interested Elektra Records and they recorded an album of his songs. Frank Prophet made banjos that were fret-less and used a squirrel skin for a head. Warner performed with one of these banjos, and around its rim were hundreds of autographs of the people from whom he'd collected songs.

Warner sang for Malcolm's Rotarians, and when Malcolm gave Don one of Frank Warner's albums it began to open up a whole new kind of music to explore. He was excited to think that you only needed to learn to play the guitar or banjo in order to perform. "I have never been good at team work. I did not want to belong to a group. So being a troubadour really appealed to me, besides folk and rock were close, in those days, as was country. All the songs had simple lyrics and could easily be played on the guitar."

Another big influence on Don's interest in folk music was a recording of *The Weavers at Carnegie Hall*. His discovery of the Weavers and their music had a lasting impact on his life and the direction he took with his music for many years. The Weavers combined music and politics. Their music was more intellectual. But Don kept rock and pop songs in his repertoire as he went along.

McLean's assessment of the Weavers influence on his music follows in his own words:

> "By the time I was twelve years old I knew hundreds of pop songs and was excited by many diverse rock, pop, and folk artists. Around 1958 someone lent me the Vanguard recording of *The Weaver's at Carnegie Hall*, recorded in 1955. That and a record by Frank Warner were my introduction to folk music. Although I started in folk clubs and played folk instruments, I was never smart enough to be a 'folk singer.' The Weavers were. In fact they were so smart they managed to get themselves blacklisted in the '50s for the organizations they belonged to, for the people they associated with, and for the music they made. From then on, groups that followed in their footsteps were careful to talk the talk but never cross the line.

> The Weavers were unlike any musical group that has ever been, or ever will be. By this I mean that the group of Fred Hellerman, Pete Seeger, Ronnie Gilbert (a lady,) and Lee Hays was not only a musical sensation with a string of strong pop hit records on Decca Records, but also their music carried with it a moral

component which spoke to the dignity of all men and the importance of all cultures — not just ours. This was a brand new idea; a radical idea, hence the need to stop them.

The musical power of this group, the drama, the harmonies, and the humor would have made them a commercial success, if they had done nothing more than sing the country and pop songs of the time, a la the movie song 'High Noon' (which they turned down) or 'The Wayward Wind.' They could have sung the hell out of folk-sounding pop songs and stayed on the good side of the government, but they had too much brainpower for that.

They single-handedly brought the music of Woody Guthrie and Leadbelly into every American home and much more. I responded to this and made up my teenage mind that I would get to know all four of them. I would study them, and maybe I could get a brain transplant. Coming from conservative Westchester County, this was a must.

Throughout the 1960's this was my goal, and by the end of that decade I knew I had come to the end of this particular journey. My musicianship and singing, as well as my writing, could not be contained with three chords on the guitar. I was growing in my own unique musical direction, and that made the folk song only a tiny, but important, part of a much bigger, broader, more personal musical picture. I have retained a political component to my music because of the Weavers. I got to know all of the members of this group. They were the brightest, most thoughtful, creative, and humane artists it was ever my good fortune to meet. I attended the Weavers Reunion Concert at Carnegie Hall, in 1963, instead of going to my senior prom. I graduated in a profound way that evening, making up my mind that music would be my way of life.

The original members of the Weavers were: Lee Hays, Ronnie Gilbert, Pete Seeger on the banjo, and Fred Hellerman on the guitar. In the 1960s Erik Darling replaced Pete Seeger on the banjo, and then Frank Hamilton replaced Erik Darling. Pete Seeger was the son of musicologist

Charles Seeger. After dropping out of Harvard in the 1930s, Pete followed in the footsteps of Carl Sandburg, crisscrossing the country collecting songs, and singing at political gatherings. Woody Guthrie said, "Pete decided to vaccinate himself with the population."

Hays was a minister's son and grew up in Arkansas. He similarly rejected his family's conservative background in favor of radical politics. He moved to New York during the Depression. McLean said that Lee told him he was so poor that he walked across the George Washington Bridge to get to New York City. The first thing he saw was a man selling dentures at a table. Such poverty was incomprehensible to Don.

Hays gravitated to Greenwich Village where he met Huddie Ledbetter, with whom he lived, Josh White, Woody Guthrie, Bess Hawes, Millard Lampell, Pete Seeger, and an ever changing crew of singers and pickers. In 1940, this resulted in the formation of a loose-knit organization known as the Almanac Singers. Their repertoire included union songs, civil rights songs, anti-war songs, and an endless variety of newly arranged and adapted older songs. It was all very informal. They hardly ever rehearsed away from the concert stage. They enjoyed brief but notable success on radio and record.

As dedicated members of Henry Wallace's Progressive Party, the Almanac Singers supported pacifism and American neutrality during 1940 and early 1941, but reversed their stance when Nazi Germany invaded the Soviet Union. This uncomfortable political position compromised their music, and the group members went their separate ways. Guthrie and Seeger joined the army and saw action in the Pacific.

Seeger and Hays spent the later war years campaigning on behalf of the causes of international peace, civil rights, and workers' rights. Eventually, in late 1948, Hays suggested trying to form a group similar to, but better organized than, the Almanac Singers, a group which would be rehearsed and use formal arrangements. This was odd, coming from the least disciplined of the four members, but Hays believed that only by being commercial could they get their message to a larger audience.

They had wanted to create a multi-racial sextet, but this gave way to the final quartet of Hays, Seeger, Fred Hellerman and Ronnie Gilbert. To begin with, they were known as the "No Name Quartet." Fred Hellerman and Ronnie Gilbert worked as counselors at a summer camp in New Jersey. Ronnie was a trained singer who performed Gilbert and Sullivan material, while Fred had studied music at Brooklyn College. They first met Seeger and Hays in the mid '40s, through Peoples' Songs, another informal group of songwriters and musicians. Peoples' Songs met in the basement of Seeger's house in Greenwich Village. Lee kept in touch with Fred through post cards, a favorite device of Lee's.

After a few months performing as the No Name Quartet, the group decided on a new name: the Weavers. During the first year it was difficult to make ends meet. The Weavers secured their first big break in 1949 with a Christmas booking at the Village Vanguard, a famous New York night club. Initially it was to be a three week booking, but they ended up staying for six months, during which time they perfected their act and became a New York sensation. While performing at the Village Vanguard, they met Harold Leventhal. He recommended Pete Kameron, their first manager, to them. Meanwhile Gordon Jenkins, a top composer, arranger, and bandleader, noticed them. Jenkins brought them to the attention of Decca Records chief Dave Kapp. Kapp wasted no time in signing them to his label, although he had his reservations about Seeger, whom he called a "Commie."

In June 1950, the Weavers had their first No.1 chart single with the Huddie Ledbetter song "Irene, Goodnight." The success of this single (really a double, with "Tzena, Tzena" on the other side) caught everyone by surprise. Ronnie Gilbert had to be recalled from her honeymoon so the group could meet their suddenly burgeoning performance commitments.

The title of the Weavers' program was *Folk Songs around the World*. Songs like the African "Wimoweh" ("The Lion Sleeps Tonight,") the Caribbean "Sloop John B," and the Israeli "Tzena, Tzena" reflected the international flavor of their stunning repertoire.

It's hard to imagine that preaching brotherhood and international goodwill would be seen as subversive, but during the hysterical McCarthy era, it was. Overnight, the Weavers were blacklisted, and, consequently, they became unemployable. No record company would touch them. Throughout 1953 and 1954 the Weavers did nothing. Pete Seeger performed at grammar schools. Don saw him at Henry Barnard. "I vaguely remember this tall, lanky guy with a long-necked banjo — He was a sight to see for the first time. He sang 'On Top of Old Smoky' with all the kids." In spite of the blacklist, even though it was considered un-American to attend a Weavers performance, the public did not turn away from them.

The tide finally began to turn in 1955 when Harold Leventhal proposed holding a reunion concert for the Weavers. He first tried to book the Town Hall in New York, but the quartet was still too controversial. Luckily, Carnegie Hall accepted the booking. Traditionally a venue for classical music, it was likely that the staff did not know about the controversy surrounding the group. Nine years later, Brian Epstein pulled off a similar trick, securing a booking for the Beatles at Carnegie Hall. On that occasion, the management assumed that the "quartet" consisted of string players, not a rock 'n' roll group.

With the booking made, the Weavers dusted off their tuxedos and performed a holiday concert to a courageous, sell-out crowd. The recording of that concert, produced with a single microphone on a wire recorder, became the album known as *The Weavers at Carnegie Hall*.

This triumphant musical recording was released by Vanguard Records. Along with Elektra Records, Vanguard Records had begun signing blacklisted performers, creating a stable of the finest folk artists in America. The release of *The Weavers at Carnegie Hall* album caused the Weavers to rise, phoenix-like, from the ashes of the blacklist, and fueled an important change in America's musical taste, from pop to folk. The

Weavers were in their second coming, performing concerts around the country once again. Carl Sandburg said, "The Weavers are out of the grassroots of America. I salute them for their great work in authentic renditions of ballads, folk song ditties, nice antiques of word and melody. When I hear America singing, the Weavers are there."

Audiences were saluting not only the brilliant music the Weavers made but the uncompromising courage of the Weavers as individuals. The drama of their story and the power of their music had a tremendous impact on Don. He decided he wanted to learn as much as he could from them and about them.

Years later Fred Hellerman remembered Don's enthusiasm for the Weavers:

> "Back in the late fifties and early sixties, Harold Leventhal's office was a buzzing hive of exciting activity. It was, after all, the management office of the Weavers, Pete Seeger, Theodore Bikel, Judy Collins, Alan Arkin and others, as well as young "wanna-bees" like the Simon Sisters (Carly and Lucy), and others who just hung out there.
>
> "It was there that I first laid eyes on young Don McLean. I didn't pay much attention to him. I can't remember hearing him sing there, although I'm sure I did. Nor did I know much about him. I knew he was a Weavers fan and that he lived in the Hudson Valley, not far from Lee Hays and Pete Seeger. I had no suspicion of the fire that was burning inside him, fire that would eventually burst into the kind of creative flame that produced some of the major songs of the seventies and put him up there with the best.
>
> "I had no occasion to be in contact with him for a number of years while he was busy making quite a name for himself, so I was surprised when I received a call from him out of the blue. No

reason. Just wanted to get acquainted. After all, he knew Pete and Lee. I guess I was a blank in his Weavers mosaic that needed filling in. He came to visit me in Connecticut and we talked of many things — music, family, love, death, things we each wanted for ourselves and others, things like that.

"And so started a friendship that has lasted more than 25 years, despite the pulling apart that geography can inflict upon our lives. The bonds have not been severed, the strands are held together by Christmas cards with proud pictures of his growing family, bearing testimony to a set of priorities that is refreshing to behold.

"But an exciting discovery was yet to come.

"The Weavers had made many records, and they all seemed to be called *The Weavers at Carnegie Hall,* or something close to it. Although they were all recorded before live audiences, they were never recordings of complete concerts, but only <u>excerpts</u> from concerts, and I felt they lacked the full flavor of what we did.

"Some of our early concerts had been taped, or parts of them were. After a while we had a considerable pile of random tapes, but we didn't have a complete, usable recording of any one concert. I thought it would be a challenge to try to <u>create</u> a concert, one that had never taken place, a song from here, an introduction to it from another performance, a joke put in there — a fictitious Weavers concert that would have the feel of a Weavers concert, complete with tunings and noises and the pointed stories of Lee Hays that put so much of the material into meaningful context and gave those concerts the overall flavor which made a Weavers concert different from all others.

Erik Darling and Fred Hellerman

(Music Inn tent, summer of 1960)

"And so, I went to work on it. And it was about this time that this baker of "American Pies" shows up. He knew a lot about those tapes through his friendship with Lee Hays. He kept urging that something be done with them. Lee used to say that Don McLean had a deeper understanding of the Weavers' significance in the history of American music, than did any of the Weavers. But Don was much more than a mere cheering section. Don's familiarity — no, make that intimacy — with those tapes was nothing short of astonishing. As often as I had listened to those tapes and worked with them, I thought I knew them inside out. A few worthwhile performances had gotten past me, but not past him. It seemed as if every Weavers song he had ever heard had been catalogued and etched into his head. He was able to call up particular performances of particular songs that were subtly different from the versions I had chosen. When I went back and listened to both performances, he was invariably right about which was better. It was the most incredible demonstration of musical memory I have ever run across."

Don was now at Albert Leonard Junior High, which he hated. The year was 1958, and discipline at school was a problem. On one occasion Don saw a teacher leave school on a stretcher after being beaten up by a student who had been held back three times. Don spent all his time listening to records, playing his expanding instrument collection, vocalizing, trying to write songs and giving lessons to earn money. He said, "Even though I didn't know much about playing the guitar at the time, there were plenty of kids who knew even less than I did and would pay to learn what I knew."

Don's academic record at Albert Leonard was poor, but somehow he scraped through. In 1960, he started high school at Iona Preparatory School, a small Catholic boys' high school located on the campus of Iona College in New Rochelle. The building was a handsome, two-story, red brick Georgian structure set back on a slight rise on the east side of the campus, and the total enrollment was around 400. The remarkably capable faculty of 16 taught a classic college preparatory curriculum — English, history, math, science, economics, Latin, French, and of course, religion. The extensive extra curricular activities included all the varsity sports, and Iona Prep was always the smallest school in the league. The next smallest school in the football league was Holy Cross which had over 1000 students. The students commuted from places like Scarsdale or

Port Chester, on the New Haven line, or drove in from Stamford, Connecticut, thirty miles away. Many came from New York City.

Iona Prep was run by the Order of Irish Christian Brothers, and the Brothers made up over half the faculty. All of the lay (non-religious) teachers were men, and they, too, wore black, flowing robes. The only women at the school were the principal's secretary, the librarian, and the cafeteria staff. The wiry, bantam-weight Brothers placed great store in the Virtue of Humility, replacing their own leaders (including the principal) every five years, and using sarcasm and corporal punishment on any back-talkers, late-comers, homework-malingerers, and other errant adolescents among the students. Academic standards were high, and knuckles were beaten with rulers until they bled.

Don attended summer school almost every year. One summer, Tony Lock, a kid from Scarsdale with long blonde hair combed in a pompadour, who fancied himself to be a pretty cool dude, baited the teacher with snide remarks all summer. Finally, on a very hot and sticky day, Lock pushed it too far. Brother Doran, who seldom lost his temper, swung from the floor and slapped Lock across the face. He slapped him over and over, each time asking him a question which Lock couldn't answer. There was silence in the classroom as the Brother asked his questions and delivered his blows. McLean said, "We all found this very frightening and a little bit satisfying. I can't think of any kid in that class who wouldn't have lined up behind Brother Doran to give Lock a shot, sort of like that great scene in *Airplane*." After that, Brother Doran never raised a hand to a student. He died seven years later in Africa.

Another student recalls being at a high school dance and seeing a couple slow dancing. The brother warned the student, in a friendly way, "Leave enough room for the Holy Ghost." To which the student replied, "He can get his own." The brother hauled off and slapped the kid silly in front of everybody.

During the years of innocence and optimism that preceded the Beatles, the Rolling Stones, and Vietnam, experiences like those at Iona Prep were supposed to build character. Over 90 percent of the students went on to college.

At home, Don's father had grown white haired, ashen, and irritable. He would come home from work and lie across the bed, exhausted. Don's grandmother, Olive, decided to buy an insurance policy from the school which guaranteed a tuition-free education should the father of a student die. This was done after Don had a dream and told his grandmother he thought his father would die soon. She laughed it off, but bought the insurance.

In the summer of 1960, Don and his father took a trip to Washington D.C. It was the first trip Don had ever taken with his father, and it was the first time his father had ever left the state of New York, except for minor excursions into New Jersey or Connecticut on business. Don was 14 years old.

They visited the Washington Monument, the Lincoln Memorial, and Mount Vernon, George Washington's home. They also visited battlegrounds of the Civil War. Don's father was very interested in history. Don was bored, but pleased to see his father happy. He said, "Seeing these places that were so important in American history delighted my father — he had read so much about them. It was his last, and only hurrah."

It gradually became apparent to Don that his father was not well. One day they decided to climb to the top of the Washington Monument. Don's father only managed one flight of steps before he sat down and said he could go no further. McLean said, "Something must have alarmed him, because he scared the hell out of me. Later, in our hotel, he took out his wallet and said, 'Look son, if anything should happen to me, here's my wallet. Call your mother; she'll know what to do.'"

This foreshadowing clouded the trip with an underlying anxiety, but without further incident, Don and his father returned home safely. McLean found out later his father knew he was dying and secretly took medication. "He was brave and gallant and did not want to frighten me or my mother."

Don's father was a typical member of 1950s middle class America. At that time, men and women retained the discipline and character that had been essential for survival during the Depression and World War II. The idea of "having it all" was declasse. People were more likely to get a sense of self-worth from getting by on less and making it seem like more. Don's father worked all his life for Consolidated Edison, taking only two weeks of vacation each year. He never complained about this or the relative lack of reward, because people didn't complain. He did not dress casually. He worked in the garden wearing a flannel shirt, tweed trousers and scuffed wingtip shoes, which he used only for that purpose, since they had long outlived their use for wearing in public.

By contrast, Don's mother had a relaxed approach to life, but could be neurotic and caustic. Each winter she went to Florida for two weeks with her sister Ann. This year, Don's father decided to take the opportunity to do some painting inside the house and have it finished by the time she returned. This was his idea of a great time and a big surprise. Unfortunately, Don had a surprise of his own: the worst school report card ever. Music had become a total distraction.

Don and his father took his mother to Long Island to meet Aunt Ann for the beginning of their trip, and returned home late that night. As they pulled into the driveway, the green radium light of the dashboard lit Don's father's face. In McLean's memory, his father seemed to have sunlight on him, as he looked at Don and said, "What would you like to be when you grow up, son? I would really like to know." Don thought he looked tired, his little wisp of white hair falling down over his eye but he had a look on his face that said: this is a beautiful moment; I'm asking my son what he would like to do with his life.

Like father, like son. Don answered honestly, "I want to be a musician." His father's expression turned to sadness, then to anger. "What the hell are you talking about? Musicians are nothing but bums. I want you to go to college." The fathers of teenaged boys in Don's neighborhood hoped their sons would take the right path in life, not the road to the circus.

When things did not go the way Donald II wanted them to, especially with family members, he withdrew all emotional contact from that individual. He did this to his children almost as a reflex. He was never able to uncouple his own desires for his children from their desires for themselves.

McLean always knew that he was destined to be an artist and that it was probably the only thing he could do successfully. It was unfortunate that the one thing Don knew he could do well carried absolutely no weight with his father. All the things that were important to Donald II, such as athletics and scholarship, meant nothing to Don. Today McLean believes that, had his father lived, he would not have become a musician, because he could not have withstood the withdrawal of his father's affection. "My father thought nothing of not speaking to me for days if I pissed him off."

As the days went by, the clock ticked, until high noon and the arrival of Don's report card, the anticipation built to unbearable, mind-bending surrealism. The mailman became the most frightening person in the neighborhood. Finally, the day came, and Don had to show the card to his father. Don expected a beating, followed by a freeze-out. His father was indeed furious, and there was a bad scene. Don went to his room, and his father continued painting the stairway railing.

Around 1a.m. Don was awakened by his father standing in the hallway in front of Don's little room crying and holding his chest. He was saying "Oh my God, oh my God." Tears streamed down his cheeks. Don knew his father needed help, immediately. He helped his father into his room and laid him on the bed and said, "Dad, I'm going to call the police and the hospital." His father begged him not to, but Don placed the calls. If word got out he was sick, he might lose his job.

Suddenly, in the early morning hours of January 18th, 1961, the house was full of strangers. The police were on the ground floor, while the paramedics prepared to take Don's father to the hospital. They put him on a stretcher, bundled him up, and put a towel around his head. It was bitterly cold out. Fresh snow was on the ground.

The local policeman, whom everyone called "Irish" because he spoke with a heavy Irish brogue, was on the telephone talking to Don's mother in Florida. She was hysterical. "Ah, Mrs McLean, don't worry," said Irish. "It's just a bit of indigestion, it'll be fine." He even chided her for not being home to cook for her husband and son. "A man can't live on peanut butter and jelly sandwiches," he said.

Eventually, the paramedics carried Don's father down the stairs to the ambulance. As he passed Don, he gave him a very tender smile. Don felt that he was saying goodbye. He was letting him know that he was a man now and very proud of him.

Arrangements were made for Don to spend the night with friends. He walked alone to their house through the crisp snow and ice. The night was crystal clear with a thousand stars in the sky. Everyone was up when Don got there.

At about 4 a.m., the door to the bedroom where Don was sleeping opened, and the light went on. Standing in his overcoat and hat and gloves, with cold air all around him, was Uncle Malcolm. With a grim expression he said, "I have some bad news for you, son. Your father died tonight." Then Malcolm took Don with him to Garden City. It was the longest and loneliest drive Don had ever taken.

The next day Don returned home to Larchmont Woods. He was shattered and could not stop crying. The window on the stair landing where Don had sat and sung as a child was flooded with winter sunlight. He could see in the blazing light the grey fibers of the hospital blanket that had swaddled his father on the stretcher the night before. The fibers were stuck to the newly-painted banister. "I was unbearably blue. I would remain so for years."

For the next four days, Don spent most of his time at the George Davis Funeral Parlor in New Rochelle looking at his dead father and receiving visitors with his mother. From time to time alternating waves of crying and disbelief would give way to hysterical laughter, and Don and his cousin, Jock, would sneak away to unknown parts of the funeral parlor to visit the other corpses.

The funeral service was filled to overflowing with hundreds of grief-stricken people who loved his father. Donald McLean had given freely of his time and energy to neighbors and family for decades. Someone said, "To know him, was to love him."

His father's wake and funeral seemed to go on forever. They were the last Don ever attended. Today, McLean says, "I decided I would never again go to a funeral." Family members were upset when McLean refused to attend his mother's funeral, 24 years later. However, he figured that she wouldn't mind. He had no desire to see her that way or to watch her put into a hole in the ground.

A few days after his father was buried, a man from the Consolidated Edison Company came to 15 Mulberry to return his father's briefcase. It made a big impression on Don that this was all his mother got for her husband's 30 years of corporate devotion. Don vowed then that he was never going to work for anyone.

Chapter 2: Castles in the Air...Musical Apprenticeship, 1960s

As the weeks passed following the funeral, Don and his mother felt as though they had survived an emotional hurricane. They were both intact, but their lives had been wrecked. Don was lonelier than ever and had to battle to contain his grief. The laughter of children coming home from school made him furious.

McLean remembers:

> I was shattered. I can't describe what it means to be shattered to anyone who has not experienced it, and I do not need to describe it to anyone who has. I was still in one piece, but there were cracks everywhere.
>
> My happiness was over, and everybody else I knew was pretty happy. I couldn't show it, so it was all inside. I kept it inside, except at nights, when I would cry a lot. I missed my father. It's hard to see your parents go. I was just 15 years old.

His mother was lonely too. Without her husband, she became displaced from their active social circle. The invitations ended; friends rarely came to visit. There was no word from Don's uncle, either. "The Malcolm McLeans dropped us."

Don's mother could be blunt, and if she decided that someone was false, she never trusted or liked that person again, even though she might be tolerant. Unfortunately, she felt this way about the Malcolm McLeans, and never really changed her mind. A lot of warmth went out of Don's feelings for the McLeans. They were always disappointing. After the funeral, they were rarely heard from again.

While the McLeans were indifferent, members of the Bucci family were strong and compassionate, offering to take Don and his mother in. Until his father's death, Don had always felt closer to the McLean side of the family. However, after his father died, Don began to appreciate people who were down to earth.

Don McLean, 1963, about to quite college.

Though his father's death was a terrible experience for him, it gave Don the opportunity to break the chains and be free from family expectations. Suddenly he had the freedom to explore his dream of following a musical career. This thought, and his general grief, made school even more difficult. He could not concentrate.

While working on his singing, Don wanted to make inroads into the musical world that he had heard about and read about throughout his childhood. In particular, he wanted to know more about the Weavers. By 1961, folk music was moving toward the peak of its popularity. Members of groups, such as the Weavers, were superstars. This did not faze 16-year-old Don McLean. He knew that Erik Darling, who had replaced Pete Seeger as the banjo player and tenor for the Weavers, lived in New York City, and he decided to call him. He found his number through the operator.

"Is this Erik Darling of the Weavers?"

"Yes."

Don started right in asking him questions about music, about himself, and about the Weavers. Erik was immediately tuned in. Rather than being annoyed by the boy's nerve, Darling was several steps ahead. He didn't mind if Don called every now and then. He was always friendly and complementary. He was amazed that Don was just 16 years old. Today, Darling remembers Don as being "a bright and creative thinker, fun to talk to about anything."

> "He was one of those people who weren't locked into one particular perspective. He was willing to think about things, to go to new places in thought. At that time, many of the folk music

people were locked into the erroneous idea of excluding the unique and creative from their music, in a futile attempt to be 'authentic.' As I recall, Don wasn't like that. He wanted to bring himself to this music, and let it run free. That made us allies."

McLean was learning a lot from his conversations with Darling, and many things left a lasting impression. For instance, one day, Darling said how great he thought Nat King Cole was. He said, "I don't keep my mind fixed on folk music, I like all kinds of music, and Nat King Cole is one of the greatest." Don, always a Nat King Cole fan, greatly respected Erik for this remark.

During the summer of 1962, Darling had a big hit record with a group he formed called the Rooftop Singers. The song was called "Walk Right In." During one phone conversation, he said, "Why don't you come over?" By this time Don was making regular train trips to New York City, trying to find his way into the very mysterious music business. Darling's invitation was exciting.

Darling lived in a pre-war, New York apartment. Off the hallway were a kitchen, a bedroom, and two big rooms which looked out over the street. One room was the living room where Darling had a sofa and chairs, a sparsely furnished, ascetic, almost monkish environment. The other room was Darling's office, where he kept all his instruments. He had a very early 000-42 Martin guitar with 12 frets, a slotted head, and a pearl inlay. Darling had obtained it from a pawn shop, and he played it on his first album with Elektra Records. He had two custom twelve-string Gibson guitars and two custom 000-28 Martin guitars. He had a custom-made, five-string Vega banjo with a long neck. The fifth string peg was set back one extra fret so that he could strap a capo on, to change the key, one fret higher. The neck was wide, and it was blonde, instead of stained. It was a great looking instrument and McLean was amazed when Darling let him take it home. On a little strip of paper, left over from his days with the Weavers, running down the neck Darling had written out the Weavers' show. Darling's notes told him what the Weavers' program was. Don saved that strip of paper. Years later, he made a collage of musical artists, and under the Weavers he put the strip of paper. Another of McLean's montages became the cover of *The Western Album,* released in 2004.

Don spent hours at that apartment, playing guitars, while Erik accompanied him on the banjo. McLean was beginning to write his first songs, and Darling wanted to hear them. It was an amazing experience. It helped Don build confidence, and he learned that if you don't ask, you don't get. By not fearing rejection and by contacting people, he found himself exactly where he wanted to be.

McLean attended the Weavers' concert at the newly opened Philharmonic Hall at Lincoln Center in New York. The concert was difficult to hear because of acoustic problems in the new hall. In 1976 the building was redesigned and renamed Avery Fisher Hall. He was particularly impressed with Frank Hamilton who had replaced Erik Darling when Darling left to form the Rooftop Singers.

After the show, McLean went backstage where the Weavers were signing autographs. Lee Hays looked a little like Elmer Gantry; "a big man, big voice, a little bit debauched, a little bit disillusioned, but with a tremendous charisma about him." Don imagined that Hays was looking down his nose and through his glasses at everybody, waiting for them to say something interesting. "You could sense that he had a tremendous mind. He was a very complicated man. He did not like fools." This was the first of many meetings, and Don got his autograph.

Don also attended the last "Hootenanny" at Carnegie Hall on September 22nd, 1962. These hootenannies had been going on since the 1940s. They featured folk singers, audience participation, and Progressive politics. Pete Seeger was often the host, as he was for this one, and he introduced a little guy wearing a checked shirt and a wool cap and playing a Gibson guitar. His name was Bob Dylan. Other people on the show included bluegrass musicians such as the Lilly Brothers and Don Stover, Scottish singer Matt McGinn, and civil rights activist and freedom singer Bernice Regan. But Dylan stole the show. McLean remembers, "He made us laugh with his drunken act, singing his 'Talking Bear Mountain Blues.' Before the laughter had stopped he was cutting deep with 'Hard Rain's a Gonna Fall' and other songs that were life changers."

The next day McLean and a friend went to Washington Square Park where dozens of folk singers were performing with guitars and banjos. Bob Dylan was among the singers. A music critic, named Bob Sarlin, who was at Washington Square Park that day, told Don that he knew there was something extraordinary about Bob Dylan and his fans when he saw Dylan light a cigarette with a wooden match, and the moment

Dylan threw the match away someone picked it up and put it in his pocket.

Don spent his weekends playing the 12 string guitar, the six string guitar and the five string banjo. He visited Erik Darling now and then. And he played in a small group with banjoist Mike Kropp and another friend. They managed to get their first professional gig at an Israeli restaurant in New York City. In 1962 and 1963, McLean played in a number of small groups in and around New York City. He seldom sang solo. He had many songs in his repertoire and had written a few of his own songs. He got permission to use an empty classroom to make a demo tape. The echo off the cinder block walls at Iona Prep created great acoustics. Don recorded songs like "Good Old Wagon," "Well, Well, Well," "Give Me a Pig's Foot and a Bottle of Beer," and "Black Eyed Susie," on that first tape.

Since his father's death, Don's mother had become much closer to her sister, Ann. Ann and her husband, Ralph always welcomed Don and his mother to their large home on Long Island. Don's mother enjoyed looking after their two young daughters, and when Ann and Ralph gave a party, Ralph would pay Don to play a few songs.

Ralph was a silk importer, and Don had read somewhere that Harold Leventhal, the manager of the Weavers and other big stars like Judy Collins and Alan Arkin, had gone back to his original trade in the garment industry during the blacklist in the 1950s. Don asked his uncle whether he knew the name Leventhal. His uncle said, "Yes, I do know someone named Leventhal." By a stroke of good fortune it turned out to be Harold Leventhal's brother. Don gave his demo tape to his uncle and asked him to try to get it to Harold by way of his brother. This was Christmas 1962, and over a year would pass before he would hear anything else about it. Meanwhile he had to turn his attention to completing school.

School had become secondary to Don. He had no interest in fitting in. All he wanted to do was get on with making music. The only thing that interested him at school was the senior talent show. To make sure he would be able to take part in it, and to keep his mother happy, Don made an effort to catch up at school.

Brother Nagle, the principal of Iona Prep, strode through the halls with his black robes flowing behind him, occasionally stopping to have a heart-to-heart talk with a student. Around exam time, Don let slip the fact that he was failing Latin III and had not actually passed Latin II either. Brother Nagle turned frosty and said to Don, "Well, you're going to have to pass two exams in three weeks, or I will throw you out of here."

Don decided to sign up for Latin study hall everyday after school in an attempt to jump the formidable hurdle placed between him and graduation. After about 10 days, Don asked his tutor, Mr Flynn, whether he thought he could pass. Mr. Flynn looked at Don and with a smile said, "Not a chance." Miraculously, Don passed both Latin classes. Now he could focus on the talent show.

The talent show was held in a Quonset hut left over from World War II, architecture that today sells for millions in the Hamptons. On talent show day the Quonset hut was filled with 500 kids and all the teachers. Anyone brave enough to perform was liable to be severely ridiculed. First on stage was a 200-pounder who played the piccolo, bringing gales of laughter and a few spit balls. The next kid did a magic act. The reaction to this wasn't much better.

When McLean's name was announced, he was ready. He hit the stage with "Well, Well, Well" and moved into a version of "Good Old Wagon" that was better than his demo. He slowed things down with a Josh White tune called "Darlin." By now the crowd was quiet. McLean picked up the banjo and frailed a wicked hoe-down, the notes shooting off the banjo like silver bullets. Don finished with "This Little Light of Mine," a song that is still a standard part of his repertoire. When he finished, the students went wild. They threw their books and chairs in the air. There was bedlam. It was something straight out of a Hollywood movie.

After the show, when Don went back to his English class, where he had often battled with the teacher, the entire class jumped to their feet and cheered. They taunted the teacher with cries of, "So he doesn't know what he's talking about?!" It was a long time before the class calmed down. The teacher realized he couldn't give everyone the strap, and he was magnanimous in his praise of Don's performance. The teacher, Thomas Draney, is in his 80s today, and still writes to McLean from Florida.

At graduation, Brother Nagle gave a speech to the parents of the graduating seniors in which he praised McLean and his talent. Don's mother thought that she was hallucinating, because the only time Nagel had called her in the past was when Don was in trouble, which was often. Now, because of his music, it seemed doors were opening.

Don had many girlfriends during high school. Claire Case and Andrea Steiner were two whose parents did not approve of him. That scored a lot of points with the girls. Their parents sensed that he would not look good in a hat and overcoat, commuting on the train to New York. McLean says, "There was something less than solid about me. However, I loved all the girls I knew then. They were all beautiful, and I hope their lives have been good." Of course, after McLean became world famous, those parents got hell from their daughters. In 1973 the *Standard Star*, Don's old paper, did a feature story entitled "Don McLean Is a Millionaire."

Since Don would be living away from home during college, his mother decided she had to leave the house. Rather than selling 15 Mulberry Lane, Don persuaded her to rent the house and find an apartment to live in. In September 1963 they moved to a two-bedroom apartment at 1815 Palmer Avenue, in Larchmont. The decision not to sell the family home proved to be a wise business decision. The feverish real estate development of the area took property values through the roof in the 1960s. By the time the house was sold, in the late 1980s, it was worth a small fortune.

Pete Murphy, Don's good friend from Iona Prep, remembers that he and McLean shared an interest in the Weavers and in Lester Flatt and Earl Scruggs. Pete just liked the way they sounded, but Don was already a talented banjo and guitar player, singing their songs. During their senior year of high school, they hung out together at the McLean's apartment next to the New York, New Haven & Hartford railroad tracks in Larchmont. Pete Murphy was the nephew of television's Ed Sullivan, and made sure Don met him at Pete's graduation party.

McLean confided to Pete that he had written to Pete Seeger several times, and Seeger had answered him. Pete was amazed to learn that Don had not written to say he liked Seeger's music, or to ask what Woody Guthrie was really like, or to ask the genesis of a particular song, but to ask Seeger to explain his stand on Communism. Pete Murphy says, "That was a pretty ballsy thing for a 17 year old to do back then, but that was one of the reasons I liked and respected Don. The really cool thing was that Seeger wrote back!" Pete remembers that he was further impressed when McLean started reading up on Communism. Don remembers, "My mother was shocked when a large box arrived from the House On Un-American Activities Committee with fifty pounds of testimony." Pete says that "Don's approach to concepts, relationships, music, or whatever was tenacious."

Don had applied to Villanova University in Pennsylvania to keep his mother happy. She said that his father would have wanted it more than anything else. With Don's terrible high school record, it is amazing that Villanova admitted him.

McLean found it difficult to settle in at Villanova. Most of the students were interested in basketball or academics, not music. After about a month, Don began to spend his weekends taking the Paoli Local to Penn Central Station and the New York Central train to Larchmont. The apartment was practically empty, since his mother spent most of her time with her sister Ann on Long Island.

It wasn't long before McLean got involved in music at Villanova, thanks to his new friendship with another student, Jim Croce. He had a curious interest in oddball novelty songs, such as: "He's got a way with women; he just got away with mine." Later on Croce wrote songs that captured some of the street-wise, bluesy humor that he was fond of at Villanova. He was a very open and compassionate person and would hold court in the campus Pie Shop (a large cafeteria), telling stories about things that happened in the South Philadelphia neighborhood where he came from. He was a "big man on campus," majoring in psychology and hoping to follow an academic career working with children. Jim liked a wide variety of musicians and musical styles and had a huge record collection. Jim was older, and he knew many people in the local Philadelphia music scene. He would say, "Hey, I know somebody that lives in a trailer and plays great mandolin. Let's go over there tonight." He would come in his car with a couple of buddies and pick up Don. Excited by Don's enthusiasm for music, Jim spent a lot of time with him. He also helped Don get his own 30-minute show on the university radio station. This gave Don access to the entire music library at Villanova. McLean remembers his friendship with Jim Croce at college with great affection. But in spite of this friendship, Don was miserable at school and conflicted. "I was so damned bored."

Other than his friendship with Jim Croce, or seeing Perry Como sitting in his limousine waiting to pick up his son, Don has few significant memories of Villanova, until November 22, 1963. While waiting for a friend in front of the administration building one afternoon, McLean saw what seemed to be the entire student body and all of the faculty come pouring out of the buildings and head in a mob towards the Pie Shop cafeteria, where the televisions were always on. As a student ran past, Don asked what was happening, and the student said, "The president has been shot." Don joined the students and teachers in the Pie Shop as Walter Cronkite told the world that Kennedy was dead.

This brought back memories of his father's funeral, for all during the funeral, Kennedy was being inaugurated. Now Kennedy was dead. Nothing in America was worth believing in. Something told Don that it was time to leave school.

Years later when McLean was asked whether he would have been a success in business, he responded:

> "No, I think I would have been a serious alcoholic if I had been in business. If I had done what my father wanted, I would have been arrested, I would have hurt someone, I would have been an alcoholic, a drug addict, or both. I'd probably be dead by now.
>
> I'm a wild person, a free person, and I don't like taking orders from people. I think it's because of how I developed as a young person. I never got accustomed to the harness like the other kids

did by going to school so regularly. There was always this wild streak within me which caused me a lot of trouble in school. Thank God, I had music. Music came along, and it suited me so beautifully, and I was able to use my abilities. You have to give a young person something they can get excited over, something that they can be competitive about, something that makes them feel, 'I can do that.'"

McLean quit Villanova in January, 1964, leaving everything he owned in a pile in the center of the room he shared with another guy. He told Jim Croce that he was going to start his career. Jim just laughed and said that was too reckless for him. Jim wanted to graduate.

Don returned home to the half empty apartment in Larchmont. There was no way he wanted to be a person who a country club acquaintance would ask to bring a guitar to the party because he had <u>almost</u> been professional in his college days. He wanted to follow Sandburg and Guthrie and write songs about the New Jerusalem.

"I was a poet. I was a troubadour. This was not an image or a fanciful, thoughtless moment when I departed from the script for a while. Fuck the script. I was going to write the rules from now on, and nobody would ever tell me otherwise. I wasn't cut out to be some wimped-out college boy from New Rochelle. I was going to be a legend. Nobody would give my wife my briefcase. I didn't want a wife anyway. I wanted women all over town, like Josh White."

Don was a college drop-out living in an apartment with no furniture. He was becoming a "show business bum," the kind of person his father had despised, except that he wasn't even in show business yet. He was unemployed, but at least he knew what he wanted to be unemployed at.

He attended many auditions and eventually began to get odd jobs accompanying other singers, but a breakthrough seemed elusive. Then one day the phone rang, and it was Harold Leventhal. Leventhal had received Don's demo tape and wanted him to visit his office in New York City.

In the spring of 1964, McLean took the train in to the city to meet Harold Leventhal at his office on 57th Street. He rode the elevator up to the top floor where "Harold Leventhal Management" was printed on the door. Don sat in the waiting room, looking at the large posters that covered the walls: Alan Arkin in Second City, the Weavers at Carnegie Hall, Judy Collins at Town Hall, and Pete Seeger in - where else - Russia. In a few years, while auditioning for various record companies, McLean would wander through a world of record executives' offices that could only have been created by Mel Brooks. Purple offices with chrome. All white affairs. White, white, white is the color of our carpet. Stun me! Shock me! I'm in the record business. But Leventhal's office looked like he was in the silk importing business.

Indeed he might have been, if it hadn't been for the Weavers' Reunion Concert at Carnegie Hall in 1955. Now, he was truly at the heart of the music business, and his artists were the best. And he had integrity. He refused to handle the Beatles when they came to New York, because he didn't handle that kind of music. He had the Leadbelly legacy and the Woody Guthrie archives to watch out for. He didn't need the Beatles. Leventhal knew how to build and maintain legends. It was his stock and trade, not music.

As a young man, Leventhal had been a song plugger for Irving Berlin, and a picture of them with Sinatra hung on the wall. Leventhal told McLean that Irving Berlin used to have him wear his new shoes to break them in, because they wore the same size. He wanted to know what Leventhal had thought of his tape. Leventhal said, "We like it. We think you're talented. One of the folks here in the office would like to work with you."

Don was amazed. He knew his tape recording was not the best, but here he was, where music had taken him, being told that he had talent and that they wanted to "work with him." He was again where he wanted to be. "Validation oils the wheels," says McLean.

Leventhal arranged for McLean to have breakfast with Alan Arkin. At this time, Arkin was making the transition from music to the stage and screen, but Arkin was a figure that Don had heard about already. During Arkin's childhood, his parents had been fans and friends of the Weavers. Lee Hays was like an uncle to Alan and like a grandfather to his kids. Lee and Alan even made several albums of children's music, which still stand today as some of the best of the genre. In the 1950s Arkin alternated between stage-work and singing with the Tarriers, a folk group that included Erik Darling and Bob Carey. The name came from an old Irish folk song, "Drill, Ye Tarriers, Drill." With their 1956 record of "The Banana Boat Song," the Tarriers became the first folk trio to get a hit single on the Billboard pop charts. Arkin liked McLean's singing and was impressed by his knowledge of music. He was especially impressed that Don had talked with Erik Darling about the importance of using mental energy to move a group beyond thinking about a song to becoming one voice.

A few days after their meeting, Leventhal called McLean and said that his assistant, Charles Close, would work with him. Close was 27 years old, a handsome, blonde graduate of Tulane University. He loved women, loved to party, and loved to have a good time. He went out with a different woman every night. He met Harold Leventhal because he was friends with Lee Hays' nephew, Bill Hays, at Tulane University. When Close moved to New York, he became Leventhal's assistant and the Weavers' road manager.

McLean visited the office frequently and sat with Close as he penciled in gigs on the calendars of different artists. Don saw the amount of work that a busy professional had to do. He also acquired a healthy respect for the frustration involved in being an agent and trying to coordinate all the appearances so that the routing is not completely insane.

As the Weavers' road manager, Close had to look after the needs of Lee Hays, who could be very demanding. Lee did not travel. He had to be transported like a large piece of furniture. He'd sit like a pasha in his hotel room and order room service. He always had a regal presence and he expected people who he hardly knew to do almost anything for him. Charles was sick of Lee but had a lot of respect for the Weavers' professionalism. There were stresses and strains that caused them to have daggers drawn, but, when show time came, they never failed to deliver.

Weavers at Carnegie Hall Reunion Concert, 1963

Shortly after McLean joined Leventhal's office, the Weavers disbanded. He received an invitation to dinner from Hays. Hays wanted McLean and Close to join him at his apartment on Cranberry Street in Brooklyn Heights. Don was unable to believe he was sitting in Lee Hays' living room. However, during the evening McLean learned that Leventhal had sent Hays his demo tape, and it was Hays who had said that they should take him on. He had liked the sound of the tape very much and recognized that Don had talent. Hays died in 1981 and left Don a box of reel to reel tapes of obscure Weaver recordings and other memorabilia. In among the tapes McLean found the original demo that he had sent to Harold Leventhal in 1962.

Charles Close booked McLean many guest appearances in clubs in Greenwich Village. After each show he would critique Don's performance. McLean began to learn how to program his concerts, how to know what to sing and when to sing it. This is the single most important thing that a musical performer can learn. In the beginning Don was not confident about programming. When he was talking between songs, he could easily be thrown, if somebody in the audience said something. He would feel as though he had lost his place in the script. He was in the long, painful process of developing his own idiomatic style as a performer. McLean watched many seasoned performers "phone in" the exact same show every night. To him, this is not art. He never sings the same show twice. He doesn't know what he is going to sing until he hits the stage. He says, "You will never find a set list taped to my guitar. Symphony performers and groups need scripting so that everybody knows what's happening. Troubadours don't."

McLean was now in show business. Charles Close was getting him frequent bookings at a range of coffee houses and clubs. This started a six year period during which Don would perform at venues like the Bitter End and the Gaslight Café in New York, the Newport Folk Festival, the Cellar Door in Washington, D.C., the Main Point in Philadelphia, the Troubadour and the Ash Grove in Los Angeles and many colleges throughout New York and New England. In 1964 he won a singing competition at the World's Fair. He brought home a huge trophy. This was the start of Don McLean's career as a professional singer and songwriter.

McLean remembers Close breaking him into show business this way:

> Charles was my first manager. For a guy who had a lot of pursuits he managed to stay quite involved with me for about two years. I

was so young and green that he had to call my mother from time to time to tell her how I was doing. My mother and my aunt even showed up, unannounced, at Charles's Greenwich Village apartment. My mother was worried about me and had no idea where I was or what I was doing in 1964. Just a few short years before we had been a close knit family in our little house on Mulberry Lane. That was all shattered now and Bleeker Street was no Mulberry Lane, but all I had eyes for was the music business. I did then, as I do now. I let the music take me where it will.

Charles could not believe how innocent I was. He was always pointing out the difference between the harsh realities of show business and my rose-colored dreams. He had a perpetual smile of semi-condescension on his face, which made me feel that, in spite of our mutual desire to get somewhere with my career, he had his doubts. However, I didn't. I was excited when the International Talent Agency, we call it I.T.A., signed me. They are a major talent agency.

I felt bad for Charles, because he seemed tortured, as if he was frustrated in some basic and serious way. Creativity on the part of show business managers is very real, and performers need other creative people to get anywhere, but managers are often very frustrated that they are not on stage, or writing something important. I don't know if this was the case with Charles, but something was eating at his insides.

Charles was my very first link to the realization of my dreams. There is no way to measure the value of someone who believes in you.

I was still unaccomplished, and many of the gigs I got were less than successful. It's funny how you can plan a performance, and when you're on stage it just dies on its ass. Flop sweat is very real. If you've every really bombed, it is not a sensation you want to repeat. But, like riding a horse, it's not a question of if, but when, you will bomb, and you must get back on the stage.

It was after many weak performances and no prospect of recording that Charles and I decided that it might be good for me to try school again. It was hard to admit defeat, to admit that I was not good enough. I decided to take a break and try college, but I never gave up inside.

Years later, in 2002, I was appearing at the West Hampton Playhouse on Long Island when who should come back stage but Charles Close. Older now, with lines on his face, he still had a young honey on his arm. He told me he was making boats and loving it. I thanked him for helping me set sail, and when we parted he said, "I always knew you'd make it."

In 1964 McLean was combining visits to Erik Darling's apartment with meetings with Charles Close. Darling was enjoying notable success with the Rooftop Singers and was often away, performing concerts across the U.S. From Darling, Don was getting to know the rhythm of being a successful artist. He was also finding out how much they earned. It seemed like a lot. Darling was producing a record with Lisa Kindred, and Don ended up playing guitar and singing background vocal. It was McLean's first time in a recording studio. "It was tremendous to see what it was like; to see how it all worked." The album, *I Like It This Way*, was released in 1965 by Vanguard Records.

Though McLean had gained a lot from Darling, their friendship was not destined to last. Darling had formed the Rooftop Singers with Bill Svanoe and Lynne Taylor. Now he had ideas about creating a new group. According to McLean, he wanted the group to wear masks and be completely mysterious. "It was a sort of fantasy of his, the mysterious, gun-slinging, guitar player who blows away the audience and rides off."

Today McLean remembers:

"Erik is a genuine philosopher and perfectionist. I learned a lot from Erik about vocal and instrumental clarity. I have always tried to make my guitar and 5 string banjo ring out with clarity. I also worked on perfecting and clearing up my voice so that it hit the notes squarely. In the beginning of my singing career my voice would waver and I had trouble controlling the vibrato and the pitch. I also worked on building the tone and "width" of my voice, since it was not big to begin with. My voice would not be thought of as big today, although it is much more powerful than it was. In addition, I learned the value of lots of practice. The more you practice, the more things become second nature and muscle memory takes over and you are able to move on to more complicated things. When a performer makes things look effortless, you can be sure that a great deal of effort went into it. I thank Erik and the other Weavers for helping me learn the deeper secrets of the music and performance craft.

Erik is still very creative. I was pleased to catch up with him recently and be able to tell him how much I appreciated the time he spent with me so long ago. Undivided mental attention to every aspect of music making and performing is a hallmark of Erik's work, and I believe some of that rubbed off on me."

In 1965 McLean decided to go back to school, at Iona College in New Rochelle, for a degree in business administration (B.B.A.) Academic work and study became important to him, and he was often on the dean's list. However, he wouldn't let college interfere with his performing. He had just signed a contract to work at Caffé Lena in Saratoga Springs on the weekends, thus starting a life-long friendship with Lena Spencer. About college McLean says:

The three and half years spent at Iona College were very good for me. My mother and I grew closer. We began to laugh again, and we fought too. My mother was a fighter, but she was very compassionate. I never remember her being less than supportive, even though most of her family and friends thought I was some kind of silly young man without any solid prospects for the future.

That was the attitude of my girlfriend's parents, too. Her name was Nancy Renneau. Her parents were Irish and German, and her real name was spelled Reno, but her father, I guess, thought folks might think they were Italian, so he changed the spelling to Renneau. Mr. Renneau did not approve of me. I can appreciate why he felt the way he did, since he wanted more for his little girl than spending time in lousy nightclubs and crummy hotels. She didn't care. She liked me anyway, and we got along very well. I thought she was terrific and the fun we had healed me. I felt like I belonged. When I got into the Columbia University Graduate School of Business, she and her folks thought they had me roped into a real job in the city someday. They didn't know me.

As I got closer to graduation, I changed girlfriends and headed up the Hudson River to begin my odyssey with Pete Seeger and the Husdon River Sloop. My music took me to every stop along the Hudson River, to Washington D.C. for the anti-war rally, to basement concerts where the building was crawling with FBI agents, and to the Newport Folk Festival, as a man landed on the moon. Everything that I knew I was destined for was beginning to unfold, and I could feel that I was exactly where I was supposed to be.

McLean had developed into a handsome, charismatic, young man, and he was attracting beautiful women. He was earning enough money to pay the rent and give his mother some spending money, as well. He was able to put himself through college and move his mother back into their house at 15 Mulberry Lane. He was happy, he was relaxed. He saw the Beatles at Shea Stadium and the Rolling Stones at the Brooklyn Academy of Music. "Satisfaction" was No.1 at the time. This is still his favorite rock 'n' roll song. He says, "We don't rock 'n' roll much any more. We just rock. I read where Dylan said that the roll has gone out of today's music. There doesn't seem to be the syncopation there used to be. Now it's balls to the wall and guitars in the face. And that has morphed into rap which has no melody. Bring back the roll. Let the good times roll."

In 1966, Charles Close got McLean a summer job at the Music Inn in Lennox, Massachusetts. The Music Inn was an old estate that had been converted into a resort. A striped tent, like a circus tent, that held 500 people, stood on the grounds. Also on the grounds, an old greenhouse, originally used to grow perennials so that the owners could have cut flowers all year round, had been converted into a club called the Potting Shed. The Music Inn was owned by Donald Sauviero, who also owned the Shaw Booking Agency, which handled stars like Ray Charles. Sauviero's wife, Louise, was beautiful and vivacious. She ran the Shed and did the cooking. The cuisine was always excellent. Sometimes Don helped her prepare the pasta.

McLean worked the Potting Shed, two shows a night, for six weeks. Sometimes he performed solo, other times he worked on the bill with a jazz trio or blues legends Brownie McGhee and Sonny Terry. Don lived with Brownie and Sonny in a converted chicken coop for that summer. Brownie and Sonny were together so long they bitched like a married couple over how they had screwed up the night before, or how they wouldn't get hired anymore if they didn't quit drinking. But they were amazing musicians and were always in demand, drunk or sober.

Sonny was swollen all over with arthritis and usually stayed in bed all day. Finally, McLean told him that if he didn't start moving, he wouldn't be able to. Don told him to take aspirin four times a day and walk. McLean got his point across, and before long Sonny was strolling and tapping his cane, all around the grounds. As he felt better, he and Don became good friends. That summer, Sonny met a high school teacher, and they later married. She gave Sonny the best years of his life.

Brownie wrote songs from time to time, and he would sit in the summer sun in front of their humble dwelling and moan and scat the blues with a partial lyric here and there. Brownie played a D-18 Martin guitar that had been given to him by Andy Griffith, after they appeared together in the movie called *A Face in the Crowd*.

On the weekends, the tent featured big-names such as Thelonias Monk, Dave Brubeck, Carlos Montoya, the Modern Jazz Quartet, Josh White, the Buddy Rich Orchestra and Fats Domino. The tent was popular with a young singles audience, who frequently stayed the night at the resort and kids who came from summer camps by the busloads.

Nancy Renneau and her father came to pick Don up after visiting her younger brother at camp in the Berkshires. On the way home there was thick fog on the Taconic Parkway. Nancy was driving, and the station wagon went into a spin and rolled down an embankment. Nancy was taken to the hospital needing plastic surgery, and her father was taken to the emergency room with a broken back. Don crawled out through the windshield with four broken ribs. A week later he was back on stage at the Potting Shed, his chest bandaged.

During this summer at the Music Inn, McLean met Carly Simon. She was a counselor at a music camp for gifted children who wanted to become symphony musicians. The camp was run by bass player Chuck Israels, and Don was pleased to accept an invitation to play a few songs for the kids at the camp. He sang some of his own songs that he had been writing, including several that would end up on his first album, *Tapestry*. Carly Simon often visited the Music Inn to see a show, and she became friends with Don.

McLean met many musicians at the Potting Shed. Jazz trios were popular, and Ken Ascher, a piano player from one of the trios, became a good friend. At the time, Kenny was a struggling musician, taking work wherever he could find it. In the 1970s he would win an Oscar for a song he composed with Paul Williams, called "Evergreen." Barbra Streisand sang it in the film *A Star Is Born*. But during the summer of 1966 Don and Kenny would wander over to the piano on the stage under the tent, and Don would sing the standards he'd learned on his late night walks in New Rochelle. "Only Kenny knew all the right chord changes." They spent hours doing this. Don loved the old songs from the 1930s and '40s, and in the 1980s he recorded an album of old standards called *For the Memories*. "And I Love You So," "Empty Chairs," and "Vincent" trace their style back to the old fashioned pop music.

In 1967, McLean worked several weeks at the Main Point with Janis Ian who had a big hit with "Society's Child." One evening, Jim Croce appeared in the audience. It was the first time Don had seen him since leaving Villanova in 1964. Jim invited Don and his girlfriend to visit his home in Media, Pennsylvania. Jim was at a crossroads at this time, and

McLean remembers that "people thought of Jim Croce as this sort of truck driving hipster with a cigar, but he was really the straightest guy I ever knew. He always wore a blazer in college, and on the cover of his album with his wife, Ingrid, he's wearing a white suit."

In 1967, Lena Spencer invited him to perform at a high school in Saratoga as part of a fund raising event for Caffé Lena. Don planned to sing four or five songs, but as he was busy preparing backstage, he noticed Bob Dylan, wearing a big hat and granny glasses, sitting quietly in the corner. "There was the man himself. I wondered what he would think of my songs."

McLean sang a bunch of new songs including, "Sure to Be Love," "Aftermath," "I Want Her," and one or two others that ended up on the *Tapestry* album. Bill Spence, who owns Front Hall Records, recorded the performance, and the tape still exists.

At the party after the show, Dylan told Don that "The Circus Song" was a very inspiring song, one of the most inspiring songs he'd ever heard. He asked, "How many verses were you sick for?" This was praise from Caesar. It was a magic night and led him to include "The Circus Song" on *Tapestry*, his first album.

The Circus Song

> Cotton candy, two for a quarter
> See if the fat man can guess your weight
> A big stuffed tiger is what I bought her
> And I'm going home 'cause it's late

Roller coasters make me dizzy
And cotton candy makes me sick
I wish I had some Bromo fizzy
Now that would do the trick

Everyone knows that the clowns aren't happy
And everyone knows that the people don't care
I wish I could laugh at the way that they're acting
But I'm so sick, I just don't dare to

High wire dancers kick and balance
White silk horses step in time
The tattooed man displays his talents
I'm not the talented kind

I always go to the circus on Sunday
And there I can laugh at the people I see
But when I leave home in the morning on Monday
Everybody laughs at me

I make other people nervous
I guess that's why they laugh at me
But to me my life is a three-ring circus
And I can see it for free

Have you seen my wife Elvira?
She can tame a lion, you know
Well, I once had a bushy mane
But that was so damn long ago

Tight-collared clowns in plastic buildings
Have happy families as their fate
Happy jobs and happy clubs
And happy people they hate

Everyone's juggling and everyone's acting
With smiles of grease paint three feet wide
Everyone's caught on a carousel pony
And one time around is a lifetime ride

McLean performed often during his college days. At one point he became hoarse and went to an ear nose and throat doctor. The doctor told him he was developing a node on one of his vocal chords and he must not talk or sing for one month. Don did as he was told, and his voice came back, as good as new. His singing and playing were getting better and better. He was more confident on stage. He was making demo tapes, auditioning, writing songs and trying to find a record company. He had signed an agency deal with the William Morris Agency in New York, the biggest booking agency in the world. The many agents of the William Morris Agency specialized in a variety of talents, booking clients into all kinds of music venues: nightclubs, concert halls, TV shows, TV specials, movies, theater; they even represented authors and publishers.

Don's manager was now Herb Gart. Gart managed Buffy St. Marie and another American Indian named Patrick Sky. Patrick Sky was born on the same day as Don, and they became good friends. Gart also managed a group named the Youngbloods who had recorded the No.1 single "Get Together." By 1969, Don got more and more bookings, and had to work as hard as he could to keep up. He toured on the road with Blood, Sweat and Tears, Ten Wheel Drive, the James Gang, Laura Nyro, Steppenwolf, and Sly and the Family Stone, and many others. The *Tapestry* album was begun at this time, as well.

McLean's favorite singer and guitarist of all was Josh White. White had an electricity and charisma unlike any other performer. He began his musical career as the lead boy to Blind Boy Arnold and other blues singers in the South in the 1920s. Although these singers guarded their guitar tricks selfishly, Josh began to pick up more and more. He had started playing at the age of 6 and had a head start on his contemporaries. According to Brownie McGhee, Josh couldn't understand why everyone liked Leadbelly. "Josh thought Leadbelly was a handkerchief-head."

In the 1930s Josh was an influential and popular blues star. By the 1940s his audience had widened, and he was regularly performing alongside jazz singers, like Billie Holiday, in top New York venues. Josh was so popular that Pete Seeger called him "Mr Folk Music." His recording of "One Meat Ball" was a smash, and he became one of the few black figures to star on Broadway and appear in Hollywood films. In the 1950s he conquered Europe, becoming a major star in England. His life story is told in Elijah Wald's definitive biography, *Society Blues.*

You couldn't start much farther down than Josh did, and you couldn't get much farther up than he did. Sadly, Josh saw his achievements and status collapse during the McCarthy era. In testimony, he dismissed his leftist background by declaring that he had been a "sucker for the Communists," while maintaining his outspoken stance on civil rights.

Josh White

Because of the blacklist, Josh left America and moved to Europe. He was more comfortable in England and Scandinavia where there was less of a color barrier than back home. He was free to perform for all audiences since most Europeans were unaware of the controversy back home. Josh was angry with America. It would take him nearly a decade to re-establish his position at the top in America.

By 1963, at the height of the folk music revival, Josh was one of the three most popular folk singers in America, alongside Pete Seeger and Harry Belafonte. He was a featured performer at Martin Luther King's March on Washington. He sang at the White House for FDR and JFK. But there were still hard feelings about his testimony during the McCarthy hearings. In the late 1960s when Don first met Pete Seeger, Seeger didn't want to hear anything about Josh White.

In the spring of 1968, Don graduated from Iona College with a bachelor's degree in Business Administration. He passed the graduate entrance exam and was admitted to the prestigious Columbia University Business School in New York. But he turned it down and headed to Washington D.C. where Josh was singing at a club called the Cellar Door.

Once, years before, in his office, Charles Close had shown Don Josh White's guitar. Josh played a pearl 00-42 Martin guitar. The guitar, made in the late 1930s or early 1940s, would be worth more than $50,000 today. Josh could probably have used the money. He often had to pawn his guitars. He stretched himself to the limits of his abnormal energy, driving his Lincoln at top-speed from club to concert on his itinerant odyssey. Women loved him. Weeks before he was scheduled to appear, they would start phoning the nightclubs. He was known for his prodigious sexual energy. It permeated his music. It was the defining characteristic of his persona.

Ed Murphy, Pete's brother, managed to get Don an audition to be Josh's opening act at the Cellar Door. McLean got the job, and they played together for nine shows. Sometimes Josh had pain shooting down his arm and had to go to the hospital. Then he would feel better and swagger in like his old self. He died on the operating table during open heart surgery, later that year. Before the operation, Josh asked for his guitar and sang "Goin' Down Slow."

At the close of one of their shows, Josh told the crowd, "This boy is going to carry my music on. I think he's great." They closed the show with "The Midnight Special."

In the 1980s McLean suggested that Harry Belafonte make a documentary film about Josh. But Belafonte rejected Don's idea, because too many of his friends had been hurt by Josh's testimony. But at the end of the conversation, Belafonte said, "By the way, Don, Josh was the best."

Don receives honorary doctorate, Iona College, May 2001.

Chapter 3: Tapestry...The Hudson River Troubadour

The word *troubadour* comes from the 12th and 13th centuries and refers to the lyric poets who roamed between the courts of southern France and northern Italy, singing songs they had composed in complex metric forms, songs that were musical commentaries on the times. The "Hudson River Troubadour Project" was a major landmark in McLean's early development as a singer and performer. In 1968 the New York State Council on the Arts decided to engage a musician to walk the entire length of the Hudson River, singing three concerts in three river towns each day, over a period of about six weeks. The arts council wanted to provide summer entertainment for local families and kids. They envisioned a troubadour, dressed as jester, an all-around singer and entertainer. McLean had recently graduated from Iona College and was a regular singer at Caffé Lena in Saratoga Springs. The State Council on the Arts approached the club's owner, Lena Spencer, and asked her to recommend a performer to serve as the Hudson River Troubadour, and Lena suggested Don.

It seemed like a great opportunity, not much like work. Don was immediately interested, but one thing was certain: there was no way he would dress like a clown. When the council sent him a costume, he threw it in the incinerator. He had a clear idea of who he was and what he would or would not do. That had not changed since he was fifteen. But, with zero dollars in his bank account, McLean needed the job. He accepted without delay, and when he met with the arts people he told them what he had done with their costume and announced that he would turn the project into something more educational. In each town he would sing and talk about pollution and the environment and the history of the Hudson River. He set about learning as much as he could about the Hudson River, getting books from the library in Cooperstown, N. Y., and talking to a lot of interesting people. The arts council got more than a New York State Ronald McDonald.

To begin his trek, McLean was flown to Mount Marcy where the Hudson River rises from Lake Tear of the Clouds. As soon as he arrived, he headed for the general store with a guitar and a banjo. The locals were noticeably quiet. McLean says, "At that time, country folks, no matter where they were in America, were uniformly opposed to long-haired, guitar-playing kids." Don took out his instruments and began singing. He soon had his small, stiff audience singing along with him. Then he spread the word that he would be giving a show at the local beach. This became his standard procedure in every town he visited. The state took out ads in the local newspapers, giving his schedule, and McLean did occasional radio spots. He gave three performances a day, in three different towns. He sang in every town along the river, from Mt. Marcy to Riverside Park in New York City.

Don loved the singing, but he endured a sketchy relationship with the arts council reps. They were unhappy when he refused to sing if no one was there. He told them, "I don't mind a small crowd, but I won't sing to nobody." Because he wouldn't take orders, the council decided to bring in a new singer to replace him. The new recruit arrived as Don was singing to a group of drunken poker players. He and Don sang some blues together, but the guy quit when he realized what the job entailed. He said that no singer in his right mind would do that job, after all, someone had been killed in that same park the previous day. By the time McLean reached Newburgh, toward the end of the summer, council members had to admit that what he was doing was working well.

The Troubadour project was a great success. It gave McLean excellent publicity. CBS did a piece on the "Hudson River Troubadour" for the evening news, and local papers in every town along the Hudson River, including New York City, had front-page articles about his appearances. Even the *Wall Street Journal* mentioned him on page one.

The project enabled McLean to avoid Vietnam for a year, and he was eager to skip that experience, altogether. He discovered that if he took a "cultural trip" the summer following graduation, he would qualify for an automatic deferment until the fall. This may have been why a large number of Americans went to Europe to soak up some culture immediately after graduation. While he was the Hudson River Troubadour, McLean received a lot of draft notices. Then, all of sudden, a light went on in his head. He thought, "Well, my God, I'm a one man cultural tour." He called, his contact with the New York State Council on the Arts, and said, "These guys are going to draft me. Why don't you ask John Hightower [head of the New York State Council on the Arts] to see if he can get me a deferment?" And sure enough, they did.

McLean had no interest in killing or in being killed, and that critical summer gave him time to think about ways to avoid the situation. He hoped that his asthma and the fact that he was the sole support of his mother would help. On August 12th, 1970, he went for his Army physical. He had all the paperwork necessary to prove that what looked like a perfect male specimen was, in reality, a broken-down shell of a man. The experience reminded him of some kind of cattle auction or slave sale. The draftees were given a choice of lines to stand in with their paperwork. McLean instinctively chose the line with a young doctor. When the doctor looked at his paperwork, he said, "You've claimed quite a few things here. Can you prove any of it?" Don provided the letter from his doctor about his asthma, to which the doctor replied, "OK, you're out." He was out! Those were the most beautiful words he had ever heard. He still hears them, from time to time. When he boarded the bus for home, he noticed that he was the only guy on the bus.

Later that year McLean was singing at an anti-war rally, and as he concluded his show and walked among the crowd, he recognized the doctor who gave him the deferment, with his baby on his back. Don said, "I know you!" The doctor looked him in the eye and said, "No, you don't."

Spending the summer of 1968 along the Hudson River convinced McLean that the Hudson River Valley was where he wanted to live. He began looking for a house and finally found a gatehouse in Cold Spring, New York, just north of Westchester County, available for $100 a month. European colonial settlers and their descendants had populated the Hudson River Valley in the 18th century. The valley became a center of considerable wealth, as many of the aristocratic landholders were descended from the Dutch and British gentry who had been granted manorial charters. They spent considerable money on architects and landscape designers to help them realize the country estates of their dreams, and by the mid 19th century the valley was the center of American Gothic Revival architecture. The magnificent Hudson River Valley, with castles overlooking the river and dramatic Gothic architecture, had become "America's Rhine River Valley." Cold Spring is listed on the National Register of Historic Places and is one of the best-preserved 19th century Gothic townscapes in the Hudson River region.

Cold Spring was a sleepy, conservative, right wing settlement, an unusual location for a budding music star to settle, but it was the area that Don loved. The wide open space, the fresh air, the hills, the castles, and the gatehouse on one of the valley's most beautiful 19th century estates intoxicated him. It was a major change. The gatehouse in Cold Spring was McLean's first home, after he left the apartment he shared with his mother in Larchmont. His sister had come home with her infant son, which made that two-room apartment unbearable.

The gatehouse was a Victorian Gothic cottage, with gingerbread trim, located at the end of a long, private road. It had served as the caretaker's home for the surrounding large estate. The estate, owned by Jim Benenson and his wife Sharon, contained seven acres, including a beautiful apple orchard, set in a large, natural, stone canyon extending down the eastern bank of the Hudson River. The caretaker's house had four rooms and some land, but it was a mess. Don refurbished the property, sanding the floors and painting the walls and trim, until it shone like a jewel.

Jim Benenson was a Wall Street investment banker with an engineering degree from MIT and a masters degree in English literature from Yale. He took a liking to his hippy tenant, and they became friends. Jim was a brilliant businessman and helped Don apply some of what he had learned in college to his own business affairs. After McLean achieved commercial success, he was fortunate to have Jim to advise him. Jim even served as his business manager for several years, and Sharon did his books.

The Benenson Gate House, circa 1969
Cold Spring, NY.

McLean also became friends with Jim's mother, Mamie, who lived in the main house. Sometimes she would cook breakfast for him and they would go "junkin," poking around antique shops. During those excursions Mamie taught him many things about antiques, what was good and what was not good. Jim gave him books to read on the subject, and sometimes they would all go hunting for treasures. Jim Benenson reminded Don of the Great Gatsby, because he lived with a Gilded-Age sense of style. McLean admired Jim's refined taste. The Hudson River castles floated like they were in the air on mountain ridges.

Castles in the Air

And if she asks you why
you can tell her that I told you that I'm tired
of castles in the air, I've got a dream
I want the world to share and castle walls
just lead me to despair.

Hills of forest green
where the mountains touch the sky a dream come true
I'll live there till I die, I'm asking you
to say my last goodbye, the love we knew
ain't worth another try.

Save me from all the trouble and the pain
I know I'm weak but I can't face that girl again
Tell her the reasons why I can't remain
Perhaps she'll understand, if you tell it to her plain

But how can words express
the feel of sunlight in the morning in the hills,
away from city strife, I need a
country woman for my wife, I'm city born,
but I love the country life.

For I can not be part
of her cocktail generation, partners waltz
Devoid of all romance the music plays
and everyone must dance I'm bowing out
I need a second chance.

Save me from all the trouble and the pain

I know I'm weak but I can't face that girl again
Tell her the reasons why I can't remain
Perhaps she'll understand, if you tell it to her plain

And if she asks you why
you can tell her that I told you that I'm tired
of castles in the air, I've got a dream
I want the world to share and castle walls
just lead me to despair.

In the years that McLean lived in the gatehouse (1968-1972) he wrote some of his most famous songs, including songs on the *Tapestry* and *American Pie* albums, and part of "American Pie" itself. There were also some unhappy times.

But, in general, 1968-1969 was extremely busy. Besides the Troubadour project there was a hectic schedule of concerts booked by the William Morris Agency. It was at this time that he met Pete Seeger. Seeger was promoting a project to build and launch a boat that would sail along the Hudson River, and, at every port of call, its crew would disseminate information about the environment and the perilous state of the Hudson River. McLean says: "This boat is an example of the Seeger genius because it combines the fun of boating with the seriousness of environmental degradation and gets everyone involved at the same time while also being a public relations dream."

The Hudson River Sloop Clearwater Organization was founded in 1966, with the aim of defending and restoring the environmental quality of the Hudson River. By the mid-1960s, the 315 miles of river, extending from its source in the Adirondacks to the New York Harbor, was suffering from the careless development of energy resources and industrialization which caused pollution, especially down river at New York Harbor. Coal burning power plants emitted a lethal cocktail of substances including sulphur and nitrogen oxides and potential carcinogens such as cadmium and arsenic. Heavy industry was discharging a range of unsavory substances, including PCBs, into the waterway.

At the Gate House, Cold Spring, 1969

At the beginning of the 20th century the valley glistened in near pristine condition, and Dutch-style sloops were a common sight, cruising the river. The Clearwater organization hoped to restore the river to its former glory by promoting legislation to prevent pollution and encourage management policies that would sustain the environment of the valley. What better way to launch the campaign than aboard a traditional Dutch sloop? Seeger asked McLean to join him, to be a member of the first crew of Sloop Singers, and to help raise money for the project.

In February 1969, the Sloop Singers went on a short tour of several cities from Maine to Massachusetts, to announce the existence of the boat and to test the musical concept of the Sloop Singers. The shows were reminiscent of the Almanac Singers. Seven or eight singers sat in chairs in a row, with two or three microphones covering the line of chairs. The seven or eight Sloop Singers rose and sang an opening sea shanty or two in harmony, with different singers leading on different shanties. After the opening shanties, the Sloop Singers sang an acappella version of "Lord Nelson,"an old English shanty:

Lord Nelson

Come all ye bold seamen
Wherever you're bound
And always let Nelson's
Proud memory go 'round
And prey that the wars
And the tumult may cease
For the greatest of gifts
Is a sweet lasting peace.
May the Lord put an end
To these cruel old wars

>And bring peace and contentment
>To all our brave tars

The singers took their seats, and Pete Seeger acted as a master of ceremonies, talking about one thing or another and playing a song. He then asked one of the singers a question, using this as a theatrical device to allow that person to respond with a song. As time went on, the group worked out special parts for certain songs. In the tradition of the Almanac Singers, the group was rehearsing in front of the audience. McLean has retained an element of this stagecraft in his performances ever since.

The Clearwater Sloop, with its crew of sailors and singers, was launched from the Harvey Gamage Shipyard in South Bristol, Maine, in May, 1969. The sloop sailed along the Atlantic seaboard and up through Sheep's Head Bay, docking at over twenty coastal destinations. It entered the mouth of the Hudson River at New York City, in time to join hundreds of other Tall Ships in a special festival. At each port, the Sloop Singers were transported to a local concert hall or outdoor venue to perform a mix of traditional music, ecology and anti-war music, novelties, ditties, lullabies, old rock 'n' roll tunes, and new songs. Many of the new songs were written by Don McLean. Each concert ended, as it had begun, with several rousing sea shanties to which the audience sang along, and finally, a cathartic "This Land is Your Land."

Rather than staying in a hotel, the Sloop Singers would head back to their floating home. Weeks passed like this, and the togetherness, the creative energy, and the endless learning changed everyone. McLean spent the summer of 1969 being bombarded with ideas by interesting people who knew so much music that he did a lot of growing that summer. He also became friends with artist Thomas Allen on this tour. Allen's sketches appeared in a book about the first Clearwater crew that Don edited in the seventies.

The Sloop Singers, summer 1969

Pete Seeger, Don McLean, Gordon Bok, Alan Aunupu, Frederick Douglas Kirkpatrick

On June 7, 1969, Don McLean married Carol Sauvion in Germantown, Pennsylvania. He was 24, and she was 23. Two weeks before the wedding, her brother was killed in an automobile accident in Wisconsin. He had been the first child in the family to graduate from college. It would have been better if the wedding had been called off, but it went ahead in a strange environment of grief, joy, apprehension, and confusion. Everything from that moment on was off balance.

Don and Carol rejoined the Sloop on its voyage from Maine to New York City, just as it stopped at the Newport Folk Festival. The festival was a dream come true for McLean, and his lack of interest in anything besides the music annoyed his bride. Prior to the marriage they had been great friends, and her appreciation of his music was keen. But now, to make matters worse, Don's guitar was stolen. When Carol said he could get another one, he blurted out, "I loved that guitar more than I love you." Hot summer days and cold hearts don't make for great memories. Johnny Cash said he divorced his first wife because she hated the music business, and if she hated the music business, that meant she hated him.

Even so, the highlight of the trip was when the Clearwater Sloop docked in Newport, Rhode Island, as part of the last Newport Folk Festival. The program included the Everly Brothers, their father Ike Everly, Johnny Cash, Muddy Waters, Joni Mitchell, Merle Travis and, making their debut performances: James Taylor and Van Morrison. If this wasn't enough for one weekend, Neil Armstrong and Buzz Aldrin landed on the moon. There was palpable creative energy in the air. Everyone was in a heightened state of creative exhilaration.

When not performing or watching someone else perform, there was a lot of hanging around, talking and making music. Artists wrote about everything that was happening, including the historic moon landing, and new music was being performed on stage each night. McLean sang some of his new compositions, including "Orphans of Wealth" and "Castles in the Air," written in 1968, and "Color TV Blues" which he had written in college. He was well received, with many rapturous ovations. Woody Guthrie's widow, Marjorie, was in the audience, and after the show she threw her arms around him and kissed him and told him she loved his music. The kid from New Rochelle was in the very spot he had dreamed of.

During the festival, McLean had a chat with the Everly Brothers, and conversation soon turned to one of his favorite subjects, Buddy Holly. Phil Everly said, "You know, Buddy died because he had to do his laundry." It was the first time he had heard this, and the casual way Phil said it suddenly changed the Buddy Holly story in Don's mind. He asked, "What do you mean?" Phil answered, "Well, Buddy took the plane so he could go ahead and do his laundry before the tour bus got to their next stop." This was the beginning of McLean's emotional and intellectual return to Buddy Holly.

One of the last stops of the Clearwater Sloop was at Nyack, New York. During the summer of 1969, PBS television had produced a series of concerts called "Sounds of Summer," and the final show was to be the Sloop Singers at Nyack. Called "The Sloop at Nyack," the show was recorded on the Hudson River landing. During the rehearsal, Pete Seeger's wife, Toshi, told Don that they didn't want him to sing "Color TV Blues" for the show. He couldn't believe it. Here was a woman who complained constantly about censorship telling him to censor himself! The song includes a reference to the Pope that is really the incorporation of a silly Catholic high school joke. The joke goes: "What's the Pope's phone number?" Answer: "Et cum spiri tu tuo," which comes from the Latin mass and means, "and with your spirit."

> Did you read the encyclical written by the Pope sayin' folks
> With private property got no hope

The rich ain't welcome in the heavenly palladium but the
Knights of Columbus own Yankee Stadium
Now I ain't sayin' that the Pope was wrong but he can easily
Afford to sing that song
And if you'd like to call him up when you need some dough
His number's et cum spiri tu tuo.

"Toshi is one of the hardest working people I ever knew and I learned a lot about the healing benefits of work. I guess she thought my song was offensive."

That night in Nyack, McLean sang "Color TV Blues." When he got to the lyric about the Pope, a bolt of lightning flashed across the sky. As he continued the verse, thunder crashed, loud and continuously, provoking gales of laughter. By the end of the song, rain was pouring down, and the show finished with a soggy, but spirited, "This Land is Your Land."

After the show, the crowd was hysterical. The production crew was elated, because they had captured it all on film. The program was broadcast nationally a few weeks later. Don received mail from all across the United States. Offers came in for appearances at nightclubs and concerts everywhere with him as headliner. This began McLean's association with Public Broadcasting which frequently found him performing on the Great American Dream Machine and the early Sesame Street. It was one of the many odd phenomena that have shaped his career.

The Clearwater Sloop's activities acquired national media attention. The interest surrounding the old fashioned sailing ship and the group's unique musical presentation caused crowds to grow larger with each docking. Their appearance at the Commons in Boston attracted an audience of over 20,000. However, a warm welcome was not always guaranteed. When the Clearwater Sloop sailed up the Hudson the following summer and made a stop in Cold Spring, New York, it was met by an angry mob that didn't want any "God-damned, long-haired hippies and commies" in their town.

With Pete Seeger at Nyack, 1969.

McLean's work along the Hudson River in 1968 and his experiences with the Clearwater Sloop in 1969 proved an inspirational learning experience for him. He was constantly learning and teaching about environmental degradation and the problems facing the Hudson River Valley. He is particularly proud of a song that he wrote aboard the Clearwater Sloop, called "Tapestry." Its powerful lyrics are as relevant today as when he first wrote them. They provide a powerful warning of the consequences of humanity's exploitation of the environment. *"If man is allowed to destroy all they need. He will soon have to pay with his life, for his greed."* Despite its powerful message, it has remained one of Don' lesser known compositions. It is overshadowed on the *Tapestry* album by the giants, "Castles in the Air" and "And I Love You So." It is remarkable that Don McLean does not see himself, despite all he did from 1968 to 1975, as an environmental activist. He has avoided becoming a spokesperson for the environmental movement. He says, "Political people bore me, and I don't want to be one. I'll settle for being a decent citizen."

Tapestry

Every thread of creation is held in position
by still other strands of things living,
In an earthly tapestry hung from the skyline
of smoldering cities so gray and so vulgar,
as not to be satisfied with their own negativity
but needing to touch all the living as well.

Every breeze that blows kindly is one crystal breath
we exhale on the blue diamond heaven,
As gentle to touch as the hands of the healer,
As soft as farewells whispered over the coffin.
We're poisoned by venom with each breath we take,
from the brown sulfur chimney and the black highway snake.

Every dawn that breaks golden is held in suspension
like the yoke of the egg in albumen,
Where the birth and the death of unseen generations
are interdependent in vast orchestration
and painted in colors of tapestry thread,
When the dying are born and the living are dead.

Every pulse of your heartbeat is one liquid moment
and flows through the veins of your being,
Like a river of life flowing on since creation,

Approaching the sea with each new generation.
You're now just a stagnant and rancid disgrace
that is rapidly drowning the whole human race.

Every fish that swims silent, every bid that flies freely,
every doe that steps softly,
Every crisp leaf that falls, all the flowers that grow
on this colorful tapestry, somehow they know
That if man is allowed to destroy all they need,
He will soon have to pay with his life, for his greed.

After the first Clearwater Sloop voyage in 1969, McLean left the crew. Before he left Pete Seeger told him, "Don, I think you're a genius. You're like a wonderful chef who serves a great meal once and never repeats it." Don returned from time to time to perform at Sloop concerts. He also recorded a version of "Tapestry" for the 1974 *Clearwater* album and edited a book entitled *Songs and Sketches of the First Clearwater Crew*, with sketches by his friend Thomas Allen.

Chapter 4: Magdalene Lane...First Record Deal

McLean wrote a number of powerful, new songs, besides "Tapestry," during 1968 and 1969, including "Respectable," "Orphans of Wealth," and "General Store." He wanted to replace some of his original material like "Milkman's Matinee" and Bessie Smith's "Good Old Wagon" with stronger material. (These two recordings were released in 1992 on the *Favorites and Rarities* album). The introduction of the new songs not only gave the album a title, but made it into a powerful record, "the kind of thing that I wanted to write."

During 1968 and 1969, Don attended many recording sessions at the Sierra Sound Laboratories in "occupied" Berkeley. Student protests against the war in Viet Nam were a fact of life in California from 1964 to 1974. By 1967, demonstrations were getting more violent and police routinely used Chemical Mace to control the crowds. In mid-May 1969, matters came to a head when Governor Ronald Reagan called in 2,000 National Guard troops to confront 30,000 students and demonstrators who had assembled to protest against the development of a plot of land called the "Peoples' Park."

The recording studio was located in the midst of the unrest, so session musicians could blame their bleary, red eyes on the tear gas, rather than the excesses of the night before. Recording the album was not an enjoyable experience. At the same time, McLean was negotiating with record companies in a never-ending search for a record deal. A sense of nervousness pervades the music on the *Tapestry* album, a sound that became a feature of the early albums. Don likens his early sound to that of a hummingbird or a butterfly. "It was difficult for me to get over being excited, anxious, terrified and thrilled after all the years of thinking and dreaming and working toward this goal."

Herb Gart had asked Jerry Corbitt to produce McLean's first record. Corbitt played bass and rock 'n' roll guitar and had founded the Youngbloods with Jesse Colin Young. Gart had managed the Youngbloods, and Corbitt wanted to produce. Corbitt, provided support and experience and insisted that Don stay with him and his wife at their house in the hills above Point Reyes in Marin County. Corbitt admired McLean's talent. He said, "He has an enchanted way of having us see things through his eyes in a way we have never seen before. His understanding of the human heart is a gift that has produced some of the most deeply moving compositions of our times. Don is right up there with Dylan as a poet, and he is in league with the best as a tunesmith."

McLean and Corbitt assembled an eclectic crew of musicians. Pete Childs, who played bass on the album, was a "New Wave" musician with folk roots. He wrote liner notes for the album that both provided an accurate reflection of Don McLean's developing musical qualities and identified the album's potential importance in a wider context. In the liner notes of 1970 Childs said:

> "I think we are all aware that something pretty big is going on in the world, but we certainly aren't sure what it is. I believe that it's for everyone, and that in order for us to get it together, we're going to have to pick up on a lot of things (many of which we don't really want to hear.) This is where the artist has his

function. Perhaps never before has the artist enjoyed a position of so much influence and responsibility, with mass communication in its present, highly-developed state. I see a growing number of young artists understanding and expressing the things that need to be said, and it fills me with hope. Surely Don is one of these people. I can't imagine anyone listening closely to his songs and failing to come away the better for it. If we are going to save ourselves from the desperate situation into which our ignorance leads us, it will be through the work of people like this. Press on!"

McLean says, "Working with such people on the *Tapestry* album gave me confidence. I think it helped me realize that what I had in mind, and what I was doing, was bigger than I thought it was. Jerry and Pete made me realize that I would touch people that I never thought would be interested. I was even surprised that Jerry liked a song like 'And I Love You So.'"

Even though the recording of the album was proceeding, Don did not have a record deal at this point. Polydor had indicated interest in a deal, but then pulled out. Pete Seeger did his best to help, by writing letters of recommendation to several record companies. He took McLean to New York to meet John Hammond, a senior executive at Columbia Records. Don's music failed to impress Hammond, and after the great success of "American Pie," Hammond said, "I'm sorry we passed on him. It's a brand new ball game."

McLean had been rejected by over 30 record companies, when Alan Livingston's Mediarts Records finally offered him a deal. The deal actually came about by accident, since Don had contacted Mediarts about a completely separate project.

During 1969, Bob Elfstrom, a filmmaker from Ridgefield, Connecticut, was making a movie about Pete Seeger called *A Song and a Stone*. Elfstrom followed Seeger around, filming him at rallies and concerts. Since Don was close to Seeger at this time, he was frequently present. At a party hosted by the Seegers, McLean sang the "Circus Song," and Elfstrom filmed his performance for the movie. The performance so impressed Elfstrom that he said he would like to make a feature film about Don. He would call it *Till Tomorrow*. This development was quite something, considering McLean was still trying to get his first album released.

Elfstrom approached Alan Livingston at Mediarts for funding for the *Till Tomorrow* project. Livingston was a legendary figure in the music industry, having been president and chief executive office of Capitol Records from 1960 until 1968. He had signed such stars as Frank Sinatra, Nat King Cole, the Kingston Trio, the Beach Boys, and the Beatles to the Capitol label. With Bob York, from RCA Records, Livingston was attempting to make Mediarts into a high quality, boutique label. When Elfstrom approached Livingston about the *Till Tomorrow* film, he also sent a tape of more than forty of Don's songs. Livingston was not interested in supporting the film, but on hearing the tape, he was anxious to sign McLean to the Mediarts label.

Livingston offered McLean a contract that ended his long struggle to secure that first record deal. Mediarts cleared up Don's $20,000 debt with the studio and gave him a favorable publishing arrangement with Livingston's Mayday Music. McLean had been unhappy with the way management was always pushing him to "do the album and then get the deal." And Don was delighted to be associated with a record producer who had worked with Frank Sinatra.

Thinking of Alan Livingston makes McLean think of Sinatra, and that led him to write these thoughts:

> We all love the career and the life story of Frank Sinatra, the little Italian guy who fights for every scrap of success and dignity he ever gets, who has only one gear — forward. This is the great post-war story and the perfect star. The idea of having Dylanesque angst or doubts of any kind was just too European for America at that time. Most of the performers I grew up watching on TV and enjoying were this sort, and I admire them for it. There is a kind of complete surrender to the public and to the career which transcends divorces, death, kids falling down the stairs, or any other distraction.
>
> There is part of me that is like this, but if it's only part, it don't count. The part of me that is like this is the part that says: "the show must go on." I will do anything to make the gig and so will the guys who work with me. With terror on the rise and bird flu in the skies, most young performers seem willing to blow off whole tours if they have gas pains. Frank wasn't like that. In fact, he once wrote a letter to George Michael telling him to quit complaining about how hard success was and start being real thankful for it. Continuing, Sinatra said there were many times he had to do a show when his throat was killing him, but he knew what it meant to his audience for him to be on stage at show time.
>
> The last time I saw Sinatra, he introduced a song by saying it had been written by Buck Jones and Tom Mix, western heroes who

kept their word. And Frank kept his. That's really what it's all about — keeping your word and being a stand-up guy.

For me, the angst crept in when the lawyers and oily record execs and promoters were crawling all over me. I felt like I needed to take a shower all the time. I knew they were smiling because they were stealing me blind. Frank knew it too, but he just went bankrupt and started over.

Fortunately, this is another time, and angst is allowed, in fact, it's required. So I'm OK. But sometimes I wish that my gears were all forward and life could be more ring-a-ding-ding.

Following the agreement, Mediarts took an active interest in the songs that would appear on the album and those that would make good singles. They added songs McLean had written around the time of the Hudson River Troubadour project, such as: "And I Love You So," "Bad Girl," and "Castles in the Air." Songs, such as "The Wrong Thing To Do" and "I Want Her," were recorded but were not used on this album.

McLean was experimenting with a form of lyric writing, and the album evolved as he wanted. He wrote ten different songs in ten different styles and made them fit together around a general theme. Each song told an American tale, creating characters that allowed the listener to understand the story, but each song also allowed the listener to use his own imagination to see other aspects of the story. He did this in "Magdalene Lane," a song he wrote after a trip to California in 1969, when he attended the auction of MGM film artifacts:

MGM Studios can't make the nut,
They're auctioning Dorothy's shoes.
Gable is gone, the Good Witch is a slut

And I've got the parking lot blues.

"Magdalene Lane" was the beginning of McLean's attempt to do a song like "American Pie." "General Store" is based on a real life incident that happened in Cold Spring, New York. "Three Flights Up" is a song that Don considers to be one of his most ambitious. "It's almost like a French movie, a little bit maudlin and over-done, but I like the concept. It would make a nice video."

Musically, the album is diverse. On "General Store," McLean used only his voice and his guitar. He sang "Magdalene Lane" with a group. "And I Love You So" has a full string orchestra, a mixture of synthesized and real strings, arranged by Edward Bogas. Strings are also used on "Bad Girl," "No Reason for your Dreams," and "Castles in the Air." Don used two Martin guitars on this album, an 00-21 and a D-28. He later used his 00-21 on "Vincent," and his D-28 on "American Pie." He gave his 00-21 Martin guitar to the son of the captain of the Clearwater Sloop, who calls now and then to ask if Don wants it back.

McLean has continued the musical diversity evident on *Tapestry*, because he believes it is the most artistic way to make a record.

> "It allows me to express myself fully, but it is a problem from a commercial standpoint. If a song becomes a hit, and there's only one song like it on a record, it makes it difficult for the record company to create a consistent image with the public. This has cost me quite a bit. But I have to separate my desire to be an artist from my desire to be a success, and hopefully, a few things will come along that will be commercially successful and will allow me to do other things that are worthwhile."

Tapestry was released in April, 1970, and received excellent reviews from trade magazines, including *Billboard, Cash Box,* and *Disc Magazine.*

Cash Box wrote:

> "Don McLean is one of the most brilliant new songwriters around. His music is fresh and inventive, and his lyrics, frightfully realistic. Don sings of love and castles and dreams, and is equally convincing with all. The album contains eleven magnificent tracks, all woven together by voice and music to produce, indeed, a tapestry. 'Castles in the Air,' 'And I Love You So,' 'No Reasons for Your Dreams,' 'Circus Song,' and 'Magdalene Lane,' must be heard. This album is destined to become a musical landmark."

Disc Magazine wrote:

> "This album gets through to you more and more with every play. The songs reprimand the world's errors - vaguely reminiscent of Dylan's attitude; straight, sad, love songs, experimental songs like 'Three Flights Up' and 'General Store.' Also listen to his crisp confident guitar style."

In *The New York Times* of February 28, 1971, Don Heckman wrote:

> "Don McLean's record has been in the stores for a couple of months now and hasn't received nearly as much attention as it deserves. One of the problems is that his folk-based songs make few concessions to commercial topicality — to plastic country rhythms or queasy electronics. He is, quite simply, a contemporary troubadour, and one who, despite his relative anonymity, can produce music which is easily comparable to the best of such current heavies as James Taylor, Neil Young, and Elton John.
>
> McLean is still a few songs from the consistency that will keep him around long enough for his music to sink into the public's consciousness, but at least four or five of the songs included here

— especially 'Castles in the Air,' 'Magdalene Lane,' 'Three Flights Up,' 'Circus Song,' and 'And I Love You So' — are nearly perfect marriages of music, lyrics, and ideas. 'And I Love You So," if perhaps a bit too sweet for some tastes, strikes me as the kind of simple, uncluttered love song that opens the heart and renews the spirit.

My criticisms are simple enough: McLean tends to stuff his songs too full of demanding ideas and colorful imagery. His problem at the moment is finding an appropriate editorial funnel for his cornucopiac imagination (would that more songwriters had the same problem!) His singing is gentle, folky, a bit reminiscent at times of the sound that Peter Yarrow gets when he is sounding particularly good and on the verge of becoming a genuinely personal expression. His guitar playing is excellent, and the instrumental backgrounds of Edward Bogas are just right.
Obviously, I like Don McLean's music. I doubt that anyone will find all of his tunes to their taste, but, as I said, there are a few pieces here that shouldn't be overlooked. Don't let this one pass you by."

From the beginning, McLean was surprised at the positive critical reviews he received for his song writing and performing. Lee Hays of the Weavers, who wrote liner notes for *Tapestry*, immediately understood the fusion nature of his music:

"If the lore of our culture helps keep the past alive, then it makes Don's present life and art more solid. One wishes that more young singers would be more radical — that is, to find and to cling to their roots. And if they can't find any, grow some.

The poetry of earth is never dead. It's a theme in Don's music and in his life. I'm all for him."

It was Don McLean's first album. It is most well known for its two pop classics "Castles in the Air" and "And I Love You So." It was rejected by

34 record companies before being released on the Mediarts label in the fall of 1970. Don still remembers the day it arrived in the mail at his house in Cold Spring, New York. "There it was. It was a reality. It was an album. It was in my hand. Next to the birth of my children, the release of *Tapestry* by Mediarts Records had to be the most exciting moment of my life." It was the culmination of the hardest, most important years of his career, which began when he assumed the role of the Hudson River Troubadour.

On stage Massey Hall, Toronto, 1970, opening for The James Gang

Mediarts promoted the release with a beautiful press kit and associated publicity. It was difficult to attract publicity for a new album by a relatively unknown singer, but they succeeded in getting the first single, "And I Love You So," on to the *Billboard* chart. In so doing, they attracted a lot of FM radio airplay for the track. The song quickly became a concert favorite, and within a couple of years it had been recorded by many other artists, charting each time.

Those other recordings actually hurt McLean's recording. He remembers:

"My first release on the Mediarts Record label was 'And I Love You So' which immediately charted on all the pop charts of that time. The record label was small, and the song was immediately cut by people like Bobby Goldsboro at United Artists Records and Ed Ames at RCA Records along with other recordings I can't remember. The Ames version took the steam out of my recording and prevented me from having a Top 40 record. This was because RCA has much more clout with radio stations than Mediarts did. RCA spent lots of money on the Ames version. The song came back to No.1 and sold millions when Perry Como recorded it, five years later, also on RCA. At this time I was the victim of what some in the music business call 'covers.'

Back in the days of black radio and white radio (i.e. segregation), if a black act had a hot record, the white kids would find out and want to hear it on 'their' radio station. This would prompt the record company to bring a white act into the recording studio and cut an exact replica, a white version, of the song for white stations to play, thus keeping the black act where it belonged, on black radio. The Crewcuts were cover artists. A 'cover' of a song was a racist tool. The term was not used to describe a new interpretation of an old song. Today the term 'cover' is used in the music industry to describe any time a performer sings someone else's song.

My next and most damaging experience with cover records was when my own record label in Germany covered 'American Pie.' It was outrageous. If you can believe this, the German affiliate of United Artists made a decision to cut 'American Pie' with a German guy who looked like me. They shot the same cover for the album with him and recorded the song, part in German and part in English. When I arrived in Germany they gave a luncheon at which they informed me that the guy sitting at the head of the table had my hit in Germany. At that point I got up, cursed the bastards, and walked out. The damage done to me by my own record company was huge. I have had no German record sales and no concert career there, to this day. The German affiliate obviously wanted to promote their artist, and nobody could stop them.

Lastly, I heard that when 'Crying' was moving up the charts, the original Orbison version was re-released to cover my version, because it looked like my version would take off, and it did. The Orbison version got no traction, but today you mostly hear Roy's version of that tune, which is as it should be."

In 1973, Perry Como took "And I Love You So" to the top of the pop charts in America and around the world. He recorded his version for Chet Atkins in January, 1973, and three months later it was No.1 on the Adult Contemporary chart and No.3 on the UK singles chart.

The early stage of McLean's career with Mediarts was positive. He was getting a taste of what happens when a record is actively supported by a record company, and he liked it. The William Morris Agency kept him busy touring the United States throughout the early 1970s and secured star billing for Don, as his status rose above that of an opening act.

In 1971, McLean did a breakthrough stint at the L.A. Troubadour, along with Carly Simon, which helped to lift off both their careers. Robert Hilburn, music critic of the *Los Angeles Times* wrote a sensational review, titled "Twin Bill Strikes Legitimate Sparks." In the 1960s and 1970s the Troubadour and the Whiskey A Go-Go were the top clubs on the Sunset Strip. The Troubadour was the place where actors like Richard Harris and Anthony Hopkins drank at the bar and spouted Shakespearian doggerel. The waitresses were tough. When John Lennon put a Kotex on his forehead and asked a waitress, "Do you know who I am?" She answered, "Yeah, you're an asshole with a Kotex on your head," and threw him out. McLean signed a five year contract with the club in 1969, beginning a long association there. Many stars, including Natalie Wood, Rock Hudson, Brian Wilson and Steve Martin came back to his dressing room. Pat Boone came with the whole damn family. Don enjoyed working at the Troubadour, even though his contract prevented him from working at other places in L.A.

Natalie Wood, Don McLean & Alan Livingston at the Troubadour, Los Angeles, California, 1970

As his musical tastes evolved, McLean found himself drifting away from folk music, back to pop and rock. Although Don still has great admiration for Seeger, his constant preaching about the end of the human race, the end of the world, the end of everything, had become tiresome. Don was writing a great deal and easily filled his concerts with his own compositions. He still valued folk music, but no longer saw himself as a folk singer. He did not want to start again from scratch, but to move towards the true essence of his music. The folk influence would still be present, but as a foundation upon which to layer many influences and experiences. He was developing a more quintessential and musically valid repertoire.

Today, McLean says of folk music:

> "In the old days, working men and women of a rural nature, sang old songs they learned from friends and relatives on the farm, and these songs were changed, by accident probably. Many versions would result, influenced by Shakespeare and the Bible, as well as by common sense. These people were folk singers. They were folks, and they sang.
>
> The current use of the term 'folk singer' is for anyone who plays acoustic guitar and everyone who plays the banjo. It is a wonderful, fun thing to be able to make music on a guitar without having to read music and without all those damn lessons. But in my case, other, more complex, kinds of music began to interest me. They were not political; they were pure, musical entertainment. They required me to sing in tune and to play more than three chords on the guitar. As I moved toward more sophisticated music in my writing and singing, I outgrew folk music.
>
> I still run across "folk singers" I knew forty years ago, and they still sing the same songs. Today it seems absurd to hear them sing, with authority, about things they never did. I could go on and on about this but I think you get my drift. Pete Seeger, the daddy of the folk singers of the 1960s, went to Choate Prep School and to Harvard. He fell in love with the banjo and folk music through his father, Charles Seeger, the Harvard musicologist. Today, Seeger lives in a log cabin. I find it interesting that Glen Miller was actually born in a log cabin. Only in America can you be whatever you want.

My philosophy of music can be summed up by saying that I am only interested in singing and writing good songs. I do not care whether a song is a hit song, an old song, or even a famous song. It only has to be a good song and suit me."

Chapter 5: American Pie…Something touched me deep inside…

By the end of 1970, McLean had written many of the songs that would be featured on the *American Pie* album, including "Vincent," "Empty Chairs," and "Crossroads." But he had not yet written "American Pie." Within twelve months this song would propel him from the relative obscurity of touring with acts, such as Blood, Sweat and Tears, to worldwide fame. It would move him to the head of the singer-songwriter movement of the seventies and confirm his status as a true original, a great poet and performer.

"American Pie" is partly biographical and partly the story of America during the idealized 1950s and the bleaker 1960s. It was initially inspired by Don's memories of being a paperboy in 1959 and learning of the death of Buddy Holly. "American Pie" presents an abstract story of McLean's life from the mid-1950s until the end of the 1960s, and at the same time it represents the evolution of popular music and politics over these years, from the lightness of the 1950s to the darkness of the late 1960s, but metaphorically the song continues to evolve to the present time. It is not a nostalgia song. "American Pie" changes as America, itself, is changing. For McLean, the transition from the light innocence of childhood to the dark realities of adulthood began with the deaths of his father and Buddy Holly and culminated with the assassination of President Kennedy in 1963, which was the start of a more difficult time for America. During this four year period, Don moved from an idyllic childhood, through the shock and harsh realities of his father's death in

1961, to his decision, in 1964, to leave Villanova University to pursue his dream of becoming a professional singer.

The 1950s were an era of happiness and affluence for the burgeoning American middle class. Americans had a feeling of optimism about their prospects for the future, and pride in their nation which had emerged victorious from World War II, setting the world free from the tyranny of Nazi Germany. Popular music mirrored society. Performers such as Buddy Holly, Elvis Presley, and Bill Haley and the Comets churned out feel-good records that matched the mood of the nation. Sinister forces such as communism were banished, and serious folk groups like the Weavers were being replaced by the beat poets who, as members of the intelligentsia, were excused their lack of optimism.

The 1960s was the antithesis of the previous decade. The exuberant simplicity of the 1950s was displaced by a much more volatile and politically charged atmosphere. People were asking questions. The cozy world of white middle class America was disturbed, as civil rights campaigners marched on Washington, D.C., and Martin Luther King Jr delivered his "I Have a Dream" speech from the steps of the Lincoln Memorial. The following year saw the 1964 Civil Rights Act become law. On the world stage, America's leading super-power status was being challenged by the Soviet Union, and its military might was being tested by the Vietnamese. Even in music, America soon found itself overrun by a British invasion. The 1960s was a turbulent time for McLean's generation. By 1971, America was still deeply troubled. The Vietnam War was out of control. The anti-war movement was gathering momentum and being listened to. On April 22, 1971, former naval officer, John Kerry, stated to the Senate Foreign Relations Committee:

> "...In our opinion, and from our experience, there is nothing in South Vietnam, nothing which could happen that realistically threatens the United States of America. And to attempt to justify the loss of one American life in Vietnam, Cambodia, or Laos by linking such loss to the preservation of freedom, which those misfits supposedly abuse, is to us the height of criminal hypocrisy, and it is that kind of hypocrisy which we feel has torn this country apart..."

Other events of the time, such as the successful launch of Apollo 14, did little to restore national pride. "American Pie," in the opinion of the song's producer, Ed Freeman, was the funeral oration for an era: "Without it, many of us would have been unable to grieve, achieve closure, and move on. Don saw that, and wrote the song that set us free. We should all be eternally grateful to him for that."

"American Pie" was one of the last songs McLean wrote for the *American Pie* album. He had started writing it in the gatehouse in Cold Spring, New York. Sitting in his office, aimlessly strumming the guitar, he started to think back to his childhood, the neighborhood where he grew up, and being a paper boy for the *Standard Star*. He remembered Buddy Holly. He remembered the day he cut open the bundle of papers that had been deposited on the doorstep for him to deliver, and there, on the front page, was the story of the death of Buddy Holly, Richie Valens and the Big Bopper. It was a small column on the right hand side. He remembered being in shock while he delivered the papers on his route.

He wrote:

A long, long time ago, I can still remember how that music used
to make me smile
And I knew if I had my chance that I could make those people
dance
And maybe they'd be happy for a while
But February made me shiver, with every paper I'd deliver
Bad news on the doorstep I couldn't take one more step
I can't remember if I cried when I read about his widowed bride
But something touched me deep inside, the day the music died.

McLean would later write:

"Of all the unique oddities of my career, I am perhaps proudest
of the fact that I am forever linked with Buddy Holly. I bet if you
ask any guitar player, he will tell you that he looked at record
jackets and guitar catalogs more than anything else while growing
up and dreaming. I have heard it said that children dream in a
different way than grown-ups. To them, the dreams they have for
themselves are as real as reality is for grown-ups. With this in
mind, I can say that Buddy was a huge part of my childhood
dream. Long before I decided how I would use music or what
kind of artist I would be, Buddy was there. When I listened to his
music, a mood overtook me which was both happy and sad, and I
often looked at the record covers while the music played.

Buddy's music is so musical. The number of great recordings he
made in his very short life places him at or beyond the level of
any musical artist in almost any category. Elvis never wrote songs,
while Buddy composed a huge number. In my opinion, looking
back, no rock act, not the Beatles, not the Stones, nor anyone
else, can top records like "Peggy Sue" or "Rave On." They are
rock mountains that nobody has climbed. The diversity of
Buddy's music is also profound. "Moondreams" and "True Love
Ways" are musically as advanced as anything by the great popular
composers. Gershwin or Berlin would have marveled at these
compositions.

His electric guitars were raw, but controlled like bullwhips. They jingle and jangle freely in "That'll Be The Day" and "Oh Boy," and they snake around in "Words of Love." The Beatles and the Stones became the behemoths they are on the back of Buddy Holly and the records he made before anyone made records or wrote songs like his. Aside from his geek image and his sudden and cruel death, his music is a wonder which still contains the potency of its original magic. Buddy was a genuine original. He was a genius.

Buddy's death, for me, an impressionable thirteen year old, delivering papers, was an enormous tragedy. The cover photo of the posthumously released *Buddy Holly Story* and the *Buddy Holly Story, Vol. 2*, coupled with liner notes written by his widow, Maria, created a sense of grief which lived inside of me, until I was able to exorcize it with the opening verse of "American Pie." Through my relationship with Buddy, I was able to discover my peculiar writing talent and, much to my amazement, help bring Buddy and his music back from the dead. In a sense, "American Pie" contains the spiritual connection to Buddy Holly which was always in me. It's as if we both gave each other new life.

Music is about many things which music critics and historians can discuss forever, but what I think interests an audience about any form of music is its excitement. Opera excites some people (not me). Rock is all about excitement on a sonic, as well a fashion and musical, level. Pop music carries a kind of emotional impact, and, in its day, folk music had a political and intellectual excitement. I have tried, without really knowing it, to practice my craft in all these areas at once. Buddy Holly did the same thing without the politics. Had he lived through the '60s, I'm sure he would have continued to grow and lead with music that was revelatory."

Two months went by before any further progress was made. Then one day, again in his Cold Spring gatehouse, and "from God knows where in my head," McLean came up with the catchy chorus:

So bye, bye, Miss American Pie
Drove my Chevy to the levee
But the levee was dry
And them good old boys were drinkin' whiskey and rye
Singin' this will be the day that I die,
This will be the day that I die.

In the thirty or so years since the chorus was written, the term "Miss American Pie" has come under close scrutiny. An urban legend grew up claiming that American Pie was the name of Buddy Holly's plane that crashed, killing Buddy and his companions. In fact, there is no truth to the story. Buddy and his friends were in a chartered plane. Don McLean created the phrase "American Pie;" it did not exist before he wrote the song. Like much of the song, McLean says the chorus is about America.

> "I saw the implication of America going bye-bye, since by 1971 we were a horribly divided country with tremendous anger being directed at the government over the Vietnam War, whether for or against it. Death was everywhere. Spin control had not been invented, and things had spun totally out of control. Was America dying? My country is always reconstituting itself and being reborn."

The notion of America dying had already been featured in a song on the *Tapestry* album called "Orphans of Wealth:"

And the rain falls, and blows through their windows
And the snow falls in white drifts that fold
And the tides rise with floods in the nursery
And a child is crying, he's hungry and cold
His life has been sold
His young face looks old
It's the face of America dying

McLean grew up as part of the American middle class society of the 1950s, and it was no accident that the only trip he took with his father had been to Washington D.C. His father wanted him to feel the grandeur, power, and history of his country. In contrast, the country that America had become was deeply upsetting to Don.

> "To many of my generation, brought up on Norman Rockwell and Christmas and Hopalong Cassidy and the Lone Ranger, America must always occupy the high moral ground. We are heroes. As Roosevelt would say, 'We face the future with confidence. We are Americans.'"

The image of America evolving from a savior of the free world during World War II, to a bullying military giant in Vietnam, meant to McLean, and to many of his generation, that his country was most definitely lost.

By January 1971, McLean had enough songs available to start planning for the creation of his second album. No-one involved at the start of the project had any idea that the outcome would be so remarkable. Initially, it was difficult for McLean to secure a producer, since Jerry Corbitt was booked to work with Charlie Daniels. Don really wanted to stay in New York, rather than return to California where *Tapestry* had been recorded, so he decided to contact Ed Freeman. Freeman was based in Greenwich Village and had worked with artists like Carly Simon and Tim Hardin. McLean thought Hardin was a great singer and songwriter; he especially liked Hardin's *Bird on a Wire* album produced by Ed Freeman. In fact, Don thought Hardin was every bit as great as Dylan. Freeman was fast developing an excellent reputation in the industry, and Don was excited by the possibility of working with him. However, Freeman was initially wary of working with someone who was still obscure compared to stars like Hardin and Simon. But Freeman agreed to meet with him.

At that first meeting in Ed Freeman's apartment on Fourth Street in Greenwich Village, Don sang the first verse and chorus of "American Pie." Impressed, Ed told him to finish writing it, because it sounded interesting. Freeman recognized the strength of McLean's other songs and agreed to become his producer.

Bassist Rob Rothstein (who later changed his name to Rob Stoner) was also present at that first meeting. Rothstein had worked with Tim Hardin, Pete Seeger, and John Herald's Greenbriar Boys and later Bob Dylan. He and McLean had never met, even though they had both grown up in New Rochelle and were around the same age. They had even bought records from the same House of Music on Main Street in New Rochelle. According to Rothstein:

> "When we met, we found that we had a lot in common musically. That surprised me, because I had assumed his acoustic guitar persona would put him into the Guthrie-Seeger realm. But he was into the early R&B and Rockabilly stuff that I was. We both liked Sinatra, Nat King Cole, Hank Williams, all the great ones. We'd sit around and jam on those tunes for days at a time. I was like his sparring partner. He knew most of the classics, and what he didn't know, we figured out."

They frequented the clubs and bars of New York and enjoyed top gigs at Max's Kansas City, like Waylon Jennings and the newly emerging Bruce Springsteen. Together they practiced harmonizing, filling in the missing third parts on Everly Brothers songs. Eventually, Rothstein became a regular accompanist to McLean in concert. He is featured in the credits of all of Don's studio albums up to, and including, *Prime Time*. In 1974, Rothstein changed his name to Rob Stoner and joined Bob Dylan's Rolling Thunder Review. He can be heard on the Dylan album *Desire* and the Dylan single "Hurricane."

Now that Don had a producer he liked it renewed his enthusiasm for the "American Pie" project. He had an opening verse and a chorus, but he had no real idea where the song was headed. Then, suddenly, it came to him. "I decided to try to create some kind of dream about America using biblical and musical imagery." McLean sat down and wrote the remaining five verses in an hour. Philadelphia would be the place where Don McLean first performed the song in public on a bill with Laura Nero at Temple University.

American Pie

A long, long time ago
I can still remember how that music used to make me smile
And I knew if I had my chance
That I could make those people dance and maybe they'd be happy for a while
But February made me shiver, with every paper I delivered
Bad news on the doorstep, I couldn't take one more step
I can't remember if I cried when I read about his widowed bride
But something touched me deep inside
The day the music died

Chorus:
So bye, bye, Miss American Pie
Drove my Chevy to the levy but the levy was dry
And them good old boys were drinkin' whisky and rye
Singin' this will be the day that I die, this will be the day that I die

Did you write the book of love

And do you have faith in God above, if the Bible tells you so?
Do you believe in rock and roll
Can music save your mortal soul and can you teach me how to dance
real slow?
Well I know that you're in love with him 'cuz I saw you dancin' in the
gym
You both kicked off your shoes, man I dig those rhythm and blues
I was a lonely teenage broncin' buck with a pink carnation and a pickup
truck
But I knew I was out of luck the day the music died, I started singin'

Chorus

Now for ten years we've been on our own
And moss grows fat on a rolling stone but that's not how it used to be
When the jester sang for the king and queen
In a coat he borrowed from James Dean in a voice that came from you
and me
And while the king was looking down, the jester stole his thorny crown
The courtroom was adjourned, no verdict was returned
And while Lenin read a book on Marx, the quartet practiced in the park
And we sang dirges in the dark the day the music died, we were singin'

Chorus

Helter skelter in a summer swelter
The birds flew off with a fallout shelter, eight miles high and fallin' fast
It landed foul on the grass
The players tried for a forward pass, with the jester on the sidelines in a
cast
Now at half-time there was sweet perfume, while sergeants played a
marching tune
We all got up to dance, but we never got the chance
'Cuz the players tried to take the field, the marching band refused to
yield
Do you recall what was revealed the day the music died, we started
singin'

Chorus

And there we were all in one place
A generation lost in space, with no time left to start again
So come on Jack be nimble
Jack be quick, Jack Flash sat on a candlestick 'cuz fire is the devil's only
friend

And as I watched him on the stage, my hands were clenched in fists of rage
No angel born in Hell could break that Satan's spell
And as the flames climbed high into the night to light the sacrificial rite
I saw Satan laughing with delight the day the music died, he was singin'

Chorus

I met a girl who sang the blues
And I asked her for some happy news, but she just smiled and turned away
I went down to the sacred store
Where I'd heard the music years before, but the man there said the music wouldn't play
And in the streets the children screamed, the lovers cried and the poets dreamed
But not a word was spoken, the church bells all were broken
And the three men I admire most, the Father, Son, and the Holy Ghost
They caught the last train for the coast the day the music died, and they were singin'

Chorus
Bye, bye, Miss American Pie
Drove my Chevy to the levee but the levee was dry
Them good old boys were drinkin' whiskey and rye
Singin' this will be the day that I die.

Ed Freeman immediately recognized that "American Pie" would make a dynamite recording, even though it was nearly nine minutes long. "I realized that it was a classic, but obviously not single material — it was way too long." He quickly scheduled a taped rehearsal at a make-shift recording studio in an apartment owned by jazz legend, Cannonball Adderly, on the Upper West Side in New York. Dick Cutler, a friend of Freeman, ran the studio and gave them a discount on the hourly rate. To create a sound that was more unique, they spent two weeks at the studio working out head arrangements with Rob Rothstein and a drummer, neither of whom were session players; rather they were members of performing bands. McLean was firmly in charge of these sessions, getting his ideas across, while Ed refined the loose arrangements.

When they started working on "American Pie," McLean wanted the final verse to be up-tempo, much like Madonna's version recorded 29 years later. However, the piano passage that opens the song sounded so beautiful that he decided to slow down the last verse too, while letting the four central verses move out at a rock 'n' roll speed. McLean liked the music produced in this converted bedroom. It was why he chose Ed Freeman to produce the album. "We were creating a setting for this new music of mine which I found extremely satisfying."

Everything was going better than could have been wished for. Don sensed that something extraordinary was developing. Then a phone call from Ed Freeman brought him back down to earth with a thud. Mediarts was going out of business. This could have been a complete disaster, but, fortunately, United Artists, the main distributor for Mediarts, announced, one month later, they would take over the smaller company. Therefore, recording sessions could go ahead. The takeover also meant that McLean was able to re-negotiate his contract. His strong publishing agreement remained in place, and he secured significant control, though not ownership, of the master recordings of his songs. So the demise of Mediarts actually opened the door to a much larger organization and afforded McLean the opportunity to negotiate an improved contract.

Before the United Artists takeover, not everyone at Mediarts felt they were getting "the next big thing." According to Ed Freeman, before they started work on the album, Nik Venet, head of A&R (Artists and Repertoire) at Mediarts, called Freeman and said that McLean had no talent. "He told me that if I could come in under the agreed-upon $25,000 budget, he would cook the books and split the difference with me." Freeman rejected the offer. As it turned out, they went over budget anyway. Nik Venet had a good record of picking hit artists, but not at Mediarts where Dory Previn and Spencer Davis went nowhere with him. All the same, Freeman was unnerved by Nik's negative assessment of McLean.

With everything in place, recording began at the Record Plant in New York. The Record Plant was the first studio to cater to a new generation of rock musicians. It had designer control rooms, mood lighting, hip decor, and cutting edge technology, instead of the industrial, fluorescent-lit barns of mainstream studios. The Record Plant was owned by Chris Stone, a man who, according to Freeman, knew very little about music but a whole lot about how to deal with the crazies in the music-business. Chris played a behind-the-scenes role. He and Tom Flye were instrumental in quieting the troubled waters in the recording sessions. Tom Flye was a superlative engineer who worked on McLean's next two albums and went on to produce many other records. Also present were two assistant engineers: Jack Douglas, who later became Aerosmith's producer, and Jimmy Iovine, who, according to Freeman, was "a smart-ass little brat."

> "I threw him out of the studio after a couple of sessions; I figured any kid who wore platform shoes on a recording date wasn't serious about actually working. He's now president of

Interscope, filthy rich, and one of the most powerful people in the business."

In the three months they worked on the recording, Ed Freeman only asked Don one question about the lyrics of "American Pie." Out of the blue, one day, he said, "Who are the 'father, son, and holy ghost?'" McLean paused for a minute and said, "I dunno, just 'the three men I admire most.'" The line in question caused offence in Spain, where the song was banned for a time.

Soon the relationship between McLean and Freeman became tense. They had different backgrounds and different ideas about how things should be done. Don liked to sing live, while Ed felt that convention dictated that vocals be over-dubbed. According to Freeman, McLean wanted a stripped-down, bare-bones production. "In spite of his pop influences and sophisticated material, that's what he understood musically and felt comfortable doing." On the other hand, Freeman wanted to make a highly produced pop record, because that was musically challenging to him, and that was what was currently fashionable. Freeman later said, "Don was an enormously gifted and technically proficient singer; he could have done any of the vocals on all his albums in one take... I loved his voice."

McLean remembers their work together this way:

> "As an artist with only one album out (*Tapestry*) and no radio track record to speak of, I was subject to the opinions of all the people around me. I had my goals, and I really didn't care what anybody thought, but naturally I was pleased if the musicians

liked the songs. I had hoped that Ed would be my George Martin or Pete Ascher. He could not do that for me, but when the chips were down, Ed came through for me. Does anything else really matter?

A producer works for a record company; his world is the recording studio. He knows all the side men and recording engineers. He puts the musicians together; he mixes; he edits. He knows the *sound* he is looking for. A producer creates the personality of the record company; and if he is good, he sells a lot of records. No matter how good a producer is, he seldom goes outside of his "bag" (country, pop, some kind of rock, etc.) If he finds the right artist for what he does, the two of them will have a lot of success, as long as they stick to the formula and stay with the kind of tunes they do best. Producers do not like to do things other than what they know.

McLean fought with every producer he worked with. There were some songs the producers could "hear," and other songs they hated. What mattered to Don was to make the record he had in his head. He could spot a "formula" producer, one who took a listen and then decided to give him the standard treatment which tossed him off, because he was not really interested and not really listening. It was just another project he was doing for the money. Nik Venet was such a character. McLean was assigned to Nik, but he immediately saw he was wrong and would have nothing to do with him. He had heard other albums Nik did for Mediarts Records, and none were successful. Don was rocking the boat by not using the producer Mediarts wanted, and it no doubt made Vinet mad..

One explosive argument between McLean and Freeman concerned Don's guitar playing. As far as Freeman was concerned, "Don's finger-style playing was decent enough, but I thought his flat-picking was too broad and sloppy for the recording studio. For rhythm section dates, I wanted to replace him with a studio guitarist." This annoyed Don, and from this point on he started to fight Freeman. McLean was furious and made it clear that he, and nobody else, would be playing rhythm guitar.

They did approximately 14 takes of the rhythm track on "American Pie," with the takes getting hotter and hotter as the musicians got into the groove laid down and enhanced by Paul Griffin's outrageous piano playing. Paul had not been at the rehearsals. He came in just for the session, and when he heard the song, he jumped all over it. After the last take everyone was excited, and McLean thanked him for playing such great piano. He said, "Man, I couldn't help but do it with your acoustic guitar in my earphones." McLean's driving acoustic guitar is at the center of the "American Pie" track.

For the last chorus, it was decided that a whole bunch of people would sing it one more time, just as it might sound in a bar or at a football game, like a sea shanty. It was Ed's idea for the record to go from mono to stereo. This helps to create a subliminal sonic representation of moving forward, as the song progresses and the instrumentation spreads further and further across the listener's speakers. In the end, the final piano solo was in full stereo.

Ed Freeman came to value McLean's talent. The fights they had forced Ed to get out of his bag and make the album Don wanted. Every producer McLean worked with was willing to THINK about the songs and the overall project in a different way from what they were used to. It took effort on their part. McLean never worked with a "formula" producer. He insisted that they show his music the respect it deserved. Don says, "You can't get there without a fight. If you don't stand up for yourself, nobody will, and you will get pushed around by strong, creative personalities."

McLean believes the *Tapestry* album was the musical footprint for *American Pie*, and he, not the producer, created the sound heard on each track: some with full orchestra and strings, others with just his guitar. There were some songs that needed less adornment than others. McLean sees producers as wanting to do each track their way, which usually means with full musical production and arrangement that points to them and not the artist. While Don approved of arrangements produced for "Magdalene Lane," he found those proposed for "Orphans of Wealth" to be completely inappropriate. He got his way with Jerry Corbitt on the *Tapestry* album, and, with Ed Freeman, on *American Pie*. To producers, McLean's desire for control was hard to take. He said, "I hate to tell a producer who I know knows how to produce, how to produce. I knew Ed could do it. I rejected many of Ed's musical ideas, not because of instrumentation, but because his ideas seemed sometimes musically inappropriate for me. He never grasped that distinction. However, he has great sensitivity and talent. He is singular."

Besides the collection of excellent songs, the album cover, itself, proved to be noteworthy. Don's famous painted thumb was actually created before recording of the album began. Mediarts sent McLean to Los Angeles in January, 1971, to do some cover shots with photographer George Whiteman. Whiteman had a suave look and expensive tastes. A Rolls Royce Silver Cloud was parked outside his apartment. McLean describes his first impression: "While I waited, models were calling, and a very beautiful girl, who looked unlike any woman I had ever seen in my life, dropped in, lots of hugs and kisses, and I thought, "Man, I'm in the wrong business."

George said to Don, "Let's paint your thumb." He took McLean into his studio where he had everything ready on the table: a little white star, a little paintbrush, and tubes of white and blue greasepaint. Don said, "I stuck my thumb out like Little Jack Horner. It was the kind of paint that didn't dry quickly, so I had to avoid touching anything as we began the photo session. We settled on a photograph of me resting my fist, thumb up, on the bridge of my guitar and looking down at my thumb. I probably should have used George for every cover I did."

They had created an exciting package for a legendary album. On the inside sleeve, along with album credits, was a poem that McLean had written to Hopalong Cassidy, a TV western hero from his childhood, with a photograph of William Boyd, who played Cassidy. Don called Boyd on the phone and asked for his permission to use the photograph. Boyd died in 1972 after a long struggle with cancer and Parkinson's disease. A plaque containing McLean's poem hangs in the hospital where Boyd died. Don said:

> "I felt that Hoppy symbolized much about the world my generation grew up in. Things in America were so simple then. Things are so complicated now. Dressed in black, on a white stallion, with white hair and ivory-handled guns, even his color scheme suggested that there were no grey areas. William Boyd is very special to me. He's always there."

So Long Hopalong Cassidy

No matter how scary life got I could depend on you
You had that easy smile and white, wavy hair
You were my favorite father figure with two guns blazing
Not even Victor Jory could stand up to those 44-40s you packed
And that stallion you rode, I think his name was Topper
He was so beautiful and white he even came when you whistled
I've always liked black and I loved your clothes
Black hat, black pants, and shirt
Silver spurs and two guns in black holsters with pearly-white handles
Black and white, that was you Hoppy
The bad men fell the good guys lived on
The ladies touched your hand but never kissed
Whenever John Carradine asked a question you'd say
"That comes under the heading of my business"
Then you'd call for another sarsparilla
I believed in you so much that I'd take my Stetson
Off and put it over my heart whenever anybody died
My hat's off to you, Hoppy
Say good-bye to all the boys at the Bar-20
The black and white days are over
So long Hopalong Cassidy

After all the hard work, it was up to the marketing department at United Artists to come up with a catchy slogan to grab the public's attention.

After several brain storming sessions, they came up with: "American Pie – Love it or Eat it." Now Don was dealing with real corporate stupidity.

When executives at United Artists heard the finished version of "American Pie," they knew they had something hot. But there were problems. First of all, it was nine minutes long, and radio stations only played three minute songs. Besides that, it was a rock 'n' roll tune, but what the hell was it about? They decided to create a three-minute single by cutting out the opening and closing piano passages and one of the middle verses. Their version began with the fast chorus and ended with a fade out. When "American Pie" was released, the single was played on radio stations across the country and sparked instant album sales. After hearing McLean's full version on the album, listeners phoned radio stations and demanded that the entire song be played. The single version of "American Pie" was quickly discarded in favor of a two-sided single containing "American Pie, Part One" and "American Pie, Part Two." The album, released October 13th, 1971, charted on November 13th and rose to No.1 on the American charts. The two-sided single charted on November 27th and quickly rose to No.1.

In the summer of 1971, "American Pie" received its first airplay on Pete Fornatel's show on WNEW-FM in New York, to mark the closing of the Fillmore East, a famous Rock venue. This was a live acoustic version (not the forth-coming hit record) which received an immediate and intense audience reaction. A few months later, in October, the first *American Pie* LP was delivered to WNEW-FM. Pete Fornatel played side-one non-stop.

"American Pie" reached No.1 or No.2 in every country in the world. In Britain the album remained a chart topper for 54 weeks, from 1972 to 1974.

Ed Freeman's uncle, Harry Levin, taught modern languages at Harvard University. His literary snobbery was the stuff of legend, yet he was profoundly moved by "American Pie." Ed asked Don to write out the lyrics to "American Pie" in longhand and autograph them for Harry. Ed presented them to his uncle, who promptly put them on display at Weidner Library at Harvard, quite an honor for a pop poet. It was years before Freeman realized how insightful his uncle had been.

When "American Pie" was released, critics transformed Don McLean into a prophet and a superstar, overnight. *Time*, *Life*, and *Newsweek* ran major stories on McLean and his remarkable song. During January and February of 1972, "American Pie" was the most played song on radio. Twelve months later, it was still going strong. The song had touched a nerve, yet no one was sure what it was about. Was it about Kennedy, or Buddy Holly? Was it a biblical prophesy, or an ecological protest song? *Life* magazine called the lyrics "a melodic and melancholy summing up of the recent history of pop music." McLean refused to help, saying, "I can't interpret 'American Pie' any better than you can."

Bob Dearborn, a disc jockey on Chicago's WCFL-AM, decided to write his own interpretation. His analysis was too long to read on the air, so he invited listeners to write for a copy of his interpretation. Arriving at the station, he was greeted with boxes and boxes of mail from listeners requesting a copy of the "American Pie" analysis. WCFL's night-time signal reached more than thirty states and several Canadian provinces, so mail was arriving from all over eastern North America. After the first few days, it was obvious he needed help with the mail. A publicity firm in the Chicago Loop put five people to work all day, every day, handling the mailing of the Dearborn analysis.

In his analysis Dearborn guesses that Don McLean is in his late twenties and grew up with the fun rock 'n' roll music of the late fifties. Dearborn surmises that the day the music died was February 3, 1959, the day Buddy Holly, Ritchie Valens, and the Big Bopper died in a plane crash. He says that McLean employs titles and lyrics of popular songs to show that he was typical of his generation, and Miss American Pie represents the girl next door. Dearborn assumes that the "King" is Elvis Presley, the "Queen" is Connie Francis, and the "Jester" is Bob Dylan. He says McLean uses images from Beatles songs and Rolling Stones songs to imply that the 1960s were a musical dark ages when dancing was no fun. The California drug scene was the death of rock 'n' roll, and McLean longs for the happier days of his youth.

Dearborn said:

> "No matter how you slice it (please forgive the pun), "American Pie" is quite a song. Even if you don't agree that music died with Buddy Holly, you have to admire the clever way its author put his thoughts together musically. It's a catchy little song that you can appreciate even if you don't understand or listen to the lyrics. In that respect, it's much like the music of the late 1950s."

Dearborn's analysis has been the blue-print for hundreds of spin-offs. The great "American Pie" debate continues today on the Internet, but most analyses ground themselves in Dearborn's original. The Dearborn analysis attracted national attention. CBS News broadcast a feature story about it on the evening news. The US Information Agency sent a film crew to do a 10-minute piece on the analysis. The piece became part of the weekly television show about the good things happening in America that airs in 104 countries around the world.

Dearborn also made a half-hour radio show based on his interpretation. He played some of the vocal, and then had the music continue in the background without vocal while he explained the meaning of the part of the song that had just played. He syndicated the half-hour show to commercial radio stations across North America and to countries as far away as Australia and New Zealand. It became the most requested show on Armed Forces Radio in Europe and Asia. McLean thought, "The whole thing this guy did was to appropriate the song for himself. He was just another blabber-mouth who annoyed me a lot."

Though McLean does not discuss the lyrics of "American Pie," he has said this about his song:

> "How I wrote it... When I wrote it... Why I wrote it... Is it about Buddy Holly? Is it about Kennedy? Do I get sick of singing it? Didn't I stop singing it for a while? My life and career have been great, but my interviews have been a little like the movie 'Groundhog Day.'
>
> I have always sung 'American Pie.' In fact some nights, people liked it so much I sang it twice, just because it made them happy.

I have continued singing it in concerts when the sound has gone out, the lights have gone off, through bomb scares, through broken guitar strings, through thunder and lightening storms with rain pouring down, and while dodging all sorts of debris at outdoor festivals.

I was told by a family who visited Africa in the early 1970s, that upon disembarking from their plane tribal warriors in full dress banged out the song on their native instruments. Israeli soldiers have told me that whole bus loads of soldiers sang the song on their way to conflicts, as well as another song of mine called 'Babylon.' I can still recall a stadium show I gave in Ireland in the early 1980s. As I sang my song, large pictures of hunger strikers in prison were held up by members of the audience.

'American Pie' is about my life, what I've lived through and what I've experienced as a participant and witness to American music and politics. My intention was never to be evasive, or to create some sort of guessing game. 'American Pie' is not just a *roman a clef*. It is an American dream. It is an allegory. And it has become an anthem. I have always resisted discussing the lyrics of the song, even though I am often asked to. There have been many awkward moments when interviewers thought that because I was a guest on their show, I would engage in a discussion of the lyrics of my song. My refusal to discuss the lyrics usually resulted in several seconds of dead air, and then the interviewer would realize that he should move on to the next question.

I think it's fine for others to take enough interest in what I've done to ask questions about it. But, in my opinion, to write lyrics and then stand around telling people what you mean is tacky.

I'm proud and amazed that college courses are taught on my lyrics and masters theses have been written about them. They have been quoted and referred to for decades. But they do not come with an owner's manual. All that is required is imagination. Besides, when I have occasionally said that the first verse was about Buddy Holly, I have been contradicted by fans who say it's about Kennedy. So I stay out of it.

The success of this song symbolized more than I realized it did, because trade publications like *Billboard* and *Cashbox* put my picture on the cover and wrote long articles about how my phenomenal success was signaling a turn away from the British rock that had predominated in the mid-1960s. American music was taking over again. I was proud."

With Buddy Holly's widow, Maria Elena, in Sherman, Texas, 1977

"American Pie" also turned the spotlight back on to an almost forgotten star of the 1950s. John Goldrosen wrote the definitive biography of Buddy Holly a couple of years after "American Pie" was released, in which he said: "No tribute to the legacy of Buddy Holly had more impact than Don McLean's 'American Pie.'" While the album was openly dedicated to Buddy Holly, the song never mentions him by name. However, anyone familiar with the story of Buddy Holly has little trouble understanding the first lyrics:

A long, long time ago I can still remember how that music used to make me smile....the day the music died

In a matter of weeks, Holly received more publicity and recognition than he had received in his lifetime. By 1973, McLean's view of rock history had become so standard that it was reflected in the popular movie, *American Graffiti*, when hot-rodder John Melner turns off the radio in disgust and says: "I can't stand that surfing shit. Rock 'n' roll's been going downhill ever since Buddy Holly died."

"American Pie" was not a hit record in the normal sense. It was as if one song pulled a lever which changed the rails of America's musical train tracks. After "American Pie," the music business and radio became conscious of 1950s rock 'n' roll as they never had before. Whole radio formats were devoted to it. "Oldies" stations, which were not considered commercially viable before the "American Pie" phenomenon, thrived. John Goldrosen's book, *The Buddy Holly Story*, was the basis for the hit movie of the same name which broke '50s rock wide open. In 1975 he wrote McLean about the musical debt owed to "American Pie."

Brockton, Mass. October 4, 1975

Dear Don,

I got your letter, and I thank you for it. In writing my book, I was exposed enough to the world of show-biz to know that I wouldn't want to be part of it, but I retain enough innocence or naiveté to find it a thrill to get a letter from someone like you.

In December 1971, I had just arrived in Lubbock, Texas, and was beginning to work on a draft of my book. The first thing I did was to write a sort of introduction — a justification for writing seriously about a rock 'n' roll singer from the Fifties. After all, the prevailing orthodoxy was that early rock 'n' roll was primitive and meaningless, and that things had been improving ever since. If you've even seen collections of articles by critics put out around then, that's the attitude that emerges. But I know I didn't feel that way, and I knew that most of my friends had turned off their radios by '67 and were waiting for music that you could listen to and dance to and understand. They went to oldies record hops and Sha-Na-Na shows to enjoy the music, not to make fun of it. But it seemed like the media couldn't see that, and so I found myself writing an apology or defense for what I was doing. Then one day, I heard your song, and was absolutely floored. In a couple of lines, you had poetically made a point that I had spent fifteen pages trying to express. And by the time I was ready to approach publishers, I could scrap that introduction. It was unnecessary, because the "progressive" view, that rock 'n' roll was always improving, was no longer accepted. Maybe you were just the right person in the right place, but that's what history's all about.

Like you, the most pleasure I will get from my work will be the people who get exposed to Buddy Holly through my efforts. Also, there's the satisfaction of doing something that a lot of fans have been hoping would get done for some time.

It took a long time to get the book published. I sent it to a lot of big publishers, but their attitude was, "Who's Buddy Holly?" Or more gently, they didn't think there was a market for it. One editor put it more bluntly (in a memo I wasn't supposed to see): "Rock fans don't read." So that is why I wound up with Bowling Green Popular Press. The problem now is that it's a small publisher, and I'm not sure they can distribute or promote it adequately. (Indeed, my initial reaction when I got your letter was, "How did he find out about the book?" Because if there have been any reviews, I haven't seen them.) It's not important to me that the book "sell." I was lucky to have the opportunity to meet the people I did and learn as much about Buddy as I did, and that's all I need. But I do hope that the book gets some exposure, so that Buddy's fans will know that it exists. And I'm worried that might not happen. Writing the book was easy compared to all this stuff. (In England, of course, things have been easier. The book was put out in paperback there and sold 10,000 copies in a month. It had all sorts of publicity on radio and in magazines.)

Right now, I'm working as an environmental planner. As you can probably understand, I didn't write the book in order to become a "professional" writer — I never felt the need for someone's stamp of approval, and getting a book published didn't make me a better writer. I just did it because no one else had, and it was about time. So now I'm writing reports on local groundwater supplies, and even if it's not so dramatic, it has its own satisfaction.

I almost got to see you perform in Lubbock. Just before I left there in March, 1972, you were due to come in for a show, but then the show was cancelled. I live about 25 miles from Boston now, so if you're ever going to be there, let me know. I'd like to meet you sometime.

Once again, thanks for writing. I like your music, and as much as that, I like your attitude towards "stardom" and your refusal to let people make something of you that you don't want to be. Being true to yourself is such a simple notion, but the pressures to do otherwise are immense. That's one thing I'd like to have people learn from my book on Holly — that he grew with success, but was not destroyed by it. He had a sense of personal responsibility, and he wasn't scared off by how tough it was going to be to do what he wanted to do.

Thanks for singing our song, and best wishes in all you do.

Sincerely,
John Goldrosen

Later that year, Gary Busey and the producers of the movie, *The Buddy Holly Story*, visited McLean in his dressing room at the Troubadour in Los Angeles. He said, "We're going to make a movie about Buddy Holly, and it's because of you that we're doing it. Without 'American Pie,' there would be no Buddy Holly Story."

While "American Pie" had become a worldwide phenomenon, questions were being asked about how McLean would follow it. From nowhere, he had reached a pinnacle of achievement. Surely nothing could be as successful, certainly not his next single, "Vincent." Musically, it was diametrically opposed to "American Pie."

Germany, 1973

Chapter 6: Starry, Starry Night…Vincent and the Grammys

Released on February 25th 1972, "Vincent" reached No.12 on the US charts, and No.1 in almost every other country. "Vincent" was an even bigger international seller than "American Pie." Whereas "American Pie" only reached No.2 in Britain, "Vincent" was a chart topper.

Most producers would have been tempted to lay the strings on with a trowel and cover the song with violins from beginning to end, so it was a credit to Freeman's musical taste and sensitivity that he did not. Freeman wasn't convinced it was a good idea to release "Vincent" as the second single. He bet Herb Gart's assistant, Alan Miller, $500 that it *wouldn't* be a hit.

McLean wrote "Vincent," also known as "Starry, Starry Night," in the fall of 1970, while he was working for the Berkshire School District. He was living in the Sedgwick House, a beautiful Federal style house in Stockbridge, Massachusetts. The Sedgwick family included Edie Sedgwick, a colorful figure whom Andy Warhol had filmed in the 1960s. McLean wrote "Vincent" in his apartment full of antiques. The inspiration came to him one morning while he was sitting on the veranda looking at a book about Vincent Van Gogh. As he studied a print of Van Gogh's painting "Starry Night," he realized that a song could be written about the artist through the painting.

> "The more I thought about it, the more interesting and challenging the idea became. I put down the book and picked up my guitar, which was never far away, and started fiddling around,

trying to get a handle on this idea, while the print of "Starry Night" stared up at me. Looking at the picture, I realized that the essence of the artist's life is his art. And so, I let the painting write the song for me. Everyone is familiar with that painting."

Van Gogh painted "Starry Night" during one of the most difficult periods of his life, while he was locked up in an asylum at Saint Remy. He had to paint the scene from memory, not outdoors as he preferred. Van Gogh mentioned "Starry Night" only twice in his letters to his brother, Theo. It is therefore one of the more mysterious and intriguing Van Gogh compositions.

The tremendous increase in value of Van Gogh's works during the Seventies and Eighties may not have been caused by McLean's song, but "Vincent" has become a permanent part of the Van Gogh legend. When the Van Gogh Museum opened in Amsterdam in 1973, a time capsule, containing a collection of Van Gogh's paint brushes and a copy of the sheet music for "Vincent," was buried beneath the museum. In addition, the museum staff plays "Vincent" for visitors each day, despite the fact that the original painting of "Starry Night" is owned by the Museum of Modern Art, in New York.

South Street Seaport, New York City, 1973

McLean's friendship with Lee Hays of the Weavers led to the inclusion of "Babylon" as the closing track of the *American Pie* album. In 1968 Hays had moved to Memory Lane in Croton, New York. Croton was not far from McLean's house in Cold Spring, so Don made regular visits. Hays had changed a great deal since 1962 when Don first met him at Avery Fisher Hall. He had mellowed. His health was deteriorating, but he still loved to sing and talk about music. Occasionally, he would ask McLean to join him in singing "Babylon," a short tune based on Psalm 137. It is a "round," sung in three parts, with a delay between each part. Don worked out an arrangement on his banjo, and on the album, he sings all three parts himself. However, in concert appearances, he would get the whole audience to sing the song in three parts. The dramatic effect can be heard on his 1976 *Solo* album.

> By the waters the waters of Babylon
> We lay down and wept and wept for thee, Zion
> Thee remember thee remember thee remember thee, Zion

With Lee Hays at Lee's home in Croton, NY, 1974

Other songs on *American Pie* match the quality of the album's two big hits, "American Pie" and "Vincent." McLean wrote "Till Tomorrow" in the studio during the final recording session, in 1971. It was the year that people were screaming at each other over the Vietnam War, and he wanted to ask, "What's happened to us? Where has the love gone in America?"

"Crossroads" and "Empty Chairs" were two of the best songs that Don McLean ever wrote. Nik Venet, at Mediarts, even liked "Empty Chairs," except he wanted to change its name to "I Never Thought You Would." McLean wrote "Crossroads" on his guitar, but it was when matched with Warren Bernhardt's piano solo that the song seemed inspired. The song has a number of biblical references, and although Don was raised in a religious home and attended a Catholic school, he has never been overtly religious. It is coincidental that religious references are featured in so many of his songs. He says,

> "After eight years of theology in high school and college, and the interesting study of philosophy as my minor, I no longer felt the need for institutionalized religion. Whether I believe in God is not important. I would probably be classified as some sort of pantheist, since, to me, God is in the forest and the world of nature which has always been my home. I live with God all around me, and I hope that spirit will bestow its blessings on anyone who lives with me or visits me. The idea of knowing what lies after death, or of what is in the mind of God, is ridiculous to me. I have given my children the right to take religion or leave it alone when they are old enough to decide what their spiritual needs are. To indoctrinate a child with religion is intellectually dishonest and unfair, since it burdens the mind with guilt which can only disturb and hinder a healthy character."

The inspiration for "Sister Fatima" came from a leaflet that McLean found at the top of the subway steps in Greenwich Village. He picked it up, and read, "Sister Fatima will do this for you, and that." He loved the name, so he went home and wrote the song about her. "Winterwood" also came about during his travels. One winter day in 1970, he was driving alone, and he noticed birds sitting on a tree. "I thought they looked like leaves – 'birds, like leaves, sitting on winterwood.' I invented the word 'winterwood.' I'd never seen it before."

The other two tracks on the album, "Everybody Loves Me Baby" and "The Grave," couldn't be more different. "Everybody Loves Me Baby" was just a crazy, fun idea about a guy who has everything, but can't get the woman he wants. "The Grave," on the other hand, is far more solemn and provides a haunting commentary on the darkness of war. It came to McLean in a dream. In 2003 George Michael recorded "The Grave" as a protest against the US-led invasion of Iraq. The song achieved renewed fame, as Michael's version was featured in worldwide media coverage of the war and was played repeatedly on MTV.

The success of the *American Pie* recording sessions prompted United Artists to look again at *Tapestry*. After taking over Mediarts they had acquired the sound recording masters for this album, and they decided to re-issue it. One or two changes were made. Ed Freeman re-mixed the entire album. For "Castles in the Air," he replaced the synthesized strings with real ones. The *Tapestry* re-release hit the stores in August 1971, but it wasn't until the success of "American Pie," that the public's interest in Don McLean's music made it climb the charts.

For the 1972 Grammys, McLean was nominated for four awards: Record of the Year, Song of the Year, Album of the Year, and Pop Male Vocalist of the Year. However, "The First Time I Ever Saw Your Face" won record and song of the year, "The Concert for Bangladesh" by George Harrison and friends won album of the year, and Harry Nilsson won pop male vocalist for his rendition of "Without You." This song was No.1 in Britain and had kept "American Pie" in the No.2 spot there.

After the show, Roy Orbison called and said, "Don, you was robbed!" And a year later, the critics were still writing about it. Robert Hilburn had a big headline in the *Miami Herald* that proclaimed: "MCLEAN WUZ ROBBED OF AWARD." He wrote:

> "With all due respect to the voting members of the National Academy of Recording Arts and Sciences and to Ewan MacColl's 'The First Time Ever I Saw Your Face,' everyone knows the best song of 1972 was 'American Pie.'"

After the Grammys, Johnny Cash invited Don to come back to his house in Hendersonville, Tennessee. McLean reminisces about Johnny Cash and those two days:

> I remember the first Johnny Cash album I ever heard. The year was 1957, and I was 12 years old. The album was titled simply *Johnny Cash Sings the Songs That Made Him Famous*, and it belonged to a friend of mine in New Rochelle. It had all the great songs: "The Ballad of a Teenage Queen," "I Guess Things Happen That Way," "Big River," and "I Walk The Line." It was the Johnny Cash Rosetta Stone on Sun Records. I always thought Sun could have been a bread company with its breakfast graphics and primary colors. Sun seemed to belong with Wonder, not with RCA and Columbia. The sound was flat as a communion wafer, yet just as spiritually vital for music worshipers.
>
> I kept up with Cash from that day on, as he moved from Rock to Country to Folk on the charts, and as he moved to Columbia

Records in the early 1960s. Columbia was the big time. Cash was ever the traditionalist and ever growing. He played the Newport Folk Festival in 1964, and then I saw him on a little known cable TV show, called *Rainbow Quest*, hosted by Pete Seeger, a fellow Columbia artist. It was a black and white show broadcast from New Jersey, and I had to drive over to a friend's house to watch it each week. It was on the same channel that broadcast Zacherley, the Ghoul, and his horror movies. It followed the bullfights from Spain. Each week, after a bull was tortured and slaughtered, Seeger came on strumming his banjo and singing about peace and love. When Cash appeared, he took off his shoes and sat with a vague sense of fatigue and insouciance, not quite blasé. I studied him carefully, because in those days you seldom saw extended interviews with music stars on TV. I had read stories of depression, drug use, and jail. Cash was an outlaw. That was fine — even necessary. Around that time he played Carnegie Hall, a very big deal for a country artist. Robert Shelton of the *New York Times* gave him the worst review I had ever read. He said Cash was an amateur who should go back to Dyess, Arkansas, where he came from. Ouch!

During his early years with Columbia Records, Cash pioneered and released many "concept" albums, albums with songs around a single theme: hobos, trains, gunfighters, Indians, etc. This was a whole new approach from other artists, and they sold. In 1968 Cash appeared at Carnegie Hall for a second time, and I was there. I saw the show of a lifetime. Later that year the Johnny Cash Show took off on TV, and Cash exploded, hotter than a four ball tomcat.

Meanwhile, back at the ranch, my mother and I were living in a two-bedroom apartment by the railroad tracks in Larchmont, New York. I was going to college and singing here and there. In 1968 I moved to Cold Spring on the Hudson River, and in 1969 I began singing with Pete Seeger and the stimulating collection of singers, artists, and scientists gathered around the Hudson River Sloop Clearwater Organization. In 1969 we played at the Newport Folk Festival, as a man was landing on the moon. Johnny Cash was headlining that night, and the atmosphere was charged with a strange energy, as we watched the moon landing on a portable TV and listened to the live sounds of 'Big River' in the background.

In 1970 my first album, *Tapestry*, was released, then *American Pie* was released in 1971. While I was working with the Sloop Clearwater I met film maker Bob Elfstrom. He was fresh from making a film about Johnny Cash, and he was working on a film about Pete Seeger. He wanted to make one about me, and he did. It was called *Till Tomorrow*. At that point I had crossed the Seeger - Cash axis for real, and I had fought quite a few bulls to get there.

1971 saw me explode. I was in a killer maelstrom of deadly travel schedules which I knew had claimed the life of my inspiration, Buddy Holly. It would soon claim friends like Harry Chapin and Jim Croce. In February, 1972, I was nominated for several Grammys (which I lost) and the show was broadcast from Nashville and hosted by none other than Johnny Cash. Cash invited me to visit him the day after the ceremony. He sent a black Rolls, piloted by his armed Italian bodyguard, and I spent two days with Johnny and his family. It was not something I would normally do, since I don't like to rely on anybody, but, as you can understand, this I had to see.

We drove over to his recording studio, and I sang and yodeled some, which inspired him to write a song called "I Wish I Could Yodel." Cash had a great sense of humor.

The Cashes had invited Robert Hilburn, the music critic from the *Los Angeles Times*, to do an article on Cash and his new album and new career. Hilburn had written a review in which he liked my music but piled on the "he can't follow it" routine. So I called him a jerk in front of Cash. Later Cash told me a critic had hated his show in Shreveport, and fans burned the critic's house down. We laughed, but I thought it must feel good to have fans like that. He mentioned his catastrophic Carnegie Hall review from 1964 and said it still hurt to think about it. He said that he had been so messed up in those days that he had taken a fire axe and chopped down the door and the doorway we were standing in because someone had locked him out. He had changed.

Johnny loved the gospel song 'I Saw a Man.' The song says: 'If I be lifted up, I'll draw men to me.' And Johnny was lifted up and drew men to him. Upon finally seeing him up close, standing in his own living room, he reminded me of Frankenstein. His head was huge, and he had an outsized pompadour of preacher black hair piled high. Then there was the fatigue, the fluttering eyelids, the shuffling, the fear of my direct gaze, and the voice — soft and wide with bass undertones. He had a beautiful southern accent and a unique way of saying words like "more" which came out sounding like "mower." He had a vibrato like the mighty Mississippi, which sometimes overflowed its banks. I loved the way Johnny always saved the special low note in his show for the right moment, the 'I Walk the Line' moment, the fastball, the money note, the note that dipped you, just for a second, into the scary blackness of his mental echo chamber.

Cash was a rebel soldier, a patriot, an authority-hating revolutionary, a bottomland cotton picker, a gigantic star with gigantic appetites, a man upon whom poverty had left its mark. No matter how much he had, there would always be black Arkansas dirt under his fingernails. He was also a gentle giant who could grow and change. He had a code. I don't know what it was, but I know he worked like hell to stick to it.

Johnny and June were the most attentive and gracious hosts I have ever experienced, and they had excellent taste. Their home was large and modern and beautiful — all stone and glass and natural wood. It had a huge, curved, glass-enclosed, main room that overlooked a lake. Johnny liked to fish, often with his neighbor, Tex Ritter. Imagine the conversations between those two big ol' country boys.

The rooms were large and had high ceilings with dentil molding. Each room was furnished in the English Regency style and elegantly decorated. June Carter knew her antiques as well as any Newport socialite. Their home was the perfect blend of rustic elegance and Gilded Age grandeur. It was perfect for country music royalty.

During my visit I met the family: Johnny's brother, father, and others. There were fans, like the large matching lesbians dressed in black, and another man in black, Roy Orbison. Orbison had called after the Grammys to say, 'Don, you was robbed!' He came over and talked at length about my songs and my singing. I told Roy that I loved his song, 'Crying,' and although I felt I understood it, I didn't think I could sing it. In 1980 I would have a No.1 record of Roy's song, and it would foreshadow the final comeback of Roy Orbison.

After saying our goodbyes, I continued to follow Johnny Cash as I always had. I watched him soldier on after his TV show went off the air and Columbia let him go after more than thirty years on the label. Johnny said he had a No.1 record every five years and he was about due for another one. He never had another No.1 record, and I watched as the big time buzz morphed into iconic heavy rotation. June and Johnny toured the country and the world like whirling dervishes and gypsies in love. As Johnny grew older he aged swiftly and badly from 60 to 70. It was as if the polypharmacy loan sharks had used his last years as collateral, and payback was brutal.

In 2002 Johnny was too sick to travel, but June came to Atlanta to sing on a TV show with me. She kissed me and said that she and Johnny were proud to have known me. I sang 'Crying' on the show, and June cried at the memory of Roy, whom she loved. Not long after that, both June and Johnny were gone.

By the summer of 1972, "American Pie" and "Vincent" were international hits, and there was a great demand for McLean to visit countries around the world. After Canada, the next foreign country that he visited, and the one he has since visited the most, was England.

McLean's first concert appearance was at the Great Western Express Festival in Bardney, Lincolnshire, on May 29th, 1972. The festival promoters were remarkably optimistic to hold an outdoor rock festival on a holiday weekend in May. A British holiday on a weekend usually doubles the chances of rain; add a music festival, and the chances increase ten-fold. 1972 was no exception. A continual downpour resulted in appalling conditions. Fans' tents blew away, and some walked three miles to sleep in a church hall. Meanwhile, the police maintained an enthusiastic presence, detaining a sizeable crowd for drug offences. The officer in charge said, "You should have seen the degradation we saw amongst the people we had to arrest. Young people were out of it on LSD and stinking of cannabis."

Reporters in the press dugout in front of the stage did not help matters by obstructing the view. The master of ceremonies struggled to maintain order. Joe's Café, an unauthorized, off-site eatery, provided a ray of sunshine by serving generous portions of vegetables, brown rice, and an orange for less than the authorized booth charged for a boiled hamburger on a bun.

On day four of the festival, McLean followed Status Quo on the main stage, and the omens did not look promising. However, his performance was the highlight of the concert. The enraptured audience enjoyed a great set that ended with "Vincent," as the sun broke through for the first time all weekend. Other notable acts at the festival were Genesis, Joe Cocker, and the Beach Boys. *Melody Maker* called it "One of the most successful of all British Festivals."

A concert in Croydon followed on June 4th. McLean visited Paris on the 5th for interviews, followed by television appearances in Holland on the 7th. On June 8th and 9th, he recorded two television shows in England —

Top *of the Pops* and, in Manchester, The Old Grey Whistle Test, where he performed "Yonkers Girl," a track that was eventually released on the 1992 *Favorites and Rarities* album. McLean said, "The audience was tremendous. I have always found that they get more upbeat the further north you travel in England. By the time you get to Manchester and Liverpool they act more like an Irish audience."

McLean's schedule continued with a major concert in the prestigious Koncertgebau in Amsterdam on the 11th and his first appearance at the Royal Albert Hall in London on the 12th. A few months earlier, he had performed for the first time at Carnegie Hall in New York and had received disappointing reviews. The concert at the Royal Albert Hall was twice the size of the one at Carnegie Hall, and it was a triumph.

Disc Magazine wrote:

> "In every way it was nothing short of a masterful performance by McLean whose status as an artist seemed to grow with each song. As easy as flicking channels on a television, he possesses the uncanny ability to shift moods at will, enabling him to drift an audience through an entire range of emotions."

The Record Mirror wrote:

> "...Last week's Albert Hall concert proved beyond doubt that Don McLean is a masterful performer... He is certain to be one of the important singer-songwriters for a long time."

McLean had conquered one of the world's major concert venues with only a guitar and a banjo for support. His first two-week tour of Europe generated a wave of publicity that helped carry his single, "Vincent," to

No.1 across the continent. From that moment on, his visits to the UK became major events for his fans.

Back in the USA, McLean withdrew from the spotlight to work on his house in Garrison, NY. After four years in the drafty little gatehouse in Cold Spring, he was a star known around the world, but still he had no desire to leave the Benenson cottage. Then one fateful evening, he rescued a small dog from the George Washington Bridge and brought her home. That small black and white dog was named Sasha. In a photograph on the insert in the *Homeless Brother* album, she is standing on the railroad tracks next to Don. She was a wild street dog, and she bit everybody. Besides that, Mamie Benenson had made one firm rule: no dogs. Therefore, Don had to move. Much to his surprise he found the Garrison house almost immediately. It was located on a dirt road he had passed a hundred times, but never noticed. He ended up living there for twenty years, and he owned the place even longer. Sasha settled down and became a beloved member of McLean's household. She is buried on the Garrison property in her favorite coverlet.

Unlike the gatehouse in Cold Spring, the house in Garrison was a fairly sizeable, 19th century farmhouse situated on four secluded acres. McLean purchased it from Gladys Shultz, a former writer for *Ladies Home Journal*. He allowed her to live there while she sorted out her affairs, and while workmen were renovating the house. It needed everything — new floors, a new roof, new wiring, new plumbing, and a new heating system.

Garrison N.Y. home. Purchased 1972, sold 2001.

His home in Garrison soon became the most important spot on earth to Don. There he was free to do as he pleased. His land was surrounded by hiking trails owned by the Nature Conservancy on property donated by his neighbor and friend, designer Russell Wright. Wright was something of an innovator. In the 1930s the Russell Wright Company had designed fabrics, furniture, dinnerware, and cutlery for American homes still in the post-Victorian era. Wright championed the principles of informal living. He was one of the first to explore the use of aluminum as a decorative material rather than merely functional. He also designed the first "sectional" sofa, manufactured by Heywood-Wakefield for Bloomingdale's in 1934.

McLean was interested in architecture and design and continued his education with Wright as his neighbor. They both shared a love of the Hudson Valley. Both were concerned that a population explosion would destroy its pristine beauty. They even organized a benefit concert for the campaign to prevent Stewart Air Force base from converting to a commercial airport. The concert was held on March 22, 1974. Ultimately the campaign failed, and as the Garrison area grew it lost its semi-rural charm. Eventually McLean moved to Maine to escape the people who were escaping the city.

During his time in Garrison, Don developed a passion for riding horses. His first Appaloosa was named Papago Warrior and was an Indian pony raised on the Papago Indian Reservation. He was ten when McLean got him, and he was so fast that he could have been on the track at age two. He was a "barrel horse" who could turn on a nickel and give you some change, as the old song says. He taught Don how to ride, as the two of them rode the hills of upstate New York together. He gave Don a love of horses which is with him today. Papago was very flashy, and because of his high strung personality, he burned out early and died at 19; the day Liberace died. He is buried on the Garrison property.

Suraz was a beautiful Polish Arabian horse who won medals and ribbons as a first class jumper. McLean loved to fly through the woods on Suraz and jump any obstacles in their path. Suraz was slow to heat up, but when he got going there were times when he and Papago would fight for the lead as Don and a friend rode, hell bent for leather, over long mountain trails. McLean rides in all kinds of weather, and his horses wear special shoes with tungsten spikes when there is ice and snow. A rider has to be careful in the winter, because if he is stepped on, toes will be broken.

Don learned as much as he could about horses. He was mystified as to how a good rider could ask a horse to do things and be obeyed. He developed mind control with his animals, which is how it's done. He put this expertise to novel use at a concert at the Cincinnati Zoo in the mid-1980s. He entered the arena on an elephant, and it was not easy to figure out his rhythm. He dismounted and the trainer had the elephant sit and do some tricks. By all accounts it was one of McLean's better opening acts.

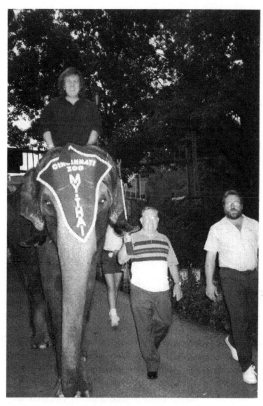

Entering Cincinnati Zoo

McLean hired a road manager in 1972. His first road manager, and probably his favorite, was David Hooten. Hooten was very musical, loved to sing, loved to talk and loved to have a lot of fun. He had a heart of gold and would do anything for Don. The two of them had a lot of laughs, getting drunk and rambling around the country, foot loose and fancy-free. At times, Hooten also acted as a bodyguard. At an Attica benefit at Queens College in May 1972, McLean was attacked by a number of hard hats. He had joked about Presidential candidate George Wallace, saying "Stone Age Man had 38 teeth, while we have 32. George Wallace must have about 600." It was a stupid joke, and the next thing he knew, a hard hat flew by his head and seven or eight guys tried to reach him on stage and knock out his teeth. It was lucky Hooten was there.

But McLean had hired Hooten reluctantly, because he felt that road managers work for themselves, not their employer. He was afraid that he would be cajoled into doing things he didn't want to do, and he wasn't happy about the added expense. He was also unwilling to delegate.

McLean learned quickly that, as a superstar, any off-the-cuff remark could soon become headline news. At a concert hall one evening, a young girl asked if he was going to sing "American Pie" that night. Jokingly, Don replied that he wasn't going to sing that song anymore. He did sing the song, but he did not realize that an Associated Press reporter had heard the exchange. The next day the AP wire ran a headline that said, "McLean refuses to sing American Pie." Within a couple of days it had been reported in every major newspaper in the world. It gave the damaging impression that Don had turned his back on his most famous song. No retraction was ever printed. Consequently, McLean is still asked today why he did not sing "American Pie" for a while. To that he says, "Whenever I make an appearance I am happy to perform those songs that people have paid to hear and that I know they love. I have always disliked ungrateful and unprofessional performers, and the AP article made me appear to be both these things."

1972 was relentlessly busy. During that year, McLean performed 85 concerts in the United States including a concert at Carnegie Hall on February 18th. Media interest in "American Pie" and in Don McLean was sky high. Each personal appearance in New York resulted in a feature on the evening news. Flocks of reporters and adoring fans followed him everywhere, day and night. Journalists filed any story about him, whether it was true or false. Reporters searched his trash and planted women in his hotel rooms and dressing rooms. He received death threats, neighbors received poison pen letters, and associates were offered money to provide "behind the scenes" insights into his life. The pressures associated with success were a million times more intense than anything he'd experienced before. At times, he found it difficult to cope.

On stage, Central Park, New York City, 1972

Chapter 7: Dreidel...My world is a constant confusion...

It is easy to imagine that the time immediately following the success of "American Pie" was a time of celebration and happiness for McLean. Almost overnight he had broken through and secured international stardom and financial security. The reality was quite different. "I wasn't sure, number one, that I was worthy; number two, that I could sustain what I had begun; and number three, that I even cared as much about music as I had prior to becoming a star." Some of the songs written for the *Don McLean* album reflect his inner turmoil at that time and his reaction to those close to him who found it difficult to come to terms with his success. "I was pretty embarrassed about my success, and people around me didn't do anything to alleviate that. They often made snide remarks that hurt me very much." These feelings are expressed in "The Pride Parade." McLean wanted his third album to be named "The Pride Parade."

Pride Parade

It started out quite simply as complex things can do
a set of sad transparencies 'till no one could see through
but least of all the one inside behind the iron glass
a prisoner of all your dreams that never come to pass
a prisoner of all your dreams that never come to pass.

Alone you stand corrupted by the vision that you sought
Blinded by your hunger all your appetites are bought
But in spite of what becomes of you, your image shall remain
a reminder of your constant loss, a symbol of your gain
a reminder of your constant loss, a symbol of your gain.

Chorus:
Your friends are together

where the people are all gathered
all along the road you traveled
all your days.

And soon you have succumbed to what others all believe
And though the lie affects them still it's you that they deceive
And all at once you're lost within the emptiness of you
and there's no one left who's near enough to tell you what to do
there's no one left who's near enough to tell you what to do.

You're left with nothing but yourself, potential in the dark
like tinder resting on a rock protected from the spark
Your fire just consumes you, you alone can feel the pain
And you stand in all your glory and you know you can't complain
you stand in all your glory and you know you can't complain.

Chorus

You are surely just as evil as the worst my tongue can tell
for you'll never face my heaven and I'll not endure your hell.
You have lost the chance to mingle by your constant quiet lies
deception hidden with the lips and spoken with the eyes
deception hidden with the lips and spoken with the eyes.

But I know you for what you are not, for that's really all you are
your talents of a minor order seem to stretch too far
and we both know that this masquerade can't carry on too long
you're deep inside the pride parade, but where do you belong
you're lost inside the pride parade, but where do you belong?

Production of the third album, the *Don McLean* album, took place during October, 1972, at the Record Plant in New York City. In contrast to the business-like atmosphere of the *Tapestry* and *American Pie* sessions, the *Don McLean* sessions combined the pressure of wishing to produce a second "phenomenon" with the drug-fueled confidence that everyone was involved in producing a sure-fire hit. McLean said, "I think a lot of the budget on that record went up people's noses." He didn't get involved in the copious consumption of cocaine. He was under a lot of pressure, and he was not working well with Ed Freeman.

Freeman acknowledges that he was facing difficulties at this time:

> "By the time we set to work on our second album, Don had clearly asserted his right to be in control, and I was too awed by the sudden status we had achieved to put up much of an objection. But there were other problems. Success was a difficult burden for both of us, and neither of us handled it well. I was increasingly unhappy in my role of producer, and I could now afford an ample supply of drugs to anesthetize that unhappiness. The drugs also managed to anesthetize my objective ear and any trace of an ability to think rationally. I was simply not in any condition to be doing much of anything at the time, let alone being responsible for bringing a major artist's vision into being."

McLean had difficult working relationships with a number of producers. He probably could have taken direction more often if he had worked with people more suited to him. This almost happened in 1975 when he met with the legendary Beatles producer, George Martin, in Ireland. McLean says, "I wish I could have worked with him. I know that it would have been a tremendous opportunity for me. I would have been more than happy to surrender any kind of control to a guy like that."

Other personnel from the *American Pie* album were retained for the *Don McLean* sessions. Rob Rothstein played bass, and Warren Bernhardt played piano. They were joined by Christopher Parker on drums and Tony Levin, both of whom went on to be very successful. Even with the thread of continuity from *American Pie*, the feeling of the record turned out to be radically different. Freeman tried some experimentation, bringing in Ed Trickett to play a hammered dulcimer on "The More You Pay The More It's Worth." But Don said:

> "Even the EQ, the equalization, the echo, on my voice was flat. It sounded like the recordings weren't even made in a studio. Everything about this record was a downer. I was down, the music was down, and the relationship between myself and just about everybody else in my life was down. In conveying that, the album succeeded."

Freeman is similarly negative:

> I wasted huge amounts of time and money on experiments that didn't work. Neither of us paid attention to the material that was not up to par. Don needed someone with perspective, experience, and wisdom to bounce ideas off of, someone who understood the pressure he was under, the challenges he faced, and the fears and uncertainties he must have felt. I was not that person.

The end product was rush-released in November, 1972. It was a complete change from McLean's first two albums. He had resisted record company pressures to produce an album that sounded just like *American Pie*, and instead he had produced something just as far from what he hoped to achieve. His mood was not improved when Stephen Holden wrote a vicious review for *Rolling Stone* magazine. Following the AP news story that claimed "Don McLean no longer performs American Pie," it was the last thing his career needed. Don believes that the Holden review started a wave of negative publicity that lasted for years. Three years later on November 24, 1975, Holden wrote Don a letter of apology, which in part said:

"...I regret especially the review's loathsome political comparisons, since I admire (and share) your political views and your selfless dedication to them. Though I eventually grew tired of hearing it, "American Pie" is a fine work — the closest thing to Eliot's "The Waste Land" that any pop writer has produced. Today "Vincent" not only strikes me as a well made song, it touches me. And in retrospect, "The Pride Parade" seems a sincerely painful, moral self-dialogue, the meaning of which I completely misunderstood..."

McLean says: "I respected Holden for trying to correct his mistake. It takes a big man to do that."

Most reviews of the *Don McLean* album were more favorable than Holden's, and fan demand was high. A special airlift of 100,000 copies had to be arranged for the UK, where the album and two of its tracks became hits. *Stereo Review* wrote:

> *American Pie* was no fluke, and Don McLean is a major writing and performing talent. His second United Artist album, *Don McLean,* not only confirms that, but suggests that still better things will issue. McLean give you flashes of not-quite-harnessed brilliance that are pretty damned dazzling. A writer tuned up on old fashioned craftsmanship, he handles a wide variety of melodic and rhythmic ideas with ease and plays the English language like a pinball machine. Nor is there ever a lapse in his vocals; he's so well equipped, such a natural, that technique takes care of itself while he concentrates on the interpretation... Drive your Chevy right on down to the record store; the music's still alive.

Don McLean climbed to No.23 on the Billboard chart and made the Top 30 in the UK. "Dreidel" peaked at No.21 in the USA, and "If We Try" reached No.58. "If We Try" has increased in popularity. Today a leading pop star could probably have a successful hit with it. "Dreidel" has maintained strong favor, and, like "The Pride Parade," deals with Don's reaction to international superstardom:

> My world is a constant confusion
> My mind is prepared to attack
> My past, a persuasive illusion
> I'm watchin' the future it's black
> What do you know? You know just what you perceive
> What can you show? Nothing of what you believe?
> And as you grow, each thread of life that you leave
> Will spin around your deeds and dictate your needs
> As you sell your soul and you sow your seeds
> And you wound yourself and your loved one bleeds
> And your habits grow, and your conscience feeds
> On all that you thought you should be
> I never thought this could happen to Me

Other songs on the album have also stood the test of time, including: "The Birthday Song," "Oh My What A Shame," and "Bronco Bill's Lament." "Bronco Bill's Lament" was never released as a single, but it received a great deal of airplay in the UK, where it was regarded as a "turntable hit."

Another song, "On the Amazon," came from the 1920s musical *Mr Cinders* and was an unusual choice for such a high profile album. The song has been a popular inclusion in Don's shows for 30 years. The song was featured in the documentary film about McLean that was released in New York in 1971.

The film, named *Till Tomorrow*, began filming in 1969 and finished just as "American Pie" topped the charts in late 1971. It became part of a Chevrolet commercial in 2003, broadcast at the 2003 Grammy ceremonies featuring Elton John, Prince, the Beach Boys, and Don McLean. The film shows McLean in concert at Columbia University as he was interrupted by a bomb scare. He had to leave the stage while the audience stood up and checked under their seats for anything that resembled a bomb. After the all-clear, McLean re-appeared and sang "On the Amazon" from exactly where he had left off. Music critic Don Heckman told about the bomb scare and the filming in his review in the *New York Times* entitled "Don McLean Survives Two Obstacles." He went on to say:

> "...Mr. McLean is magical.
>
> He sang his current hit, 'American Pie,' of course, but he also sang two particularly impressive older tunes, 'Three Flights Up' and 'Circus Song.' He led his listeners through an enthusiastic interpretation of the old folk round 'Babylon,' he played super guitar and banjo, and he sang beautifully. His songs — almost all of which are written with the pen of a poet and the voice of a minstrel — are the centerpiece of his art, and they have as direct and pertinent a message for right-here-today young people as those of any contemporary songwriter I can think of.
>
> The bomb scare and the distracting film lights faded quickly from my mind at the end of the program, but Don McLean's music hasn't. I expect to be hearing it for a long, long time."

Other tracks on *Don McLean* such as "Narcisissima" and "The More You Pay the More It's Worth" contributed to the impression that the *Don McLean* album represented a noticeable drop in quality. Ed Freeman was convinced that McLean didn't understand how good a writer he was. He said:

> "I imagine that stress played a part in the disintegration of his first marriage. In any case, he seemed to be an unhappy person at the time. That made two of us, although neither of us acknowledged it or even knew it consciously. Don attempted to portray himself as a musician who happened to have written a few songs, rather than as a poet who happened to be a musician as well. But his abrupt fame was due to his writing, not his performing, however masterful that may have been."

In Don's opinion, his third album was indeed an extension of the bleakness gradually taking over his life in 1972. He wanted his album to capture the darkness and confusion he felt. He felt isolated, and that comes through. Artistically, the album captured the mood exactly, and it is therefore a success.

Today it would be quite normal to capitalize on a successful album, like *American Pie,* by releasing four, five, or even six tracks as singles. However, after the first two single releases in 1972, United Artists was anxious to move on to the next hit album. This decision resulted in the overly rushed production of *Don McLean* and had a detrimental affect on Don's commercial status. In the public's eyes, Don McLean had come from nowhere to create two tremendously popular songs. There is no doubt that, had he been allowed to release another two or three singles from the *American Pie* album, they would have been hits all over the world.

Boosted by the success of the *Don McLean* album in the UK, he approached 1973 in a more positive frame of mind. For four years he had been running to keep up with recording and concert commitments. He was also dealing with the trials and tribulations in his marriage. By January 1973, the cracks were beginning to show. "People put me on a pedestal, and I had begun to wobble."

Completely out of character, on January 26th, 1973, McLean cancelled his concert at the Academy of Music in Philadelphia and was promptly sued. He realized that cancelling produced severe consequences and no promoter would touch a "no show" artist. He had to get a grip or quit, and quitting was never an option.

McLean performed 65 concerts in 1973, and he was busy with media appearances, overseas tours and the recording and release of his fourth album, *Playin' Favorites*. In January and February, songs from the *Don McLean* album, including "If We Try" and "Dreidel," were popular on the radio which caused leading TV shows to request that he appear and perform those songs and, of course, "American Pie" and "Vincent." Rob Rothstein accompanied him at such shows. Off-stage, they continued to be best buddies, raising hell in bars and clubs.

Don had acquired a Western style. He read books on Western history, Western horsemanship, American Indians, and Western artifacts (boots, silver, tack, guns, and knives). He lived in the East because he liked four seasons, and because he could be in any major city east of the Mississippi in two hours or less. He enjoyed the sophistication of New York and Boston, but often yearned for nature and open spaces. In short he was a guy with several personalities, a Westerner and an Easterner. He wore

Western clothes on stage. When he was young he favored bright, wild shirts designed by Nudie Rodeo Tailors. He always stopped in his shop in North Hollywood when he was in L.A. He had custom silver belt buckles made by the Bohlin Co. of Irvine, California, and he had many pairs of custom made boots from the Griffith-Blucher Boot Co. of Fairfax, Oklahoma. Some he wore out completely, some he never wore.

In the 1990s he would become more conservative. He would have black Western shirts made by Manuel of Nashville and Jamie Custom Tailors of North Hollywood. Like the song says, he became "Addicted to Black."

Don McLean with the Persuasions on stage

McLean explains how cowboys like John Wayne influenced his life and his song writing:

"I love interviews with great stars because they often say cogent, pithy things which spring out of their mouths as true words of wisdom. John Wayne was asked what makes a good Western star, and he said, 'You've gotta look good on a horse.' It was the perfect answer, since most of the Western stars couldn't act. But Wayne certainly could, and therein lies his story. He studied pre-law, and he was blessed with a love of the English language and the wisdom and folkways that each word contains. John Wayne never spoke a stupid line in a movie, because he knew the difference. Jack Nicholson also has that gift, and the gift transcends physical beauty every time. Paying attention to the meaning and derivation of words gives anyone a powerful tool for self expression. As a lyric writer, I can afford to make few mistakes and waste few words. I value each word I write.

I love horses, and I love Western movies because Western movies are devoted to the artistic photography of horses. John Wayne said, 'The horse when it is running is more exciting than a car or a train.' Winston Churchill said, 'Civilization began to decline when the age of the horse ended.' A horse can thrill you, it can kill you, and once you get to know one, it can change your life for the better. If you couple the beauty of the horse in motion with a fine actor and a great morality play, you have the career of John Wayne and why I love Western movies.

Doo Wop music is another McLean passion, and in 1973, McLean became friends with members of the Persuasions. He had first seen them perform in Greenwich Village in 1971. On February 8th, he was the guest host of the Mike Douglas Show and could bring on any acts he wanted. He had been rehearsing some songs with the Persuasions, so he brought them on, along with his old pals from the Music Inn: Sonny Terry and Brownie McGhee. That evening, he introduced Ed Begley Jr., who would go on to fame in movies and on the St. Elsewhere TV series. Ed is still a friend of Don's. He is a fantastic comedian and actor, known for his environmental and anti-war activism. Ed remembers how they met:

> "I used to perform comedy at The Troubadour in Los Angeles in the Sixties and Seventies, and after one such night in 1972, I found myself face-to-face with Don McLean, an artist I greatly admired.
>
> He had just seen my act and found it amusing. Though instantly suspect of his taste in comedy, I wasn't about to talk him out of it, and he arranged for me to audition for his manager the following night.
>
> Things happened quickly after that. I signed with his manager and wound up touring the country playing clubs and colleges and concerts and occasionally opening for Don.
>
> That last part was definitely my favorite, opening for Don. I was a huge fan. His songs are some of my favorites, and his beautiful tenor is the best."

On March 2nd, 1973, McLean was booked to perform "Vincent" on live television at the Grammy Awards Ceremony in Nashville. He was a nervous wreck. Various other stars were due to perform, including Aretha Franklin, Johnny Mathis, and Curtis Mayfield. Rehearsals took place the day before and the afternoon prior to the show. Curtis Mayfield was one of the first disco performers, and his act at the Grammys was a major event. During the afternoon rehearsals, when the weather was mild and the doors were open, Mayfield had smoke bombs go off during his song, which amused everyone present. But in the evening, when the doors were closed and a couple of thousand people were in the hall and the smoke bombs went off, smoke filled the auditorium. Everyone was coughing, and no one could see anything. Mayfield disappeared in the smoke. It was a complete disaster.

The pressures of that complex show, broadcast live to the nation, generated panic all around. Tuxedo-clad stage hands were frantically moving sets during the short commercial breaks, scarcely managing to get everything in place before the show was back on the air, live. The show began to overrun. Lorendo Almeda was supposed to perform but was kicked off the show because they were running out of time. No one said, "Sorry pal, you're not on tonight." The producers really gave him short shrift.

Don performed on a tiny round stage, about six or seven feet off the ground. Behind him hung a large, tilted plywood disk. Members of the stage crew were still lowering the disk into place as he went on stage. As he waited for his prompt, he heard a stage hand say, "Jesus Christ, the set is going to fall on the kid." The lights went on, and the producer gave him his cue. "People said I looked nervous, but they didn't know the half of it!"

Even so, his performance was a great success. The next morning, as he was coming down the escalator at the airport, he saw George Jones coming up the escalator towards him. As they passed each other, George said, "That was nice singing you done last night, son."

That performance of "Vincent" is a standard feature of any historical review of the Grammys. McLean's song "And I Love You So," performed by Perry Como, missed out on a Grammy, while Roberta Flack's recording of "Killing Me Softly" won two.

"Killing Me Softly With His Song" was a No.1 hit for Roberta Flack in March 1973. The real inspiration for the song was revealed when Lori Liebermann, just 20 years old, appeared on television and told her story. She had attended one of McLean's concerts at the Los Angeles Troubadour in 1972, and was captivated by his performance, especially the way his song "Empty Chairs" got through to her and moved her. She recounted her feelings to Norman Gimbel, who was writing lyrics for her first album, *Beginnings*. Set to music by Charles Fox, the resulting song painted a perfect picture of the McLean concert experience. Lori made a beautiful recording of this song, and Roberta Flack heard the song on an in-flight entertainment program. Roberta's version was produced by Joel Dorn and arranged by Eumir Deodata. Roberta's "Killing Me Softly" was released in January, 1973, and within a month, it was certified gold by the Recording Industry Association of America.

After his second Carnegie Hall concert on March 8th, McLean returned to the UK to promote his new single, "Everyday." He had recorded Buddy Holly's classic, live, in a BBC radio studio the previous summer, with only his guitar and his road manager slapping his thighs for musical accompaniment. The sound was quite different from the version he recorded later in 1973 for his *Playin' Favorites* album. This simple acoustic version of the song climbed to the Top 40 in the UK by April. McLean was so hot in the UK, that any single he released would have been a guaranteed hit.

The recording of the *Playin' Favorites* album began on April 29th with an all-night studio session with Frank Wakefield, Rob Rothstein and several other musicians. The album took over four months to complete, because studio sessions had to be woven in between Don's hectic concert schedule.

In May, he traveled to Australia, New Zealand and Japan for the first time. Australia and New Zealand were a tremendous thrill, and the sell-out crowds matched what he'd experienced in England the year before.

```
                    I T I N E R A R Y

                    DON McLEAN IN JAPAN

May 26 (Sat.)  2:30 pm   Arrive Japan by JAL #002, proceed to Hilton,
                         Tokyo for check in.

                         Meeting with stage staff.

May 27 (Sun.)  1:30 pm   Assemble at the lobby, proceed to Futako Tamagawa.
                         "Love River Campaign"

May 28 (Mon.)  2:00 pm   Press interview at "Suehiro-no-Ma", Hilton.
               3:00 pm   Interview for "Music Life", at Hilton.

May 29 (Tue.) 11:00 am   Assemble at the lobby, check out of the hotel and
                         proceed to Tokyo Central Railway Station..
              12:00 nn   Leave Tokyo for Osaka by "Hikari #35".
               3:10 pm   Arrive Osaka, proceed to Royal Hotel and check in.
               5:30 pm
                 -       Stage rehearsal.
               6:30 pm
               7:00 pm   Concert commence at Kosei Nenkin Kaikan Hall.

May 30 (Wed.) 11:10 am   Check out of the hotel, assemble at the lobby
                         and proceed to Shin-Osaka Station.
              12:12 pm   Leave Osaka for Okayama by "Hikari #27".
               1:20 pm   Arrive Okayama, then transfer train.
               1:35 pm   Leave Okayama for Hiroshima by "Tsubame #4".
               3:41 pm   Arrive Hiroshima, proceed to Grand Hotel and check in
               5:30 pm   Assemble at the lobby, proceed to Hiroshima Taiiku-
                         Kan.
               6:30 pm   Concert commence.

May 31 (Thu.)  9:30 am   Check out of the hotel, assemble at the lobby
                         and proceed to Hiroshima Air Port.
              10:25 am   Leave Hiroshima for Tokyo by ANA #676.
              12:30 pm   Arrive Tokyo, proceed to Hilton and check in.
               6:00 pm   Assemble at the lobby, proceed to Yubin Chokin Hall.
               7:00 pm   Concert commence.
```

```
1 (Fri.)   1:00 pm   Interview for "Shimpu Journal".
           -
           2:30 pm   After the interview, proceed to FM TOKYO Studio
                     at Kasumigaseki.
           4:00 pm
           -         "SOUND FREE"   Studio-In.
           5:30 pm
           6:00 pm   Interview for "New Music Magazine" at Hilton.

2 (Sat.)   3:00 pm
           -         Interview for "GUTS", at Hilton.
           4:30 pm

3 (Sun.)   1:00 pm   Assemble at the lobby, proceed to Yubin Chokin Hall.
           2:00 pm   Concert commence.
```

However, the Japanese trip was a debacle. On the plane from Australia, Don ate some sushi that gave him food poisoning which lasted the entire tour. Chastened for canceling his Philadelphia show in January, McLean felt he must go ahead with all the planned shows. However, he left the PR work to his road manager. The Japanese were fascinated by his experiences on the Hudson River in 1968 and his involvement with the Clearwater environmental group. They were hoping to film him picking up trash from a river, followed by a huge press conference. Even though he managed to sell out all his shows, and the tour was a financial success, he never went back to Japan, and he remembers the trip this way:

> "It was the biggest disaster of my international career. While we did get to fly first class on Japan Airlines, the food we ate made me so deathly sick that I could not rise from my bed. I was prostrate for several days, doing all the things you can imagine I would be doing, only with such force and lack of resolution that I wondered if I would ever get better. I remember watching a black and white war movie between bouts of whatever. It was called *All Quiet on the Western Front*, and it starred Lew Aires (a conscientious objector during World War II.) Finally, I felt somewhat better, and I walked over to another room in the hotel, and to my surprise my manager was giving a press conference, explaining how sick I was. My arrival put the lie to that. While

this was going on, the women in our entourage had been sent to do some PR clean up of a local dirty river. Everyone was into ecology in those days. To the Japanese, I was faking it and sending women to do a man's work, which was highly insulting to the Japanese. That was how the tour began.

We traveled on wonderful trains, and the tour was produced by a man named Totts Nagashema, who was actually from Pelham, New York, near New Rochelle. He had been raised in the U.S., spoke perfect English, and his parents and he had spent World War II in an internment camp, so I guess he was glad to be home.

I regret the way things turned out, but it was really all a comic misunderstanding, which the promoter didn't think was too funny. Singing in Hiroshima is something I will never forget."

Three days after his return from Japan, McLean was booked to play with Frank Wakefield and Rob Rothstein at a bluegrass festival in Warrenton, Virginia, on June 8th and 9th. He says those days were "two of the most embarrassing days I have spent in my life." The other musicians were razor sharp. McLean had only just begun to perform with Wakefield, and Wakefield had never played with Rothstein before. They did not gel as a group, and it showed. Even today, Don shudders at the memory. "It was not an experience I care to repeat."

McLean thought Frank Wakefield was some kind of a genius. Frank was one of Lena Spencer's adopted artists, whom she fed and gave money to. Lena got Frank guest slots with the Symphony at Tanglewood, where Frank performed gorgeous improvisational mandolin concertos.

Don's professional relationship with his producer, Ed Freeman, had reached a cease-fire during the recording of *Playin' Favorites*. However, even Freeman admitted, "Don would have done better with a more seasoned, more sympathetic producer at the console. If I had been Don, I would have fired me a lot sooner than he did."

Playin' Favorites was an intriguing album for a renowned singer-songwriter, since it consisted entirely of Don's versions of other people's songs. It included traditional songs such as "Mountains of Mourne" which became a No.1 single for McLean in Ireland in 1974, classic Holly tunes like "Everyday" and "Fool's Paradise," and an instrumental medley of "Bill Cheatham" and "Old Joe Clark," played Scruggs-style on banjo by Don. While some critics did not like this change in direction, the album received a good review from *Rolling Stone* magazine and made the charts in the United Kingdom and the U.S. McLean told *Melody Maker* magazine: "My last album, *Don McLean,* was a study in depression, whereas the new one, *Playin' Favorites,* is the quintessence of optimism, with a feeling of 'Wow, I just woke up from a bad dream.'"

By September, McLean had completed the recording of *Playin' Favorites.* He met with Millard Lampell, one of the original members of the Almanac Singers to plan a television special, but unfortunately it never got off the ground. He became a regular on the Mike Douglas Show, the Midnight Special, and the Merv Griffin Show. In retrospect he thinks he did these shows too often, that he should have developed his career in other ways. He was not happy with his manager, Herb Gart. But there was enough success to keep the relationship going.

Jim Benenson, the friend from whom he had rented the gatehouse in Cold Spring, was now Don's business manager. Walter Hofer, Gart's attorney, stole $200,000 in royalties while his Copyright Service Bureau was collecting McLean's royalties. Benenson corrected this situation.

McLean also separated from his wife in 1973. He didn't get divorced until 1976. Even though both parties realized that the separation was essential, it was painful, because of the public nature of the failure. The pain was powerful and lingered for years.

And then on September 20th, 1973, Don learned that Jim Croce had been killed in a plane crash. The memories of their college friendship flooded back. Just a few weeks before, he had attended Jim's show at the Quiet Night in Chicago. McLean had completed a sell-out concert for 5000 fans at nearby McCormick Place, and he had an invitation in his pocket from Hugh Hefner to visit the Playboy Mansion. Instead, he went to Jim's show. Jim had recently recorded several major hits, including "Bad, Bad Leroy Brown." It was clear to everyone that he was going to be the "next big thing." As with Buddy Holly in 1959, Jim had everything going for him in 1973 but luck.

McLean was heading towards a nervous breakdown. He was professionally and personally exhausted. His marriage had collapsed, and he was left alone in his home in Garrison. A dark depression overtook him, and for many days he could not stop crying. It wasn't that he had lost a great love. She had been the wrong woman for him. He refused professional help. Instead, stubborn and proud as always, he withdrew from the world into the forest that he loved. Later, when his problems became known, it created the false impression that "American Pie" had been too much for him. Actually, his music became the only thing that mattered to him in this confused and unhappy period.

In October of 1973, McLean completed a major tour of Europe, with shows in Holland, France, Sweden, Germany, Ireland, and Britain. Following his sell-out performance at the Royal Albert Hall in London, Bob Woffinden wrote in the *New Musical Express:*

> "After receiving one of the warmest receptions possible for a sepulchral Albert Hall audience to give, there can be no doubt about either McLean's enormous popularity in this country, or his abundant talent. It was the climax to a successful European tour which proved, for cynics everywhere, that McLean is no more dependant on "American Pie" for his reputation than Dylan is upon 'Like A Rolling Stone.'"

Don McLean UK Tour 1973

Chapter 8: Homeless Brother...There's Freedom When You're Walking...

By the standards of the previous five years, 1974 was a quiet year for McLean. He performed 31 shows and completed and released his fifth album, *Homeless Brother.* The experience taught him the importance of his work. "Whenever I don't work, whenever I find myself hanging around, I find myself shrinking. I need to work. I need the audience. I need the stage. I need to show myself that I can accomplish what it is that I know how to do." At this low point in 1974, he needed the positive effect of work more than ever.

Because of the success of Roberta Flack's "Killing Me Softly" McLean decided to give Joel Dorn, its producer, a call to see if he would be interested in producing his next album. Joel had been a producer at Atlantic Records for many years before going independent. He had earned Grammys and gold records with jazz artists like Yousef Latiffe, Rassan Roland Kirk, Les McCann and pop artists like Bette Midler.

McLean met Dorn in November, 1973, and by spring of the following year they were working together on *Homeless Brother.* Joel could see that Don was experiencing emotional turmoil (nothing new for artists) and that studio work was difficult for him. He encouraged Don and surrounded him with support, which helped him. McLean remembers:

> "Of all the producers I worked with, only Joel Dorn was anxious to try anything I wanted to do. He loved new ideas. He was completely free and took whatever I wrote and made it better than I had imagined it. In addition, he was a good friend, with

great strength. He worked with many "difficult" artists who were real pains in the ass. Joel recognized that I wasn't trying to be difficult, just specific. He really listened deeply and understood me for the mixed up, but passionate, guy I was. Joel loved music as much as I did and introduced me to many artists I had never heard of. My association with him and the record we made together will always be among my favorite memories. I can't say this about anybody else I worked with.

All the producers I worked with sweat blood over our records and did their absolute best to make a beautiful recording. For that reason I have nothing but good feelings toward all of them. But, I have only worked with two truly professional producers in my career, by that I mean producers who were very successful, winning Grammys, having big hits, etc. They were Joel Dorn and Larry Butler. The recordings we produced together were the best sounding, most cohesive, albums I ever made. They were *Homeless Brother*, *Chain Lightning*, and *Believers*."

Dorn wrote about working with McLean:

"I will never forget our first meeting... Don gave off the strangest combination of energies I had ever been around. He was simultaneously in motion and at rest, terrified and unafraid, sure and unsure. It was like meeting with a group of people, all named Don McLean, who happened to live in the same body. But more than anything, I knew he was the real thing, the brilliant, one of a kind original I've always lusted after. I really hoped he wanted to work with me, because I really wanted to work with him.

Like every one else into music at that time, I had been knocked backwards by 'American Pie.' But the one that really nailed me was 'Vincent.' The first time I heard it I was driving from St. Tropez to Paris, listening to a really hip station that was playing all kinds of great music. They played Fritz Kreisler, Muddy Waters, and 'Vincent,' all in a row. I was so knocked out by 'Vincent' that I actually pulled over to listen. When they said it was Don McLean, I was surprised, I only knew him from

'American Pie.' To this day, I believe that 'Vincent' is one of the great songs of the 20th century.

For six months we worked together in the studio on what became an album called *Homeless Brother.*

Of the more than 200 studio albums I've produced in the past forty plus years, there is a handful; maybe fifteen or so that I can actually listen to from top to bottom. *Homeless Brother* is one of them. It accomplished everything I set out to do. And it did so because it was a true collaboration. Don brought so much to the project that all I really had to do was capture what he did, and complement it properly when necessary."

The *Homeless Brother* album was recorded at the Regent Studio on 57th Street, in New York. Engineer Bob Lifton owned and operated the studio, and it was where the Flamingos recorded "I Only Have Eyes for You," one of Don's favorite songs. A friend of Joel's who was quite ill frequently visited the studio. Emaciated and crippled, he was carried from room to room, as Joel consulted him about various performances.

Homeless Brother features some fine New York session musicians, such as Richard Tee on piano, Hugh McKracken on guitar, Ron Carter and Willie Weeks on bass, and a special guest appearance by Youssef on flute. Ralph McDonald provided the creative percussion, heard best on the "Sunshine Life for Me" track. That song was written by George Harrison, but he never recorded it. McLean had heard the song on a fun album called *Ringo.* Bill Eaton provided the string arrangements. He also provided string arrangements for Aretha Franklin. These were the best, most sophisticated, session writers in New York, and it really showed.

The Persuasions sang the background vocals for "Crying in the Chapel." Cissy Houston, Whitney's aunt, sang the background vocal on "La, La, Love You." It was released as a single in November, 1974, and became a minor hit. Due to some slightly risqué lyrics, "La, La, Love You" was banned in Australia, providing excellent publicity for the tour there in February, 1975. Dorn remembers that song as a mistake: "I fucked up 'La, La, Love You.' I chased the jacket and the slacks more than the body of the song. It should have been more like a white-guy rock 'n' roll song."

Pete Seeger came to the studio to hum and harmonize with McLean on "Homeless Brother," as they used to do years before. "Homeless Brother" turned out to be the best song on the album. McLean was an avid reader of the beat poets, particularly the works of Jack Kerouac. Kerouac coined the term "the Beat Generation" to describe the social and literary movement of the 1950s whose members were "permanently on strike from life." The Beat Generation wrote about many of the things that America was trying to ignore in the 1950s. In his book, *The Lonesome Traveler*, Kerouac tells the story of America's "homeless brothers," or hobos. The book inspired McLean to write the song "Homeless Brother:"

Homeless Brother

I was walking by the graveyard, late last Friday night,
I heard somebody yelling, it sounded like a fight.
It was just a drunken hobo dancing circles in the night,
Pouring whiskey on the headstones in the blue moonlight.
So often have I wondered where these homeless brothers go,
Down in some hidden valley were their sorrows cannot show,
Where the police cannot find them, where the wanted men can

go.
There's freedom when you're walking, even though you're
walking slow.

Smash your bottle on a gravestone and live while you can,
that homeless brother is my friend.

It's hard to be a pack rat, it's hard to be a 'bo,
but living's so much harder where the heartless people go.
Somewhere the dogs are barking and the children seem to know
That Jesus on the highway was a lost hobo.
And they hear the holy silence of the temples in the hill,
And they see the ragged tatters as another kind of thrill.
And they envy him the sunshine and they pity him the chill,
And they're sad to do their living for some other kind of thrill.

Smash your bottle on a gravestone and live while you can,
that homeless brother is my friend.

Somewhere there was a woman, somewhere there was a child,
Somewhere there was a cottage where the marigolds grew wild.
But some where's just like nowhere when you leave it for a while,
You'll find the broken-hearted when you're travelling jungle-style.
Down the bowels of a broken land where numbers live like men,
Where those who keep their senses have them taken back again,
Where the night stick cracks with crazy rage, where madmen
don'tpretend,
Where wealth has no beginning and poverty no end.

Smash your bottle on a gravestone and live while you can,
that homeless brother is my friend.
The ghosts of highway royalty have vanished in the night,
The Whitman wanderer walking toward a glowing inner light.
The children have grown older and the cops have gripped us
tight,
There's no spot round the melting pot for free men in their flight.
And you who leave on promises and prosper as you please,
The victim of your riches often dies of your disease,
He can't hear the factory whistle, just the lonesome freight train's
wheeze,
He's living on good fortune, he ain't dying on his knees.

Smash your bottle on a gravestone and live while you can,
that homeless brother is my friend.
That homeless brother is my friend

Now McLean had a theme for the album, and he began casting about for other compatible topics. As he was reading the *New York Times*, a small article on one of the back pages caught his eye. The article was titled "Mummy Buried in Dallas," and it concerned a hobo named Anderson McCrew. A black Dallas hobo in the late 1920s, McCrew was killed when he leapt from a moving train. When he was found beside the railroad tracks, no one claimed him, so a carnival took his body, mummified it, and toured all over the South with him, calling him "The Famous Mummy Man." The artifacts and equipment of the carnival eventually ended up in a basement in Dallas, and a woman discovered the mummy. She was a nurse, and she insisted that the mummy be buried. Circulars and papers were included with the mummy which told that he had lost a leg when he fell to his death. When the story hit the papers, the black community of Dallas gave him a decent burial. McCrew became a folk hero with many articles written about him, including the story in the *New York Times*. Lee Hays remembered seeing the mummy down South in the '30s. McLean called the Dallas newspaper to learn more details so he could write a song about Anderson McCrew.

McLean's song, "The Legend of Andrew McCrew," inspired radio station WGN in Chicago to tell the story and play the song to raise money for a headstone for Anderson McCrew's grave. Their campaign was successful, and McCrew was exhumed and buried in the prestigious Lincoln

Cemetery in Dallas. On his tombstone, paid for by the listeners of WGN, are the following words from the fourth verse of McLean's song:

> What a way to live a life, and what a way to die
> Left to live a living death with no one left to cry
> A petrified amazement, a wonder beyond worth
> A man who found more life in death than life gave him at birth

McLean wrote "Wonderful Baby" for the *Homeless Brother* album, although he had no children at the time. He was inspired to write the song for Joel Dorn's little boy. He also had Fred Astaire in mind when he wrote the song. McLean had recently discovered the music of Fred Astaire and loved his style and sound. He realized that Astaire introduced a large number of the pop standards written from 1930 to 1950 in his movies. "Wonderful Baby" became No.1 on the easy listening charts in 1975, and Astaire danced to it when he heard it on the radio. A short while later, he decided to come out of retirement and record one final album, including McLean's "Wonderful Baby."

Wonderful Baby

Chorus:
Wonderful baby, livin' on love
the sandman says maybe he'll take you above
up where the girls fly on ribbons and bows
where babies float by just counting their toes

Wonderful baby, nothin' but new
the world has gone crazy, I'm glad I'm not you
at the beginning, or is it the end
it goes in and comes out and starts over again

Chorus

Wonderful baby, I'll watch while you grow
if I knew the future, you'd be first to know
but I don't know nothin' of what life's about
just as long as you live you never find out

Wonderful baby, nothin' to fear
love whom you will, but doubt what you hear
they'll whisper sweet things and make you untrue
so be good to yourself, that's all you can do

Chorus

Years later McLean received a letter from a fan in Perth, Australia, telling how much that song meant to a little girl and illustrating the power of music to heal.

25/10/82

Dear Mr. McLean,

At your concert here this week, attending with me will be a very special young person — Naomi — who is intellectually handicapped, and for whom I ask if you will consider including "Wonderful Baby" in your Perth repertoire.

Mr. McLean, to some extent your music has been directly responsible for Naomi's present comparatively high standard of achievement. You see, she was massively brain-damaged at the age of two and a half, yet she gradually dragged herself up from being totally "a vegetable" — mainly by her own determination and refusal to stay down — only to then be classified as "ineducable." We refused to accept that too, and we — Naomi, me, and your music — totally disproved that! By exposing her regularly, but casually, to a cassette of your *Solo* album, it was proved that she could not only soak up, but retain, information without teaching. She very quickly knew every word, every sentence every nuance — even to the little "ach" sound in your introduction to "The Legend of Andrew McCrew." (I hadn't picked it up, but she did!) Now, as a result of further essential training, she lives semi-independently, works in a sheltered workshop, and, in fact, saved enough from her pension to buy her own ticket to your concert.

I suppose all of that doesn't sound too special or important, but to me it's really remarkable. I am enormously — and justifiably — proud of my little lady, and so I dare to ask this small favor. "Wonderful Baby" is her especial favorite song, and I know how thrilled she'd be to hear it. But please be assured that she will not be disappointed if she doesn't hear it. For her the big thrill is in the anticipation of being actually at your concert.

I hope this tour has been great for you, and please keep coming back to Australia.

Sincerely,
Helen Mell (Naomi's mum)

Don McLean met with Naomi and her mother on every tour he did until Naomi's death from cancer, which he learned about from Naomi's mother on his last Australian tour in 2004.

In 1974, McLean recorded songs with the Sloop Singers for the *Clearwater* album. It was the Sloop Singers first album, and the proceeds were used to promote the clean-up of the Hudson River. McLean recorded a new version of his song "Tapestry" for the album, and he sang the chorus vocals for "The Seaman's Hymn." He also sang "Shenandoah" with Pete Seeger. The album sounded muddy, so Don volunteered to re-mix parts of it. He made it sound more than tolerable. In May, he recorded the background vocal for the title track of Pete Seeger's *Banks of Marble* album. It is the only Seeger/McLean duet ever recorded.

In 1974 McLean performed concerts at colleges and festivals, and he returned to some of the smaller venues where he had performed in the 1960s, including Caffé Lena in Saratoga Springs, the Bottom Line in New York, and the Troubadour in Los Angeles, where his five year contract was just coming to an end. At Caffé Lena he renewed his friendship with Lena Spencer.

In March, he performed at the Newburgh Airport Benefit Concert, organized by his neighbor and good friend, Russell Wright. Wright was trying to prevent nearby Stewart Air Force Base from being converted into a commercial airport. McLean and Wright shared an interest in architecture and antique furniture, and Wright's appreciation for the restoration McLean had done to his house and the furniture he'd collected encouraged McLean's passion for art, architecture and antiques.

In an attempt to smooth their permanent parting, Don took his estranged wife to see Frank Sinatra in concert at Carnegie Hall. It was the first concert that Sinatra had done since retiring from the cabaret clubs. McLean was surprised when Sinatra forgot the words to some of his songs. When Sinatra flubbed "My Way," the audience booed. But Frank just turned around, and, in a wonderful half-mocking, tone, said, "I bet you can't remember 'em."

In May McLean appeared on the Mike Douglas Show, Midday Live, the Geraldo Rivera Show and at a couple of folk festivals. In June he attended his sister's graduation from Rutgers University. He recorded "Did You Know" for the *Homeless Brother* album with a big string arrangement to complete the album. On July 15th, he did a photo session with David Gahr, who took the photograph that was used on the cover of *The Very Best of Don McLean*, released in Europe and Australia in 1980.

Homeless Brother was released in August and sold moderately well, reaching No.120 on the US album chart. McLean took time off to relax at home in Garrison, New York.

In August he performed at the Main Point and at Artpark in Lewiston, New York, near Niagara Falls. He went to dinner at Alan Arkin's house, and they laughed together at the idea that death is the best PR in show business. McLean told Arkin how he had talked to Steve Goodman just before he died, and Steve said that when his cancer came back *People* magazine did a full-page article on him. He said, "But Don, I don't want you to think that getting cancer was a career move."

1974 ended with McLean's sell-out concert at Avery Fisher Hall in New York. Though still not entirely on track, Don realized that music was the most important thing in his life, and he decided to go back on the road, to re-enter the concert arena, and resume world touring. Even though three years had passed since "American Pie" and "Vincent" topped the charts, demand to see Don McLean in concert had not diminished.

1975 was destined to be a wonderful year professionally. Media interest in Don McLean had not subsided. He was immediately thrown into a demanding schedule of concerts and PR appearances, commencing with a sell-out show at Boston Symphony Hall on January 24th, followed, the next day, by a spot on the Today Show. At this point in his career, it can be said that Don McLean was one of a handful of singer-songwriters who were international superstars. Concert tours were sellouts, and albums were sure to go gold or platinum, world-wide.

In February McLean departed for his second tour of Australia and New Zealand. He gave the first concert in Auckland on February 27th. On his first tour of Australia in 1973, he had been shown the building site for the Sydney Opera House and promised an invitation to play there as soon as the opera house was completed. On March 7th 1975, Don McLean became the first American artist to perform at the newly opened Sydney Opera House. He sang to a sell out crowd of delirious, well-oiled Australians. As at Carnegie Hall and the Royal Albert Hall, Don McLean had conquered another of the world's great concert venues, solo.

Two weeks later he set an Australian concert attendance record when 35,000 fans turned up for his free concert at Hyde Park in Sydney. The Australians showed that they appreciated him for who he was. All his early albums were gold or platinum in Australia. They have remained the most loyal McLean fans, and he has reciprocated their loyalty by returning on numerous occasions throughout his career. When his American audience showed signs of waning interest, the British and Australian fans were still as enthusiastic as ever. He has never forgotten.

Don receives Platinum record for five albums from Festival Records President Alan Healey, Australia 1975

Back in the USA, McLean recorded the Smothers Brothers Show on April 4th and 5th with Kris Kristopherson, Arlo Guthrie, and Billy Swan, who had a hit called "I Can Help." Don was accompanied by a girl friend, Kathleen Beller, who appeared on Dynasty and in the movie, *The Godfather.* The guests were expected to do a little dance at the beginning of the show, but McLean thought it was stupid and told the producers he wouldn't do it. This did not please the Smothers Brothers. Tom Smothers called him into his office and told him that everyone did the dance and there was no way he was going to get out of it. McLean said, "If you tell me I have to dance, or be off the show, then I'll dance out to the airport right now." Sure enough, Don McLean was the star of the show, and did not dance.

Lee Hays watched the show and mailed McLean a postcard that said: "You might as well have danced." It was to remind him of the time when he visited Lee and Lee offered him a big meal. Don had said that he never ate before singing, and Lee said, "That reminds me of the opera singer who never ate before he sang. After one of his shows, a friend who had seen the performance told him, 'You might as well have eaten.'"

Don's return to the US was brief. He squeezed in a few more US shows, including a concert at the Berkeley Community Theater on April 13th with Lori Liebermann. Both McLean and Roberta Flack had enjoyed a lot of publicity from "Killing Me Softly," while Lori had missed out. She did a terrific job and the audience loved her.

Then in May McLean returned to Britain and Ireland for his third tour there. This British tour was the biggest he'd done anywhere. It started at the Royal Albert Hall on May 13th and climaxed on May 31st with a free concert in Hyde Park, in London. Demand for tickets for all the shows far outstripped supply. At Oxford, McLean agreed to perform a second show the same evening. Fans queued for hours hoping to get into the second show. That show could have been sold out four times over.

Every show was recorded for possible inclusion on his next album, a live album called *Solo*. There were so many microphones at the Oxford show that McLean felt cut off from the audience. He had the microphones removed for part of the concert, but even so, parts of this concert are featured on the album.

He was in fine form, mixing his famous songs and album tracks with a repertoire of more unusual material, including "Where Were You Baby" and an acappella version of the second verse of Tom Lehrer's song, "Poisoning Pigeons in The Park."

McLean returned to London to do a free concert in Hyde Park, attended by massive publicity. Before the concert, British actress Vanessa Redgrave insisted on meeting him at his hotel. Redgrave was an active member of the Socialist Workers' Party and a vocal campaigner. She wanted McLean to use his Hyde Park concert as an opportunity to announce that he had joined her party and to encourage others in the audience to do so. No matter how many times he refused, she kept telling him he had to do it. Redgrave has often supported unusual causes. Two years later, when she received an Oscar for Best Supporting Actress in *Julia*, she denounced Zionism on live television. Don later said, "I admired her devotion to principle, and I think she is a terrific actress, but I do not like being coaxed."

Eighty-five thousand fans attended the free concert at Hyde Park. It was the second largest concert in the UK up to that time, and it was broadcast, live, on Capitol Radio, the most popular music station in London. The concert received critical acclaim, and the tour was a stunning success. But McLean describes the Hyde Park concert as torture. He regretted not performing with a band. He felt he could not get enough sound out playing solo. "However," he said, "The audience gave me so much love it made everything okay." Don was now moving toward using musicians on the road.

Leaving the Hyde Park Stage, May 31ˢᵗ 1975

While still reeling from a nervous breakdown that had been caused, to some extent, by being in the spotlight of the world, there he was, in front of 85,000 people, with millions listening on the radio. He was at the highest level of fame a music star could hope to achieve. He loved the music, not the publicity and pressure. After Hyde Park, he vowed that he would step back from the spotlight, but he was adjusting. He says, "When an artist's ambition is bigger than his emotions can handle, something gives way inside. I needed a ton of time away to let things come back into balance. That's what I was trying to do, get back into balance."

With Herb Gart (left) at the stage door of the Albert Hall, London, 1975

His 1975 British tour provided a wealth of material for inclusion in his last album with United Artists. Every show had been recorded, and parts of the Bristol, Manchester, and Oxford concerts were pieced together to form a double album called *Solo*, released in August, 1976. This album, which is still available on CD, represents the quintessential sound of Don McLean in concert. For many, his acoustic concert performances of the 1970s, when his only musical accompaniment was a guitar or banjo, are unrivaled. McLean doesn't agree. He says he has no wish to go back to performing solo.

Besides providing material for a fine album, the 1975 tour also led to the inclusion of "Crying" in McLean's repertoire. His driver on that tour was Burt Smith, a street-wise, former Teddy Boy who was a huge Roy Orbison fan. While traveling from venue to venue, McLean and Smith spent a lot of time discussing Orbison's music and listening to "Crying" more than anything else. It made Don think that perhaps he should try to sing "Crying" in his own shows. Orbison had encouraged him to perform the song, but McLean thought it might be beyond him. However, when he returned to the States, he started singing the song at some club dates. The reaction was gratifying. He said,

> "One of the reasons that I started singing this song was that I felt I had lived it. I felt that I had experienced a breakdown as a teenager. I suppose the definition of a breakdown is when you can't stop crying. I was just broken. We didn't know about therapy, and we couldn't have afforded it if we did. Music helped me fight my way out of it."

Based on his own personal experiences, "Crying" seemed to fit like a glove. McLean felt that he understood the song better than anybody other than Roy Orbison. And it signaled a turning point in his career, for it represented a change in musical style that has lasted to the present day. He said,

> "There was no way I was going to sing "Crying" and play the banjo anymore. It just didn't fit. I had refined my musical style to the point where I no longer played songs that were suited for the banjo. There were two other reasons that I stopped playing the banjo. One was Earl Scruggs, the other was Pete Seeger. I thought that I really couldn't do much that was different from either of those two guys, so there really wasn't much point in me playing it."

Though the song became an increasingly frequent part of his concert performances, it would take McLean a couple of years and another studio album before he recorded the song.

Back in the USA, McLean performed at a Democratic National Telethon in July, and then flew back to London for a special meeting with Fred Astaire at the Connaught Hotel. Astaire was a thin, dapper man. He wore a jacket, a tie, grey trousers, Gucci shoes, and a crimson and turquoise sash for a belt. He was debonair, but he wasn't loud. His silk sash was a little touch of swashbuckling romance.

They enjoyed a lengthy conversation about music and movies, and Astaire told McLean that he loved "Wonderful Baby." He found the lyrics to be thoughtful. Astaire sang the song with a little flourish at the end, which Don loved.

McLean asked Astaire why he didn't perform as a singer anymore, with perhaps a few dance steps thrown in for good measure. Astaire replied, "Because I would always be worried that some guy in the back of the hall would shout, 'Where's Ginger?'" He turned his back on a fortune in public appearances, because he enjoyed retirement, and because he feared that question. Don realized that no matter how big you get, you'll always have something that annoys you.

The rest of the summer was quiet, except for a concert on the Uses of Smallness with Pete Seeger at the Institute of Man in Renslaerville, New York. August was a time when McLean liked to kick back, unless a really great job came along. His manager would say, "You know, all the great gigs are in the summertime, in August." But McLean wanted to be at home, so he told his manager and his agents not to book anything. Sometimes they would force a gig on him, and, after a week or two of nagging, he would relent and do it. He realized later that it was not the best career move, because the best gigs are, indeed, in the summer. But for Don, summer was for kicking off his shoes, being around the house, and doing fun things. Today, his summers are busy with touring.

McLean wanted to focus on college campuses and major venues like Carnegie Hall, Boston Symphony Hall and the Philadelphia Academy of Music. He turned down an opportunity to host the Midnight Special, because, he told them, "I'm not a host. I really don't know anything about being a host."

Instead he attended several Frank Sinatra shows that were better than Sinatra's Carnegie Hall performance in 1974. The first show at the Uris Theatre on August 10th was beautiful. At the second show Frank could barely talk, but he still managed to sing through the entire show. It reminded Don of the "no cancellations" rule, of how important it is for the show to go on.

While playing two shows at Cornell University, McLean met a psychology professor named Dr John Maas. Dr Maas, who loved the song "Vincent," worked with artists and people who were emotionally troubled. He made a video which matched "Vincent" to a series of self-portraits by Van Gogh in which he becomes more and more dispirited. The last image is the self portrait in which Vincent's head is bandaged. McLean watched the video and thought it was beautiful and moving.

He returned to Ireland for a television special in December, 1975. Otherwise his schedule was quiet, except for some club dates, including the Bottom Line, a venue he did not enjoy. Where would his career go next?

Chapter 9: Prime Time...Nashville and Jerusalem

By the start of 1976 Don McLean's career was entering its third stage. The first stage began in 1961, when his father died, when he realized that he was free to pursue his dream of becoming a singer and musician. He established a notable presence in clubs and became friends with influential figures like Lee Hays, Pete Seeger, and Josh White. With the recording of *Tapestry*, in 1968, his career entered a second stage of overnight worldwide stardom. By 1976 things had begun to slow down, especially in the US where an "American Pie" backlash followed the years of constant airplay and intense scruntiny. His international audience was holding up far better. His support from fans in Holland, Britain and Australia would prove crucial.

Don McLean with Orli Sarfati, Tel Aviv, Israel, 1980.

In the third phase of his career, extending from 1976 to 1984, Don McLean could have slipped from the radar in his home country. For almost two years he was without a record deal in the US. "They were years when I was struggling to get back to recording and struggling to stay in the business. Boy, once they throw you out, they're not interested in you anymore."

The period from 1976 to 1984 was difficult for McLean, personally. In January 1976, he was sent back to drivers' school for totaling his car. In July, his long drawn-out separation from his wife ended in divorce.

With the release of *Solo* in August 1976, his contract with United Artists ended. McLean released a total of six albums with UA, but no greatest hits compilation. His albums were selling, but were no longer hit records. And then, according to Joel Dorn, "McLean's manager, Herb Gart, had a fuckin' knock-down, drag-out, screaming match with the guy who ran United Artists, and United Artists killed 'Wonderful Baby' to teach him a lesson." It was obvious why both parties were unable to agree on a new contract.

While looking for a record company, McLean continued concert performing. In April, he completed a short tour of Holland, and played the usual clubs and colleges in America. He performed a benefit in Newburgh, New York, with Harry Chapin and Harry Belafonte. At the Newburgh concert McLean and Chapin suggested the idea for Belafonte's "USA for Africa" organization and his single that raised millions for famine relief in Ethiopia. When Belafonte received a Grammy for "We are the World," he gave Harry and Don credit.

McLean had a curious relationship with Chapin. They had met three years earlier at a major music festival in Holland. Chapin approached McLean backstage and said, "I'm going to be better and bigger than you, and I'm going to take your audience." McLean answered "Good luck." After that Chapin was always calling McLean and suggesting they do things together. Chapin seemed obsessed, but he always wanted to do good in the world, so McLean enlisted him to do two shows at Vassar College for the Clearwater Sloop organization, and McLean did two shows on Long Island for World Hunger Year for Chapin.

McLean had plenty of concert dates, but by the standards of the previous five years, television appearances were thin. He did the Mike Douglas Show twice in September. Between the concerts he recorded with a number of other singers. It gave him the chance to play the guitar and banjo without the pressures of recording his own albums. He played banjo on several Leon Redbone tracks produced by Joel Dorn, and he also did session work with the Clancey Brothers and with Dory Previn on her 1976 *We're Children of Coincidence and Harpo Marx* album.

The loyalty of his UK audience goes to David New who established the Friends of Don McLean Fan Club in the UK and kept fans up to date on McLean's frequent tours of the country. David New is perhaps Don's most devoted fan. In 1976 he turned up at Don's office with his cousin. He had made the journey from England for the sole purpose of meeting

Don McLean. Though wary of stalkers, McLean agreed to meet him and was amazed to see that New had a Don McLean tattoo on his shoulder. McLean was staggered when New said he was going to have his back covered with a tattoo of the *Playin' Favorites* album cover. McLean told him that he didn't think it was a good idea, because he might change his mind about his music. But New had already booked the appointment, and the press went along to photograph. From their first meeting, McLean has remained New's close personal friend and visits his home every time he goes to England.

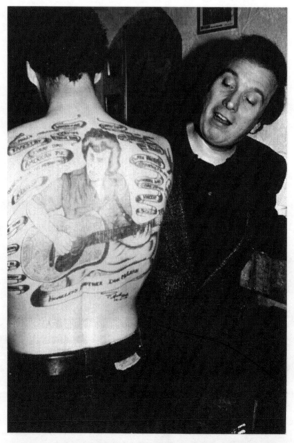

Don McLean and David New, 1990

On November 8th 1976, Clive Davis signed McLean for a three record deal with Arista Records. Davis had appeared on the Tomorrow Show with Tom Snyder and said, "I think Don McLean's a really good artist and I wish we had him on our label." In addition, McLean negotiated and signed deals with Festival Records in Australia and EMI Records in Europe. Festival Records was responsible for the distribution of McLean's first six albums in Australia. Now McLean had contracts with three record companies worldwide, and he received three sets of royalty advances. In addition, he secured the publishing rights to all his songs, except for the *American Pie* and *Tapestry* album tracks that he owned jointly with Alan Livingston's Mayday Music.

In the beginning, Davis was enthusiastic about working with McLean. He played records of songs he wanted Don to sing, and he made lots of suggestions. McLean was thrilled that Davis took such an interest. Unfortunately the material was not what Don wanted to do, and the McLean stubbornness made it impossible for Davis to get his way. McLean picked his own material for the album called *Prime Time*.

The recording of *Prime Time* occupied the first part of 1977. The songs included old songs and McLean originals like "The Statue," "Color TV Blues," "Prime Time," "Jump," "The Pattern is Broken," and "When a Good Things Goes Bad." The latter two songs are featured in the film *Fraternity Row* along with "If You Can Dream," which was recorded for *Prime Time* but failed to make the final cut. Another track that didn't make the album was "Echo," an intriguing song based on a Buddy Holly girlfriend named Echo.

Here, for the first time, are the lyrics to that song:

Echo

There is a girl who's just like me
and when I sing she sings with me
I hear her voice each place I go
Echo, echo, my love

We are as one this girl and I
a clear reflection of the sky
a universe without a lie
a mirror and a lullaby

With all I've lost it's her I've found
our spirits have a common sound
my life just seems to turn around
echo, echo, my love

She speaks in such familiar ways
of things I'm always sure to praise
I want to live out all my days
just being where her music plays

The mirror sees what cannot be
it looks at her and then sees me
there is no sounding separately
the voice I hear will always be
echo, echo, my love.

McLean wrote "Color TV Blues" a decade earlier and performed it on "The Sloop at Nyack" television broadcast in 1969. The theme of America and its decline threads its way through the whole album. "Prime Time" was a biting social commentary, years ahead of its time. By contrast, his interpretations of songs such as "South of the Border" and "Down the Road/Sally Ann" were more low key, and when he rounded off the album with a couple of banjo instrumentals, it was not destined to become a major hit. Musical fashion was leaning towards disco. Clive Davis hated the end product, so he released *Prime Time* without fanfare in October, 1977.

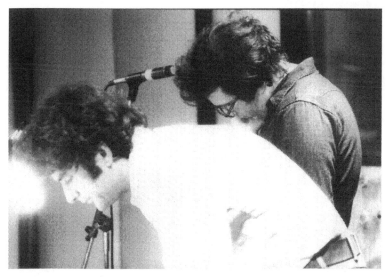

Don working with Ed Freeman on the score for Fraternity Row

McLean foresaw the beginning of robotic rock 'n' roll as practiced by groups like Devo with the song "Prime Time," which sees America as a game show with dire consequences. Upon hearing the song, Pete Seeger sent McLean a short note, which simply said, "'Prime Time' is a great achievement."

Prime Time

Chorus:
This is life, this is prime time
this is livin' in the U. S. A.
this is life, this is prime time
this is livin' the American way

I was riding on the subway in the afternoon
I saw some kids a beatin' out a funky tune
the lady right in front of me was old and brown
the kids began to push her, they knocked her down
I tried to help her out but there was just no way
a life ain't worth a damn on the street today
I passed the ambulance and the camera crew
I saw the instant replay on the evening news

Chorus

Well, will you take the car or will you take the trip
remove annoying hair from your upper lip
what's it really worth, does she really care
what's the best shampoo that I can use on my hair
hey, what's the real future of democracy
how we gonna' streamline the bureaucracy
hey, hey, the cost of life has gone sky high
does the deodorant I'm using really keep me dry

Chorus

Spin the magic wheel, try to break the bank
think about your life when you fill in the blank
here's a game that's real, if you wanna try
one spot on the wheel, says you must die
American roulette is the game we play
but no one wants to have to be the one to pay
you get to pass go, you get to pass away
but before we start the show, here's our sponsor to say

Chorus

Down in Mexico the laundry's on the line
there's where you can go if you land on the nine
Canada is nice, if you're fond of ice
if you land on the two, we'll send you there twice
we interrupt this game for a news release
a man has gone insane and been killed by police
now back to the game, that's a dangerous play
cause if they see you in Cuba, you must pass away

Chorus

My supper's on the stove, the war is on the screen
pass the bread and butter, while I watch the marine
they shot him in the chest, pass the chicken breast
the general is sayin' that he's still unimpressed
we had to burn the city, cause they wouldn't agree
that things go better with democracy
the weather will be fair, forget the ozone layer
but strontium showers will be here and there

Chorus

Livin' in the country, watchin' shadows fall
my reception ain't too good in a power stall
bombers in the air, missiles in the sea
chemicals in everything, including me
they don't keep their promise in the promised land
it's getting mighty hard to find an honest man
but coming very soon, a show you'll die to see
it's called the end of the world on the channel Z

Chorus

Throughout 1977, concert and media bookings picked up, and McLean, as always, was reasonably busy touring and doing media work. He appeared on the Midnight Special, and he recorded a radio interview with Nat Hentoff on April 1st, in which Hentoff called him a national treasure. In fact, he said McLean was one of the greatest singer-songwriters in America. He said,

"Don McLean continues to write and sing what he wants, and in the process he has transcended all the usual categories in popular music making. He has evolved into only Don McLean. He has done what few writer-performers ever are able to do: he has become an authentic original. Mr McLean is a national treasure, the most singular and durable of all our popular vocalists and writers."

Those powerful, uplifting words gave McLean quite a pick up at a low point in his career. Five days after this interview, his grandfather, Antonio Bucci, died at age 96.

McLean performed a benefit concert with Pete Seeger and John Denver in Boston at the Hines Auditorium on May 14th. At the time, John Denver was the most popular artist in America, though not to Don's personal taste. The Boston benefit was followed by a benefit in Vancouver hosted by Jack Lemmon and Jacques Cousteau. McLean sang "Tapestry," his environmental protest song, and Cousteau told him how much he loved that song. McLean did about 50 gigs that year, at various venues. He performed at Boston Symphony Hall, the Temple Music Fair at Temple University in Philadelphia, colleges, and clubs such as the Boarding House in San Francisco and the Roxy in Los Angeles (Jack Nicholson's hang out.) In August, he took a short trip to Europe to perform at the Cambridge Folk Festival and in Belgium.

The following year, in May 1978, McLean returned for a full tour of Britain and Holland and a number of other European destinations that he hadn't been to before. This tour was a big success, but during the middle of the tour Don lost his voice. He had to cancel a show and re-scheduled it for the end of the tour. On his return from England he kept quiet for about three weeks, just as he had done in college when he got in trouble vocally. When he started to sing again he found that he had an entirely new voice. It was higher. It was purer.

This change in voice came at an interesting time. McLean had selected a range of songs to record for his new album, *Chain Lightning*, some of them quite old tunes. He had done something similar on the *Playin' Favorites* album which was an album of old songs of different styles. For this new album, he was going to include his own versions of popular and country music classics like "Crying," "Lotta' Lovin," "It Doesn't Matter Anymore," and "Your Cheating Heart," combined with new pop tunes that he had written himself, such as "It's Just the Sun" and "Words and Music" and the epic title song, "Chain Lightning."

In late June 1978, McLean headed to Nashville to work on the album with Larry Butler, a new producer. He had been to Nashville for the Grammys, in 1973, when he sang "Vincent." He liked Nashville, and Nashville seemed to like him. He was teaming up with a leading producer who had enjoyed tremendous success with artists such as Kenny Rogers. McLean respected Butler which was good, and he was amazed at how easy Butler was to work with. Sessions went smoothly and work was completed in double-quick time. They recorded from June 26th to the 30th, and during that time, Don's voice was different. It was a new voice. It was fantastic, and "Crying" exploded out of the speakers on play-back.

They were working with some of the most famous sidemen in country music history including many of the musicians who had worked with Elvis Presley throughout his career. The *Chain Lightning* album was recorded less than a year after Elvis died. Bob Moore played bass, Pete Drake was on steel guitar, Pig Robbins played the piano, Ray Edenton played acoustic guitar, and the Jordanaires handled the vocal backing. They were all still in shock over Elvis' death. They took to Don immediately, and the results on the *Chain Lightning* album are outstanding. Presley had spoken of McLean on stage and in private, so the musicians respected him before they met him.

McLean remembers it all:

> "There was magic in the air when I arrived at the Sound Emporium studio in Nashville. The sun was setting and most of the guys were outside hanging around the entrance to the studio. It would take a week to list all the legendary records that these men performed on, from the earliest days of modern country music, through Kenny Rogers, with everyone from Patsy Cline to Loretta Lynn in between. These guys invented and dominated the Nashville sound for many years.
>
> And Larry Butler was a musical genius who could improve any track and any artist. I feel the *Chain Lightning* album is the best album to listen to of all the albums I've made. The rough mix play-backs in the studio were better than most of my finished albums, and the studio musicians were the best on earth. I still maintain friendships with them all. My experience with them marked a turning point in my career and in my life."

When Larry Butler remembers those recording sessions, he says:

> "There are many ingredients necessary for a hit record. A producer looks for a talented artist, a great song, and the best studio, engineer, and musicians. Even with all of the necessary tools, many times it is not successful. I have always believed the "magic" in a hit is emotion. There is no recording more evident of success through emotion than Don's recording of "Crying." He took a song of Roy Orbison's and made it his own.

Considering the fact that Roy was one of the greatest ever, this was not an easy thing to do. He did it by bringing out every drop of emotion humanly possible, through his incredible performance and fabulous voice. It is still being played on radio today. Of all the recordings I have ever been a part of, *Chain Lightning* is truly one of my favorites. Don was a joy to work with. I would do it again in a heartbeat."

McLean had followed the Jordanaires throughout his life, but he had not seen them perform since he watched Elvis on Bill Biven's kinescope in the 1950s. After the recording was complete, Gordon Stoker, first tenor and manager of the Jordanaires, invited McLean to his house. Don admired the fabulous Tudor-style mansion with the lovely furnishing and decor. Gordon told him that a journalist, who had visited Graceland for a story on Elvis, looked perplexed when he visited Stoker's house. He said, "I can't understand why you have a home that is so much more beautiful than Elvis's."

Stoker still becomes enthusiastic when he remembers recording *Chain Lightning*:

> "In the 54 years I have been singing with the Jordanaires, we have recorded and worked on stage with many great artists. We still have the pleasure of doing this. But I don't think there was ever a time when we were more excited than when Larry Butler called us to record an album with Don McLean. We recorded Don's hit, 'Crying,' for that album. We have continued to make many recordings with Don, including one of the best Christmas albums ever. Another highlight of our career was appearing at Carnegie Hall on Thanksgiving Eve with Don, his guitar, and two musicians. When Don called me about that show, I said, 'You mean you and the Jordanaires will fill Carnegie Hall?' What a joy,

to play to four sold out shows at Carnegie Hal with Don McLean. I hope we continue to make music together!"

Gordon played Don a tape of Elvis's last TV special for CBS, called *Elvis in Concert*. The RCA release of that show was the final record made prior to Elvis's death. The last song on the last side of the album is McLean's song, "And I Love You So."

McLean had frequently heard that Elvis said complimentary things about him before singing "And I Love You So." He had the chance to meet Elvis but decided against it. Don was an "Elvis '56" guy, but later regretted not meeting Presley. Like everyone, he figured there would always be tomorrow.

The song "Genesis" which was recorded with the Jordanaires on the *Chain Lightning* album came from McLean's interest in religion and the Bible.

Genesis

In the beginning there was nothingness
and God but waved his hand
And from the endless void
there sprang the beauty of the land
and high above the canyon walls
the diamond stars were new
And breezes blew from nothingness
and herbs and grasses grew.
And silent creatures roamed the Earth
and multiplied their kind
And man was but a molecule
that God had left behind.

Chorus:
We have grown, we have grown
We have captured the throne
of the Kingdom God made for our winning
We have grown, we have grown
and our children alone
have so little time left for beginning.

And mountains sprang and chaos rang
the overture of life
and rivers coursed the twisted blade
of natures sharpest knife
and cut beneath the rolling dales
a gateway to the sea,
while tidal waves and mighty gales
were heard in symphony
and sunshine fell upon the waves
and warmed the virgin land
and from the mud the drop of blood
was left upon the sand

Chorus

And eagles flew from craggy peaks above the garden wall
The drop of blood became a man, the tree of life grew tall
And perfect in his loneliness, a rib pulled from his chest
Formed sweet companion, pulchritude and breast
And from the tree of knowledge God said they could not eat
And perfect was their Paradise unto the serpent at their feet.

Chorus

Tree of knowledge, tree of death, upon the ground they trod
The Serpent said, "Your eyes will see and ye shall be a God.
Defy the Word and eat the fruit and ye will never die,
and you will chart your Destiny and rule the Earth and Sky."
And Man was banished East of Eden, see what we have lost
For though the father sets the price, the children pay the cost.

Chorus

Bill Justice did the string arrangements for *Chain Lightning*. He had a huge hit called "Raunchy" in the 1950s. He was a very funny man with a droll — "I don't get any respect"— sense of humor. He told McLean a story about how fleeting fame can be. Bald since his early 20s, Justice wore a hairpiece on stage. One night after a wild rock 'n' roll show, he went back to his trailer and removed his hairpiece and went outside to sign autographs wearing a baseball cap. One of the waiting kids grabbed his hat and threw it on the ground. "By the time I stood up with the cap in my hand, the kids had all run the other way. They didn't even want my initials."

McLean spent a week in June recording *Chain Lightning* before returning to the road. Bookings had picked up in the US, and he was busy traveling the country in a big, blue Mercedes with his road manager and his bass player or other accompanist. McLean says, "It was a great way to travel. Real style." They played many dates through the summer of 1978, including the Milwaukee Summerfest, the Ontario Palace, the White Mountain Festival and the Temple Music Festival in Philadelphia.

Although McLean was busy, his profile was low enough that a kid in Florida began impersonating him and, for a while, got away with it. He dressed like Don, appeared in clubs singing Don's songs, and he got good reviews. Finally the police told his mother to make him stop.

McLean returned to Nashville in late August to complete *Chain Lightning* and then began a tour of Australia and New Zealand on September 9th.

This tour continued until October 14th with a concert or television appearance every single day.

He still had a contract with Arista Records, and, in October 1978, they released "It Doesn't Matter Anymore" as a single in the US. This was a track from *Chain Lightning*, the album that should have been the second of four with Arista. However, the relationship had been poisoned by the disagreements and ill feelings over *Prime Time*. Clive Davis admitted that the deal was not working out, so McLean entered into negotiations with other record companies. They made an agreement with Casablanca Records, run by Neal Bogart, the former owner of the highly successful Buddha Records. They received a deal memo from Bogart and started negotiating terms of disengagement with Davis. But at this point Bogart reneged on his agreement, leaving McLean without a label. This was a disastrous blow. It started a two year period during which McLean had no record contract in the US. McLean now says, "I should never have let Bogart get away with what he did. But I didn't realize how damaging it was until later."

On the positive side, his settlement with Arista Records gave McLean ownership of the sound masters for both the *Prime Time* and *Chain Lightning* albums. This gave him an unprecedented amount of control. He was the songwriter, publisher and sound master owner. Though he was without a record company in America, he was able to lease the *Chain Lightning* album to EMI in Europe and to Festival Records in Australia. The album was released in Europe and Australia in late 1978. After that, McLean made it his standard practice to own his sound recordings and leased them to record companies. He applied this practice to all subsequent album releases.

1978 ended with another visit to Europe where McLean performed concerts in Copenhagen, Stockholm, Bergen and Oslo during December. On December 17th he recorded a TV special for the BBC called "Don McLean and Friends." The 50 minute program featured guests Elkie Brooks and the Jordanaires, who were making their first visit to the UK. The show was broadcast on Boxing Day and received such good ratings that it was repeated throughout the 1980s. It was McLean's third British TV special. In 1973 his Royal Albert Hall concert was recorded and broadcast by the BBC, and a few years later he recorded a special for the Stanley Dorfman Show.

Between his concerts in Scandinavia and Britain, McLean completed his first tour of Israel. It was a visit that made a lasting impression on him. He performed concerts in Jerusalem, Haifa, Tel Aviv and in a small spot on the Lebanon border in a building that was a reproduction of the Tanglewood Amphitheater in Lennox, Massachusetts. He received a welcome befitting a superstar. "They greeted me like some sort of biblical king."

His concert series sold out. Although the concerts occurred during the week of Golda Meir's funeral, the government requested that the concerts go ahead as planned. His song, "Babylon," took on extra significance. McLean will never forget being in Jerusalem and hearing "Babylon" sung by thousands in three parts, many with tears flowing.

During his first visit to Israel, Don met a beautiful Israeli girl named Orli Sarfati, who became his companion, off and on, for nearly four years. She was his first serious relationship in a long time. For the next year and a half, McLean would combine visits to Israel with his commitments in the States. For a time, he was living in Israel and going to his home country as a visitor. In Israel he lived with Orli's family. They took him in and treated him as a member of their family. Later, Orli and Don moved out and rented an apartment together in Kiriat Ono, a suburb of Tel Aviv. Their affair was headline news in Israel, a cause of major controversy among Orthodox Jews. Even after they split up, the publicity continued. It is talked about to this day. "Knowing Orli and her family changed my life. I saw the world situation much differently after that experience."

On one occasion McLean was nearly sent to an Israeli jail. While departing the country through a VIP airport tunnel following a particularly difficult week with the paparazzi, two of them jumped out from the shadows in the tunnel, and began snapping away in his face. McLean was not afraid to use physical force from time to time. He smashed both their cameras and punched one photographer, knocking him to the ground. Police were called, but it was decided to let McLean leave the country. His picture appeared in the crime section of the *Jerusalem Post.*

Living in Israel opened up a whole new life to Don. He will never forget the people, the tastes, the smells, the sounds, the faces, or the times spent rambling through Jerusalem alleys and backyards. "Israel was unlike anything I was used to. It was a dip into foreign water for me," he says. He was captivated by the magic and mystery of Jerusalem.

> "My theory is that there is some sort of energy in the ground in that area that energizes the human body. I believe that. I believe it's in the rocks. There was a level of energy that I had never experienced before or since. There was never a time when I could not hear from my window different musical instruments being practiced. I became less and less afraid of anything, as I became accustomed to living with war. I became aware of how precious life is, and how I wasted so much time by being self-indulgent, especially during moments when opportunity was at my fingertips. I also became thankful that I was an American. I appreciated how much these people value opportunity, how hard they work, and how they enjoy life to the fullest."

As word got out that Don McLean was living in Israel, the mayor of Jerusalem asked him if he would make a tourist information film to promote the city. McLean was happy to oblige. Israel was a country of hardship, but a place that offered Don a sense of belonging and friendship that he hadn't experienced for many years. He wrote the song "Jerusalem" especially for the tourist film and later recorded it in Nashville for his *Believers* album. He sang "Jerusalem," live, for the first time in a nightclub in Jerusalem. Footage from this show was included in the twenty-minute tourist film, which also features Don singing many of his most well known songs at spots that have historical significance or at spots that are especially beautiful. The day after the show, the nightclub was bombed.

In a Jerusalem nightclub the night before it was bombed

The song "Sea Man" on the *Believers* album was based on the life of a man McLean met on the beach in Haifa. He lived in a house shaped like a fish, and he was famous in Israel for being a "character." McLean spent an afternoon with him and listened to his life story. When he returned to his apartment, he wrote the story down, just as it had been told to him:

Sea Man

> I walked down to the sea
> And I saw this crazy man
> He was looking at me
> And he said, "I have a plan."
> Yes, he said, "I have a plan."
>
> He was black from the sun
> And his eyes were in tears
> And his hand was so thick
> From the work of the years
> Yes, his hand was so thick
> From the work of the years

He said, "Please come with me
to my home by the sea.
We can smoke, drink and eat
and you'll sit at my feet.
And I'll tell you what I know
while the sea breezes blow,
for I've tried to be free
but I'll soon have to go."

And his house was his art
And nature his wish
It was sculpted from clay
In the shape of a fish
It was sculpted from clay
In the shape of a fish

And the caves in the back
Had been arched into stone
And the creatures he kept
Made him far from alone

"I have only one son
in Chicago for life.
He is separate from me
and so is my wife.
And I live in the sun
and I hate what they've done
to my beautiful sea
and what they'll do to me."

And we walked from the house
For miles by the shore
And we picked up the trash
That they'd left by his door
Yes, we picked up the trash
that they'd left by his door

And the oil and the sludge
Got stuck to my feet
And the fish that were dead
Were too poisonous to eat

Yes, the fish that were dead
Were too poisonous to eat

And the blade cut his hand
And it's stiff from the scar
And the butchers called doctors
Leave you worse than you are
And we're all like the butchers,
We can cut into life
And we like to see blood
On the end of our knife.

And some day they will come
And bulldoze him down
For he has not a permit
From the Kings of the town
No he has not a permit
From the Kings of the town

And the doctors will come
And say he's afraid
And they'll ruin this man
And destroy what he made
And the pictures he kept
Will be torn from his hand
With the beautiful house
That he built on the sand

A third song, "Believers," sums up his experience as a resident of Israel and became the title song of the album.

For most of 1979 McLean concentrated on touring and performing as many concerts as possible. He was visiting Holland a lot — even more than Britain or Australia. He completed a short tour of Canada in April 1979, and, in June, he went back to Holland. He spent the rest of the year combining a concert schedule in the US, with living in Israel. A similar schedule continued into 1980. McLean completed another short tour of Canada and then spent much of January and February in Israel.

Most artists have a cycle of album – tour – album – tour, whereas McLean had firmly settled into a cycle of tour – tour – tour – tour. No one can count all the Don McLean shows since 1970, but they number in the thousands and range across many countries. McLean had done twelve world tours since the Seventies and managed to keep his popularity intact. Because he had different hits in different countries, he has received over forty gold and platinum records, worldwide.

Don McLean on Song Making and Recording

My approach to album making is to create a selection of new songs, or new arrangements of old songs, and treat each as a separate world. In order for the record to be complete I must be able to listen to the recording of the song and have it take me away. I must be transported to another place, a place unique to the composition and the performance of that particular tune. In short, the recording must be commanding, and all the songs must be different.

I do not like modulations (key changes within a song), unless they are brilliant, since most modulations are an admission of defeat by the songwriter. Modulations usually mean the song has gone on too long, it has become boring, so we modulate in order to wake up the tune and the listener. I do not like fade-out endings, as this is another admission of defeat. We can't come up with an ending, so we fade it out. I don't like the word "just" in a lyric unless it is essential, as in the title, "It's Just the Sun." The use here is alright, because of the understatement which is intended. "Just" is more often used as a filler word to cover a missing beat, and the use of it in this way shows me I have not written the best lyric. Often a rewrite produces a revamp of the whole song in which several thoughts are expressed more quickly and the song says more with fewer words.

For an album, I like to use solo guitar, or guitar and bass, for at least one song and a full string ensemble for half the tunes or more. I need a rock 'n' roll rhythm section with great electric guitars for the string tunes. I don't use horns much, but I love creative percussion. I love background voices: three girls, or, for a heavy sound, I use the Jordanaires. I used a blend of six — four male voices and two female voices — for my holiday recording, *Don McLean Christmas*.

With these musicians I can craft a unique track for each musical composition, but, like spokes of a wheel, all the songs must point to a central idea. This is at the heart of all the albums I have made. I am an album artist. I do not go into a recording studio with the idea of cutting a single. I come to make albums.

My song writing had nothing to do with the many older musicians I met as a young man. I see song writing as a mystical process which involves tuning something in on my psychic radio. I can't tell you how I write songs, or why I write them. For someone who is known as a songwriter, I have not written many songs, maybe 200 or so. But I was very particular about the concept behind each song and the process for each one. My songs are born from pure emotion and passion. I am not a formula songwriter, that is to say, I am not a "professional" songwriter. My songs are all, somehow, about me, not some idea which belongs to someone else or a script which needs music.

In the music business you can become known for a "sound," and, after a while, you begin to edit yourself so that you don't go outside those boundaries. I don't have a "sound." I make whatever music I please. If you are wedded to a sound, you can fall into the process of self parody. I believe the sum total of all my recordings, including songs I've written and songs by other writers that I have recorded, express the full talent I have.

As I grow older I have less desire to write songs. I prefer performing. Song writing is a little like doing homework or writing out the words: "I will not talk in class," 500 times. When things come to me, I'm stuck with them and I have to reveal them, because I can feel them there and they have to come out. But I don't like grappling with lyrics, spending a month thinking "Why isn't that lyric right?" I feel I have said many of the things I wanted to say in the best way I knew how, at the top of my powers. I do not want to repeat myself. And I do not want to write a "Don McLean" song just because people expect it of me. I have never been moved by the expectations of others.

Chapter 10: "Crying"...The Comeback

Much to McLean's surprise, representatives of EMI in Holland called in April, 1980, to say that the song "Crying" had spontaneously picked up continuous airplay on Dutch radio stations. He was urged to fly to Holland immediately and appear on several important musical variety shows to plug the song. To coincide with his visit, EMI released "Crying" as a single, and it shot to No.1 after these appearances. It was unexpected, but welcome, news. EMI executives from Holland flew to England and persuaded their British counterparts to repeat the promotion in England. The song quickly became a hit there too, reaching No.1 on the singles chart on June 21st, 1980. The same thing happened in Australia.

McLean did not follow his success in the UK with a concert tour right away, except for one appearance at the Cambridge Folk Festival in August. He fulfilled his obligatory appearance on *Top of the Pops* with a promotional video (one of the first.)

Following his No.1 single, EMI was keen to promote McLean's music and released a 15-track compilation called the *Very Best of Don McLean*. It reached No.3 on the UK chart and became a worldwide hit. The record was not released in North America. In the UK interest in Don McLean was so high that the *Chain Lightning* album, released nearly two years earlier, entered the charts and made the Top 20.

Then in September he returned and completed a full tour of the UK, traveling in two buses around the English and Scottish countryside. It was a significant tour. Every show sold out. This time he was not appearing solo. He was accompanied by a rock 'n' roll orchestra especially created for the concert series. Bob Henrit (who later played for the Kinks) played drums, Bob Metzger electric guitar, Jimmie Horowitz piano, David Wintour bass guitar, and Fred Snel double bass. Don thought that Bob Henrit was one of the best drummers he had ever heard and on a personal level thought Henrit was open to every kind of music and a hell of a lot of fun to be with. Robin Williams conducted the string section and played violin. The full orchestra sound allowed McLean to sing songs like "Crying" and "Vincent" as they had been recorded, with strings — live. With rock 'n' roll sidemen he could rock on songs like "Left for Dead," "Prime Time," and "American Pie."

The tour concluded on October 1st at the Royal Festival Hall in London. The demand for tickets was so great that an extra show was organized with only three days notice and took place at the Dominion Theatre in London, on Saturday, October 4th. This last, sell-out show was recorded, live, for the 1983 album called *Dominion*. This album was later issued in the US as *Don McLean's Greatest Hits Live*. Before the Dominion show, Paul Gambaccini, a well known disc jockey on British radio and a successful music journalist, interviewed McLean in his dressing room. That interview and the concert performance became the video release entitled *The Music of Don McLean*.

Don McLean had survived the roughest two or three years of his career. He had re-established himself in almost every major record-buying market in the world. His second career comeback had begun. All he needed to do now was re-conquer his home country.

After two years living abroad, news of Don's No.1 successes in Europe and Australia reached home, and US record companies began to take notice. McLean signed a deal with Millennium Records in December, 1980, and they released "Crying" that month. In January, 1981, Millennium Records issued *Chain Lightning*, two and a half years after it had been recorded in Nashville, and two years after its release in Europe. It charted on February 14th, 1981, and reached No.28.

Unaware that these releases would do so well, McLean began 1981 by repeating his successful overseas touring pattern. He flew from Israel to appear in Luxembourg and then made lucrative, highly publicized appearances in Ireland. However, by February, he was hot in the US, as "Crying" climbed to No.5 on the pop singles chart. Millennium Records wanted him home immediately.

The musical style of *Chain Lightning* was right for the early eighties market. Members of the media were falling all over themselves to interview him. It was like 1971 all over again. McLean was an overnight success for the second time, and he knew he had to work hard to press home his good fortune. Throughout 1981 and 1982, he toured the country, clocking over 100 appearances a year. In 1981 he completed three bus tours of the US, no longer performing solo. McLean had formed a band that included Bob Henrit, Bob Metzger and Fred Snel from his British tour the previous summer and Garth Hudson from "The Band."

On the road in 1981, McLean and his band had a great time traveling from one sold-out venue to another. They played the brand new Savoy Club, a 1000-seat auditorium in the heart of Manhattan which quickly sold out. Coming on after Don was a guy named Meatloaf, and absolutely no one showed up for his show. He had fifteen guitars on stage and ten people in the audience. Meatloaf would bounce back big time a few years later.

On the road the band enjoyed a full range of extra-curricular activities. Fred Snel recalled, "On one occasion we drove in the bus for more than half a day to visit the Tom Mix Museum, so that Don could buy some Western cowboy boots."

Towards the end of 1981, McLean was scheduled to play the Roxy Club in Los Angeles for two nights in December. However, en-route his bus broke down just outside Phoenix. Don spotted a girl with a trailer attached to her car, and he asked her if she was going California. When she said yes, McLean offered to pay her to take the band to Los Angeles. She agreed, they piled into her car, and she drove them to the club. She watched the show, and, "As far as I can remember," Don said, "she slept with the road manager. So there you go. That was California in the old days."

Bob Henrit, Bob Metzger and Don at the bar, Sahara Tahoe Casino, 1981

Professionally, McLean was on a high. Not only had "Crying" become a hit, but the follow-up single, "Since I Don't Have You," charted on April 11th, 1981, and climbed to No.13. A third single, "It's Just the Sun," also became a hit.

The recording of the next album, *Believers*, took place May 19th-21st , 1981, with producer Larry Butler and the same musicians he used for *Chain Lightning*. McLean followed a similar formula of mixing old songs, such as "Love Hurts," with his new songs like "Crazy Eyes," "Isn't it Strange," and "Left for Dead on the Road of Love." This album also includes the musical results of his time in Israel: "Believers," "Jerusalem," and "Sea Man." A re-make of "Castles in the Air" became the only hit from the *Believers* album, reaching the Top 40 in late 1981. The album itself only reached No.156 on the album chart, and it failed to have an impact in Europe.

McLean dedicated the *Believers* album to Lee Hays, who had died in the summer of 1981, after a long illness. The last time Don saw his friend was in October, 1980, at the Weavers Reunion Concert at Carnegie Hall. Throughout the 1970s, Lee Hays' health had declined, and Don could not bear to see this. Although he spoke on the phone with Hays from time to time, he avoided visiting him. Hays had many problems as a consequence of diabetes. Ulcers appeared on his feet, and gangrene set in. A toe was removed, then one leg, and then the other. Hays had a pacemaker for his heart condition and cataracts that were operated on. When he listed all of his ailments, he would laugh and say, "I'm the six dollar man." Don was shocked when he learned that a film crew wanted to interview him for a movie about the Weavers, called *Wasn't that a Time*. He remembers:

> "I was told the Weavers would sing again at Carnegie Hall in 1980, seventeen years after they had retired. If you had asked me whether an able-bodied Lee Hays would ever sing with the Weavers again, I would have bet everything I had that it would not happen. And yet a crippled Lee was going to Carnegie Hall one more time. I saw Lee for the last time in his wheelchair backstage at the hall. For a moment, he didn't believe it was me. As I looked at him, it was like seeing my father's grey eyes as he looked up at me the night they carried him out of our house. The Weavers would rise again, and I was coming back. I think we were both very proud of each other. Lee died the following year, after seeing his film triumph at the Cambridge Folk Festival."

In addition to recording *Believers* in 1981, McLean was asked by Rankin and Bass, creators of many animated films, to sing the title song to their new movie, *Flight of Dragons*. He watched the movie and liked it. He thought the song was adequate and agreed to sing it. However, after hearing the demo tape sent to him, he decided it sounded a little stilted and implemented some small melodic changes. He figured the writer would accept these modifications as artistic license.

> "When I got to the studio the writer was there and the engineer rolled the tape. I sang the song several times but the writer was not happy. I told him his song was not easy to sing as written, and if they asked an artist like myself to sing a tune, they should expect the artist to do his thing with the song. This cut no ice with the writer, who reminded me of a math teacher who had been in the eight grade too long. He annoyed me with his attitude, and I said, fine — get someone else."

A few weeks later, McLean received a letter from the song writer with sheet music for the song with all of his "mistakes" marked in red. He felt like he was in music class.

> "I told Rankin and Bass to shove the song and stop bothering me. However they kept begging me to try again. Out of the goodness of my heart I decided to go to the studio and sing the song as it was written, because I liked the movie. After many takes to the writer's satisfaction, the producer of the session came into the booth and asked me very sheepishly, 'Don, do you think you could sing it like you did before.' I laughed, did one take my way, and nailed the tune. By now I sure knew the damn song. So that's the story of the 'Flight of Dragons.'"

1982 was one of the best years of Don's career. He completed a sold-out tour of over one hundred cities in sixteen countries around the world. He received gold and platinum records for the *Very Best of Don McLean* in Britain, Australia, and New Zealand.

In February, 1982, McLean was featured in a German television special. The television crew filmed his mother, visited his old grammar school and high school, traveled around Larchmont, and did a good job of retracing his roots. It's the only film footage that exists of his mother.

Over the next couple of months, McLean completed triumphant tours of Britain and several European countries, including Holland and Finland. Later in the year, he returned to Australia and set an attendance record at the Capitol Theater in Sydney. When he toured Australia, he played three different kinds of venues: first, the halls of the small outback towns which other international stars rarely saw; second, the show rooms of the coastal casinos; and finally, the continent's major concert halls — selling out all the way.

In 1982, McLean was invited to perform on the popular television show, Austin City Limits. The show was produced by Terry Lacona, who had been a young announcer and personality on WEOK Radio in Poughkeepsie, in 1968, and had interviewed Don when he was the Hudson River Troubadour. His appearance on Austin City Limits was memorable. While he was playing "American Pie," a string broke. He had learned from a great deal of experience that when this happened, instead of stopping to change the string and then starting again, he should produce a set of strings from his pocket, continue to sing the song while he replaced the broken string, tune it up with a quick twang, and finish singing the song without missing a beat. This brought huge applause. It tore the house down.

But when it happened on Austin City Limits, Lacona took him aside and said, "Now, how about doing the song right?" McLean told him that he had just done the song "righter than it ever would be" and that he was finished. "And so, once again, I got a reputation for being difficult." However, that show is now considered one of the classic Austin City Limits broadcasts, and people still write letters to McLean about it. His road manager, who had seen him do this a couple of times, always shouted, "Break a string!" not "Break a leg," when he went out on stage.

Don presenting the Ivor Novello award to Sting, London 1981.

1982 was a fantastic touring year. McLean performed at remarkably diverse venues. In England McLean presented Sting with the Ivor Novello Award for the song, "Every Breath You Take." As he handed

Sting the award, Don said, "This is for Every Bath You Take, I'll Be Washing You." Sting was not amused, but the audience was. Later that year, McLean appeared at a gala celebration at the British House of Commons for artists who had No.1 records in the 1970s. In fact, throughout his career McLean has performed anywhere and everywhere. He says,

"Since I am basically a troubadour at heart, I can easily go from performing at the Sydney Opera House or the Royal Festival Hall in London to an Indian reservation in Wisconsin or a state fair. I have performed following demolition derbies and following aerialists that did their act from a helicopter over the audience. I sang at a German biker rally. You haven't lived until you've seen a stadium of German head bangers singing 'Vincent.' My 'Vincent' memories are among the most dramatic and absurd, from seeing bikers so drunk they were teary-eyed and urinating on themselves, to hearing country boys at Cairns Ballroom in Oklahoma yell 'Yahoo!' and jump to their feet, after every verse. I've experienced angry Indians on a Wisconsin reservation circling our wagons and threatening all kinds of violence, with black smoke rising from burning vinyl plastic lawn furniture behind us, because I'd forgotten to sing 'Vincent.'"

On November 21, 1982, McLean was presented with an award by the State of Israel for helping raise money through the sale of Israeli bonds. Film actor Eliot Gould presented the award. Then on November 26th, Don took part in the Macy's Thanksgiving Day Parade in New York. He rode in the crow's nest at the top of a 50-foot mast on a pirate ship. For the entire parade, he rode down Fifth Avenue in that crow's nest, staring at Mickey Mouse's rear end with Donald Duck near by, looking directly into windows on the eighth story of buildings that lined the parade route. Entire buildings of people waved at him, while his songs blasted from loudspeakers. When "American Pie" came on, the crowds of people lining the street sang out the chorus. Finally his pirate ship stopped before the reviewing stand and the TV cameras in front of Macy's Department Store, and he sang "Castles in the Air." At the end of the parade a cherry picker had to get him down. It was surreal.

Don McLean at Carnegie Hall, 1982.
(Rick Mullen, left on bass, John Platania, right on guitar.)

Following the Macy's Thanksgiving Day Parade, McLean played Carnegie Hall, accompanied by John Platania and Rick Mullen. He met John Platania in October, 1981, and from that point until the mid-1990s, Platania was his regular accompanist in concert. After the show at Carnegie Hall, McLean was presented with his third "Million Performance Certificate" by BMI, Broadcast Music Inc., the performing rights organization that monitors song performances. In 1982, McLean was one of only a handful of BMI songwriters who had received three or more such awards.

Even though EMI Records had released *Dominion* in the European market in October, 1981, McLean did not record new material in the US or extend his contract with Millennium Records in 1982. In fact, the Millennium Records deal ended with the *Believers* album in 1981, and the deal with EMI in Europe concluded when *Dominion* was released. EMI Records had taken over the back catalog of United Artists, and, with it, McLean's first six albums. However, they were no longer paying him to produce new material.

There was a failure of management during this crucial time. McLean had a string of hit records and had raised his profile back to where it was during the early 1970s. EMI was one of the world's biggest record companies, and they wanted to release the *Very Best of Don McLean* in North America. There was a good chance that such an album would make the charts and sell a million records. The time was perfect for the release of the record, but the deal was blown.

Don's relationship with Herb Gart had become severely strained during recent years when he had no recording contract in the United States. He said, "I was angry about it. I felt that it was time to move on." After the EMI debacle, McLean had had enough.

Years later, McLean looked back on his long-time manager:

"Herb Gart was my manager for 18 years. As I approached my 40th birthday, I decided that after many good things had happened and many good things that should have happened did not, that I did not need or want a manager. Managers are good for young artists who want to have fun and leave the business stuff to a surrogate parent, but as one reaches 40 you have to begin to act like an adult.

There is a saying in the business, that 'A manager treats an artist like a mushroom: keep him in the dark, and feed him on horseshit.' I can't say this about Herb but it is the way the business works and people do grow apart. Like Marlon Brando, who, at the end of his life, admitted that he didn't have the guts to walk away from the money Hollywood offered him. I, too, couldn't make a change because I didn't have the guts to.

As I reached the end of my thirties, I became more and more disgusted. In any case in 1983 I decided to 'clean up Dodge City,' and I fired everybody. I had no agent, no manager, no record company, no nothing. I was starting over from scratch, except everybody wanted to sue me. If I was going down, I was going down swinging. It was a terrifying, but exhilarating, time, as I gradually took complete control of my career. And at that time my career was at another standstill, only two years after my No.1 record — 'Crying.'

Today I have managed to see the earnings from my songs increase twenty-fold. Song performance income is up many times. Live performance fees are many times what they were. And I receive much better record income, even in the Napster era. Unlike Elvis, the best example of someone who should have quit his manager and saved his own life, I did both. And it was the beginning of the best years of my life."

1983 was a successful year for McLean. In August, he sang "Crying" on the Today Show, and he performed at Carnegie Hall with the Jordanaires in November to a sell-out crowd. He received an invitation from New York Mayor Ed Koch to sing at Gracie Mansion, on the evening of

November 29th, for the Chinese delegation visiting the United States. Bookings were going strong, though they were down from the levels of 1981 and 1982. McLean had no record contract in the US or Europe, and now he had no manager. He was on his own again, and it would be the beginning of a completely new Don McLean. He was in control of his personal life and his business affairs. The name Don McLean would become more famous than ever.

Chapter 11: Crossroads…1980s, Litigation

Where there's a hit, there's a writ.

UK show biz proverb

With no manager, no record deal in North America or Europe, and just one record left to produce for Festival Records in Australia, Don McLean was going to have to start again.

Alan Livingston announced that he was selling his publishing company, Mayday Music. This had significant implications for Don, since Mayday Music owned the publishing copyrights for all songs on the *Tapestry* and *American Pie* albums. When McLean signed his first record contract in 1969, the contract with Livingston's Mediarts to produce the *Tapestry* album, he signed over ownership of the publishing copyrights to Livingston's Mayday Music, in return for a favorable participation agreement. Under this agreement, he received a 50% share of the publishing royalties collected by Mayday Music. Mayday distributed income from his songs at a 50:50 ratio between the songwriter and the publisher (Mayday Music.) As sole writer, McLean received 100% of the writer's share, and, under the terms of his participation agreement, 50% of the publisher's share. This still applied after Mediarts was taken over by United Artists, because the publishing agreement had been made with Mayday Music continued to exist. McLean therefore received 75% of the income arising from songs such as "American Pie" and "Vincent." The same applied for cover versions of Don McLean songs. Perry Como's hit version and Elvis's version of "And I Love You So" were major earners.

The singer and record company earn income from the sale of records. This is very lucrative for successful artists, but the long term profit in the music industry lies in the publishing.

Since McLean did not own the publishing copyright to his songs on *Tapestry* and *American Pie*, he was not entitled to any proceeds from the sale to the new owners, Merit Music.

Merit Music was a new company formed by Guy Beatty and Herb Morgan, two successful real estate developers. They wanted to make it big in the music business, so they hired Dave Burgess to oversee their song writing and publishing activities. Their songwriters worked in small cubicles like those in the Brill Building in New York, where songwriters like Neil Sedaka, Carol King, Burt Bacharach, and Hal David, churned out rock 'n' roll songs for 165 different music companies in the 1960s.

Burgess was an original, founding member of the Champs in the 1950s and had a notable hit with "Tequila." The Champs were named after Gene Autry's horse, since Autry owned the Challenge record label. After writing a solo single called "I'm Available" in 1957, Burgess became an in-house producer for Challenge Records and continued his song writing. He worked with singers like Jerry Fuller, Glen Campbell, and Ricky Nelson. His writing was influenced by artists like Buddy Holly and Marty Robbins.

McLean met the owners of Merit Music in November, 1983, at the Essex Hotel in New York. He was anxious to hear what they could offer him and how they thought his publishing interests could be developed. Incredibly, however, they were there to offer him a writer's agreement. They wanted McLean to join Merit Music as a songwriter. Don didn't like that very much. He had been a star with hit records all over the world for the past ten years, and he was there to hear what they had to offer.

The meeting was disastrous, but McLean struck up a phone relationship with Dave Burgess, who was not happy with Merit Music, either. From time to time, McLean contacted Burgess to ask his advice. Burgess put him in contact with the Nashville law firm of Gilbert, Frank & Milom. McLean hired attorneys Mike Milom and Chris Horsnell, now with Bass, Berry & Sims. Horsnell remains his lawyer to this day.

Chris Horsnell analyzed his relationship with Don McLean:

> "I began working with Don in the early 1980s. I was a baby lawyer helping out a senior partner. Over the years, as my work with Don grew, so did my respect for him as a person and as a songwriter and artist. That is the cornerstone of our working relationship. We respect each other and value each other's opinions and ideas. Don is the creative, emotional, free-thinking side, while I am the ever cautious, practical side, the yin and the yang, of the business that is Don McLean. He feels free to throw out any idea, and he expects me to disagree with him, openly, if I do. Recently, when we had difficulty connecting to discuss a business deal, Don left me a voice-mail message at 4:00 a.m. The message was simple. "Please call me on this, because you know that if you don't, I'll probably go ahead and do it." It's never a dull moment. Don keeps me on my toes intellectually in business dealings and in philosophical discussions. He ranks in a rare category of lawyer-client relationships. He is the client-friend who does not let business get in the way of friendship. Now, if I can just get him to use email."

During 1984, Horsnell and Burgess helped McLean untangle various aspects of his professional life. Don insisted that they review and re-review every contract. He wanted everyone and every organization with a finger in the Don McLean pie to be examined closely. He was especially anxious to break free from the William Morris Agency. He had been on their books since the mid-1960s, and they took 10% of his song income. Milom and Horsnell uncovered various technical flaws in their agreement and were able to break the chains.

McLean was impressed by Burgess' advice and signed Burgess to be an administrator for his publishing activities. Burgess and Horsnell looked carefully at McLean's agreement with Merit Music and uncovered holes that would allow McLean to acquire the publishing copyright to his songs on *Tapestry* and *American Pie*.

When Beatty and Morgan acquired Alan Livingston's Mayday Music, the Don McLean revenues were relatively small. Therefore, Beatty and Morgan were keen to sell the copyrights to his songs and hopefully make a profit. They approached Universal Music Publishing, and that company was interested in acquiring the copyrights. However, the value of the deal rested on the ability to renew the copyrights. Copyrights do not last forever. Works registered prior to 1978 were copyrighted for 28 years. In the final year of this period the copyright owner must apply to renew the copyright for another 28 years (now extended to 67 years). At the end of this period, the work goes into the public domain. For works registered from 1978 onwards, copyright remains with the owner during his or her lifetime and for 70 years following his or her death. Copyrights are tangible assets that can be sold, leased, and passed on in wills.

Since the copyright for the first Don McLean songs had been registered to Mayday Music in 1969, their first renewal was due in 1997. As the new owners, Universal Music Group would expect to renew in 1997. However, a sensational loophole was discovered by McLean and his lawyer and administrator that prevented this. When McLean had signed with Mediarts, he had negotiated special terms regarding the rights to renew. Mayday Music would have to pay him a sum of money within the first three years of his contract with them in order to secure the right to renew after 28 years. With the sale of Mediarts in 1971 and the reorganization of Alan Livingston's business arrangements, this payment was overlooked and never made. McLean demonstrated that therefore, he had acquired the sole ownership of the renewal rights. Merit Music owned the copyrights, but had no way to renew them. Their value was much reduced. Universal Music had little to gain by purchasing the copyrights, since they could not renew them. Alan Shulman, a legendary New York music business lawyer, was a able to broker a deal which let Universal administer McLean's songs, satisfied Merit Music, and gave Don McLean total ownership of his song catalog.

McLean was involved in various legal actions for much of the mid-1980s. However, the outcome meant that he owned the copyrights to all his songs, including all those on the *Tapestry* and *American Pie* albums. McLean was now the owner of one of the most valuable music publishing catalogs in the world.

McLean further protected his intellectual property rights by registering several trademarks, including: "Don McLean," "American Pie," "The Day the Music Died," "Bye, Bye Miss American Pie," and "Starry, Starry Night." This move paid off handsomely when Universal Pictures wanted to use "American Pie" for the title of a movie in the late 1990s. Los Angeles attorney and friend, Bert Diexler, brokered a terrific deal for Universal Pictures to use the McLean trademark for its American Pie movie series.

The management upheavals of 1983 and 1984 signaled yet another new phase in McLean's career. The next thirteen years would be far quieter than the previous thirteen years. During this time the songs McLean had written would come to the fore, and he would be left in their shadows. This was fine with him. He was happy with what he had achieved. He said, "I want my songs to last and mean something to people. My main goal was to let the songs be famous. They've taken me a long way. I haven't changed, but the world has changed around me. In 1970, 1971, and 1972, I was on the cutting edge of what was happening. Now I'm something of a relic."

The upheavals of the mid-eighties led him to reflect on management and careers in the music business:

> "I always loved the way Elvis Presley emerged from the Deep South and presented himself to the public as if he were no different than anybody else. His love of his parents, as his best friends in this world, was touching and told a lot about what must have been a very loving, generous, and innocent personality. This,

along with his magical music, could have set him up to be turned into a clown, but he even finessed that.

One thing I understand about this remarkable man was his insecurity. I empathize with what must have been his monumental frustration with the direction of his career later on and the anger he must have felt toward himself for not having the self confidence to leave his manager and find out where he might go if he gave himself permission to grow. It is very hard to 'burn the bridge that brought you over.' Gordon Stoker told me, 'Once they wouldn't let him act in movies, Elvis took down his sign.' Took down his sign. Mr. Elvis Presley Inc. was no longer in business, but he was still alive and required to fill his time in some fashion. We all know the rest of the story.

When I fired everybody in 1983, I made up my mind that no matter how loyal I might be, or innocent, or generous, I was too old to be asking someone what I was supposed to do each day. Turning 40 saved my life, because, in some small way, I was too insecure to give myself permission to grow. Like many other performers, I was too loyal to break the mold which had been set.

The life I enjoy today is a direct result of the chance I took years ago. The cautionary tale, for me, was the story of Elvis. The artist is really the source of everything. I hope this story will encourage others to not be afraid to trust yourself.

A friend of mine, who knows the music business better than anyone, said, 'A big time career is a career that keeps going.' I have been going now for 38 years. A day does not go by when my songs are not played in every country on earth. There are many artists with less musical success who have larger, more lucrative careers, and there are some with great success for a while who completely fade away. There are some for whom an early death is the beginning of a bigger career, and others just fade in death. In short, if your career keeps going in the major leagues, it is a big time career, and you have made it.

Whatever business decisions I have made, I made to maintain the purity of my music and how it is used. By doing this I represent myself accurately, because I only care about my songs and recordings. I do not care about building an empire tangent to my music career.

One must overcome a great deal of negativity to be successful in any endeavor, but in the music business an artist must get used to overcoming personal rejection. The thought that your idea is not bad, you are, hurts, and it can make you crazy. That's why I never read reviews. If they hate me, it will hurt me, and if they love me, it will swell my head. In either case it's already old news, so why mess with it in the first place.

My career has been the product of an accumulation of accidents and minor miracles. 'American Pie' and Don McLean were pretty low in 1995, but by the end of the century on-line polls listed 'American Pie' as one of the best songs of the century. It was at the top of the list. This gave the song a new and powerful status. Madonna sang my song, because it was the 'millennium' song. In 2001 BMI certified 'American Pie' as one of the top five most played songs of 2001. At that point it was actually bigger than it was in 1972. I am a creation of the people, not of record company hype. And that is just what I was hoping for."

Relic or not, McLean re-entered his tour-tour-tour cycle with gusto in 1984, a year which turned out to be one of the busiest of his concert career. Don and his band covered thousands of miles in the US. "I toured my ass off, because I had no manager, and I wanted to hit the road. And we did. We went all over." In February, he was booked for thirteen nights solid at the Fairmont Hotel in Dallas. This was not McLean's cup of tea — seeing the same people day in, day out; eating the same food; and singing in the same room every evening. "Some performers can do this. I can't. On top of that, it was a black tie kind of place, and I'm not a black tie kind of guy. We played our instruments extra loud and tried to offend everybody."

He toured England and Ireland in March, but more down to earth and more to his liking was a special tour of small towns in Northern Ireland, July 21st to July 30th, 1984. Ireland's unrest was at its peak, and Irish terrorists made many places "no go" areas. McLean "did go," albeit under armed guard. He had a man cleaning a magnum pistol outside his door every night, because of kidnap rumors. Few, if any, other stars appeared in these towns and his tour brought admiration from more people than those who attended the shows. McLean wanted to visit these places to see what people look like when they are living in fear. The ordinary folk of Northern Ireland were happy to see him, and, for the short time while Don McLean was singing, a sense of peace reigned.

When he returned from Northern Ireland, McLean did a benefit concert for the hospital in Cold Spring, New York, the town where he used to live in the little gatehouse and where he wrote some of his best songs. He still owned his house in Garrison, New York, but the increasing development of the area prompted him to purchase a house in Castine, Maine.

Castine is a small coastal village located on a peninsula in Penobscot Bay, on the coast of Maine. The entire town is on the National Register of Historic Places and is known for its 18th century architecture. Major landmarks include Fort George, built by the British in 1779 and partially restored as a state memorial, and Fort Madison, the earthwork remnants built by the Americans in 1811, occupied by the British during the War of 1812, and reconstructed during the American Civil War. With a population of just 1000, Castine provided McLean with the peace and quiet he craved when he was away from the concert stage.

Over the years McLean had lost contact with many of the aunts, uncles, and cousins he'd grown up with. Occasionally the family would get together to celebrate a wedding, birth, or death, but Don did not always attend.

However, on Sunday, August 26, 1984, he attended the wedding of his cousin Lisa Embrendo with his mother, as a favor to her. As the bride was walking down the aisle, his mother started speaking very loudly, almost raving. Don was startled. She had never done anything like that before. The next day she called him and asked, "How did you like the wedding?" He said, "Well, I liked the wedding, but you were a little weird." She was shocked. She had no recollection of her outburst the day before. A few weeks later, when McLean visited his mother he noticed that she had large lumps on her neck. His sister told him that she refused to go to the doctor. Don pleaded with her to go to the hospital. The lumps were malignant. She was diagnosed with an inoperable brain tumor.

1984 had climaxed with a long tour of Australia from mid-September to the end of October. McLean played the Sydney Entertainment Centre, a brand new, ten-thousand-seat auditorium. The promoters expected three thousand people, but McLean performed to sell-out crowds on three successive nights. During this tour, he recorded and released "L'Affaire D'Amour" written by Beeb Bertles of the Little River Band.

After returning home, McLean boarded a plane for Holland where he played Ogala. This was followed with a few shows in England "just for kicks." Though he hadn't had a hit record in these countries for nearly four years, he was still filling the same major concert halls that he'd filled twelve years earlier, on his first visits. His British television profile was still high. He sang "Everyday" on ITV's top-rated show, "Live at Her Majesty's."

Don McLean and the Jordanaires on stage at Carnegie Hall, 1984.

On November 21st, McLean played Carnegie Hall with the Jordanaires for a Greenpeace benefit. They had only a couple of days to rehearse after his return from overseas. They got together with Don's band at his home in Garrison. The rehearsal sessions were filmed by a couple of friends, and provide the longest video film that exists of McLean performing with the Jordanaires. After the show at Carnegie Hall, David McTaggart, the Canadian co-founder of Greenpeace, came backstage and told Don that his song, "Tapestry," was one of the factors that got him involved in the environmental movement.

Backstage with the Jordanaires at the Greenpeace Benefit
Carnegie Hall, November 21ˢᵗ 1984
(From left to right: Gordon Stoker, Neal Matthews, Don McLean, Duane West,
Ray Walker)

In 1985 McLean hit the road hard in the US and overseas. His mother had died early in 1985, shortly before her eightieth birthday, and his legal team was embroiled in legal actions of one sort or another. Dave Burgess was an influential member of his back room setup. He wanted to help McLean re-develop his profile in the US, and he offered to use his contacts to secure a record deal. McLean signed a limited management agreement with him and did some demos with him. He was impressed with Burgess's production skills, so he asked him to produce his next record.

The next record was *For the Memories*, a collection of well known songs from the 1950s, including: "Wonderful World," "Crazy," and "A White Sport Coat and a Pink Carnation," and two new McLean compositions: "Slow and Easy" and "Lonely as the Night." The album featured McLean's version of "Maybe Baby," which he had recorded for the *Chain Lightning* album, but it had not been included. Therefore, Larry Butler is listed as a co-producer of *For the Memories* with Dave Burgess. This record fulfilled his contract with Festival Records in Australia. He leased the record to Festival, leaving him free to negotiate its release elsewhere. In the UK, the album was released on EMI's "Music for Pleasure" label. Both releases were low profile, and the album failed to make an impact.

For the Memories was released in the US in 1989 on the Gold Castle label. McLean had added a second album of songs from the 1930s and 1940s to the collection. He was indulging himself, for it took him back to his childhood when he spent hours listening to old records when he was home from school with asthma or pneumonia. Songs like "If I Only Had a Match," "But Beautiful," and "Someone to Watch Over Me" also represented the music he played with Ken Ascher at the Music Inn in the 1960s. *For the Memories* featured the Jordanaires providing the background vocals, and Tony Migliore, a top arranger and producer, on the piano.

After McLean fulfilled his commitment to Festival Records, he had no record contract anywhere in the world. This was good, because it allowed Burgess to negotiate a three-record deal with Capitol Records. The three records included: *Don McLean's Greatest Hits: Then and Now*, *Love Tracks*, and the *Best of Don McLean*, which were released in the US during 1987 and 1988. His first "best of" compilation in the US has since gone gold.

Love Tracks was recorded at the Nightingale Studios in Nashville, Tennessee, from March 1st through the 9th, 1987, with Dave Burgess producing and Joe Bogan engineering. The *Love Tracks* album was unusual, because it consisted of brand new songs written by other songwriters as well as new Don McLean songs. From this album, "Love in my Heart" and "Eventually" landed on the country charts, the former making the Top 10 in Australia. "You Can't Blame the Wreck on the Train," also from *Love Tracks*, climbed to the Top 50. This song and "Eventually" were written by Terri Sharp, one of the most talented songwriters of the Nashville scene. The *Don McLean's Greatest Hits: Then and Now* album was made up of McLean's original greatest hits, including: "American Pie," "Vincent," and "And I Love You So" and new songs including "Don't Burn the Bridge" and "Superman's Ghost." The album included "He's Got You," which became a minor country hit, and Jerry Fuller's "But She Loves Me," which was probably suggested by Burgess, since he produced some of Fuller's material in the 1960s.

The cover of the *Don McLean's Greatest Hits: Then and Now* album featured a photograph of a dressing table, supposedly in McLean's house, with various photos and items of memorabilia collected over the years. It also featured a Gibson guitar. McLean never played a Gibson guitar, and he was never consulted about the cover.

Despite the best efforts of both McLean and Capitol Records, these records never garnered big sales. However, Capitol Records got the compilation album they wanted, and the new releases reinforced McLean's presence in music stores.

As these albums were released, the CD was becoming the dominant music medium. Capitol Records released two albums on CD in Europe: *And I Love You So*, which was a collection of tracks from the *Love Tracks* and *Don McLean's Greatest Hits: Then and Now* albums, and a re-issue of the *Very Best of Don McLean*, which included five bonus tracks. Within seven or eight years all of McLean's albums re-emerged on CD. BGO Records released the United Artists albums in England, and Hip-o Records released albums from *Prime Time* onwards in the US. The demand for McLean's old recordings on CD has not declined, as old fans replace their vinyl collections and new fans discover his music.

McLean was much happier with the organization of his activities and his unprecedented degree of control over his publishing and sound recordings. The re-issues of the early albums continued to sell well, although album sales were less than they were in the mid 1970s. He was in demand for concert performances, around the US and internationally. He toured the UK in 1987 and 1989.

On December 19th, 1987, McLean appeared on the Buddy Holly 50th Birthday television special produced by Austin City Limits and hosted by Kris Kristopherson. He and the Jordanaires, together with the original Crickets, performed "Maybe Baby." It was the only time the Jordanaires and the Crickets performed together. Since then McLean has turned down invitations to appear at Buddy Holly tribute concerts, saying, "My music is my tribute."

Don McLean, the Jordanaires and the Crickets
Buddy Holly Tribute Show

At 42 years old, McLean was still carrying on like a 21 year old. After a fantastic couple of decades of partying, musical success, and endless concert work, every concert hall in the world displayed his autographed picture. He had made it. However, his mother's death in 1985 made him feel mortal for the first time. It wouldn't be too many years before he had lived as long as his father. He had several beautiful homes, stocks and bonds, and no one to share it all with. His parents had never been impressed by money, fame, or material possessions. To them, all that mattered was a person's character, and Don sensed that they would not be pleased with him.

His song "Crossroads" could serve as a metaphor for this point in his life. He says,

> "I wanted to retire and join a monastery, because I felt I was becoming the wrong person. I didn't like the person I was becoming. There was a part of me that was starting to use people. Part of my heart was dying and becoming cold. It was because I could do bad things that I did them. I realized that I was losing part of my sense, part of what my father had given me. I was self-aware enough to know that, and I realized that the only answer was to get out of the business and do something that could help me reclaim myself, reclaim my soul, and reclaim my spirit. I thought about joining a monastery, because I felt I would never find the right woman in my life. Leonard Cohen and Cat Stevens both withdrew to religion, and I know why. I actually asked the Lord to show me the way, to tell me what I needed to know or what I was supposed to do, because I was at a crossroads."

His parents never had the wealth and possessions that he enjoyed, but they had each other. It dawned on McLean that this is what really matters. "They were in love all their lives." This kind of love had eluded him, and it had eluded his sister, who had been married three times.

During 1986 McLean did a tour with Joan Baez that took him across the continent, from the Great Woods in Boston to Expo in Vancouver, British Columbia. Although he knew that interaction with the media was necessary to maintain his career, he never liked it. He hated the media circus and the intense scrutiny of the early 1970s, and he preferred to do his talking on stage, in concert, and then retreat to the privacy of his home in Garrison or Castine. On the Baez tour, however, an encounter with a journalist changed his life forever.

Patrisha Shnier, a Canadian journalist, began pestering McLean's agent, Bennett Morgan, for an interview weeks before the tour started, but Morgan ignored her. At a stop at the Concord Pavilion, in Contra Costa County, California, McLean received another request from the Canadian journalist. He threw it in the garbage. "I was not going to do any interviews on this tour. In fact I thought it might be the last tour I did." After the show, the persistent 27 year old snuck past the guards and appeared unannounced in Don's dressing room, with her pen and notebook in hand. It was love at first sight. McLean remembers, "I knew right away that this was the woman I would marry."

In the beginning, Patrisha traveled with Don to most American gigs and sometimes overseas. He remembers a trip to Nova Scotia and St. Johns, Newfoundland. "We barely escaped a massive blizzard. In fact, we flew out on the winds of that storm. And Patrisha began to see the kind of gonzo mentality that I have. I am very much of the school that thinks the show must go on, and the plane will be caught. There are no mistakes; everything that is to happen will happen."

On Friday, March 13, 1987, less than eight months after their first encounter, Patrisha and Don were married at his home in Castine, Maine.

McLean says, "Thus began my new life as a family man. All the old habits and several little black books went into the fire, and there arose from the ashes the pillar of the community that I pass myself off as today. My first marriage had been such a horrendous experience that I waited ten years to consider remarriage, and even with the perfect woman, I had doubts about my judgement. You never really know until the day after. Every day since my marriage to Patrisha has been beautiful. I can hardly remember the pain of those early years, and I don't want to."

Patrisha at Garrison 1987

Chapter 12: And I Love You So...1990s, Family, and the Surf Ballroom

The day Don married Patrisha, his focus shifted from his career as an international singer, songwriter, and performer to being a happily married family man. From that moment on, only his wife, and later, his children, mattered to him. He no longer worried about his career or whether he would join a monastery. From now on his career would take second place to his family, and he found that he could enjoy his work. His personality wasn't totally transformed overnight. He could still get extremely angry and lash out. Sometimes his dark moods persisted for days, but today he is a calmer and happier soul.

On February 16th, 1989, McLean appeared on the Tonight Show with Johnny Carson for the first time. Jim McCawley, a friend from the Hudson River Sloop, was working as the second in command under Fred Decordova, who arranged all the bookings for the Tonight Show. McCawley was surprised that McLean had never appeared on Carson's show, but back in 1972 his manager had snubbed the Tonight Show, thinking it was for old people, and instead scheduled Don for the hip, but short-lived, Dick Cavett Show. McCawley arranged the Tonight Show appearance, and McLean flew to Los Angeles and stayed at the Hotel Bel Air for three nights. On the show, he sang a full version of "American Pie," accompanied by the show's orchestra. Tony Migliore, Don's musical director, wrote the arrangement. Carson would invite McLean back for a second appearance on the Tonight Show a year later, on March 21, 1990.

Don describes his first appearance on the Tonight Show:

"Johnny Carson was great. Everybody was great. The show was a big success and got really good ratings. After being booked, I realized the importance of the appearance, since over the years the show's reputation for validating stardom had become the stuff of legend. As Carson's obituary in the *New York Times* said: 'a visit to Mr Carson's famous couch signaled a performer's official acceptance as a star.'

"I was invited over to the couch after I finished my song. Dialogue with talk show hosts is not my forte, but Johnny could not have been kinder, and the conversation was quite funny. During the breaks we talked about William Boyd, who played Hopalong Cassidy on TV, a favorite topic of mine. Johnny said that he had been married four times, and so had Hoppy. He thought that Boyd was the handsomest actor that ever was. He tried to get Boyd to come on the Tonight Show in 1968, but Boyd declined saying, 'I don't look anything like I used to, and I don't want to tamper with people's memory.'

"When I got home I sent Johnny a lobby card from the Hopalong Cassidy movie, "Call of The Prairie," which showed Hoppy and his sidekick, Gabby Hayes. I was surprised when Carson retired, and I received a note from him, saying that while cleaning out his N.B.C. office he came across the lobby card and would always keep it. Now that's class. Like Hoppy, when Carson retired in 1994, he meant it. I hope I can do the same thing when that time comes. It occurred to me that although millions of Americans had listened to 'American Pie' on the radio for years, the Tonight Show was important because it gave the American public a good look at me, and they liked what they saw. With Carson's validation I moved to another level with a larger and more permanent audience. Because of the excellent ratings, I was invited back the following year. And all this was because Jim McCawley never forgot our days on the Hudson River."

A few days after his first appearance on the Tonight Show, on February 22, 1989, McLean settled Herb Gart's lawsuit out of court. Around the time of his marriage, Gart issued a writ against McLean for loss of earnings. The settlement was much to Don's satisfaction.

John Platania

By the end of the 1980s, McLean was almost always performing in concert with sole accompaniment provided by John Platania on electric guitar. Together they were brilliant and conquered the world's greatest concert venues. They played London's Royal Festival Hall in October, 1989, and they played Carnegie Hall in November. McLean says, "That was the best show I ever did at Carnegie Hall. I'll never forget it. There were six standing ovations. The place was packed, and the excitement level was higher than it has ever been. John Platania has been a great friend. He was a completely reliable, fantastically inspired, hard-working, funny and wise human being. I feel very fortunate to have found him and very fortunate that he was willing to devote as much of his time to me and my music as he did."

Platania was equally complimentary:

> "I spent over 15 years with Don, traveling the world with him. And, of course, we became friends. You can't spend that amount of time with someone without becoming almost like brothers. Like friends or brothers, you butt heads once in a while, but for the majority of my time with him, it was a great experience — lots of laughs, musically fulfilling — after all, for the most part, I was the only soloist. Don is the consummate professional, so I had to be on my toes at all times. It was a learning experience, which is something I hope to have with anyone I work with. It's not always the case, but working with Don you learn. You have to, in order to keep up, because he is always learning, himself. I like that. I think that's one of the reasons I stayed with him for so long. That and loyalty. Don is a loyal guy; sometimes to the extreme. He put up with some people longer than he should have, giving them enough rope to prove themselves or hang themselves. But, at the same time, he doesn't suffer fools easily."

Platania summed up McLean's feeling about show business and fame this way: "Don's attitude toward the business is an approach-avoidance attitude."

During the next two or three years, McLean changed his concert line up. Tony Migliore began to accompany him for some shows, playing piano and keyboards. Migliore had been working on McLean's albums since producing the musical arrangements on *For the Memories*. He was a classically trained pianist, having attended the Julliard School of Music and the Eastman School of Music. He also did graduate work in performance and arranging at North Texas State University and at Columbia University. During the Vietnam War, he served as pianist and arranger for the United States Military Academy Band at West Point. Though a career as a top flight concert pianist beckoned, Migliore moved to Nashville, where he worked as a musician, producer, and arranger. He also conducted many major orchestras, including: the National Symphony, the Rochester Philharmonic, the Honolulu Symphony, the Atlanta Symphony, the Tonight Show Orchestra, and show orchestras at the MGM Grand, the Aladdin, Harrah's, and the Sands, in Las Vegas, Reno, Lake Tahoe and Atlantic City.

Don developed a great relationship with Tony in the studio, and Migliore transferred the chemistry to the stage. He provided McLean with a different concert sound and gave him opportunities to perform different songs. For years McLean had avoided singing "Crossroads" in concert because it didn't work well with only a guitar for accompaniment.

Migliore is proud to work with McLean and compares his musical performances to those of other pop stars:

> "In this age when audio and visual trickery produce supposed artistry, our audiences are fooled into thinking that what they are

seeing on the stage is greatness. The only thing great about most 'live' performances today are the special effects used to mask the fact that these 'singers' aren't singers at all. The way they survive the recording studios is through the use of electronics to tune their vocals, electronics to enhance dull performances, and electronics to add expression. Couple this with pyrotechnics on stage, and 'voila!' — David Copperfield couldn't do it any better.

When Don performs, he gives a performance of 100% music. There are no special effects on stage, just simple lighting; no smoke, no mirrors. He sometimes tells an audience, 'This is live; it's not television,' meaning he wants them to experience the music, to participate in the musical journey for a few hours. Consequently, McLean's audiences come away from his concerts feeling good, singing his songs, knowing that a truly great performer was in their midst. I cannot count the number of times that people have approached me after a show and told me that they didn't realize what a truly great singer he is. They 'have always loved his songs but never realized what a voice he has.'

Having been a studio musician for many years, I have worked with many singers of varying degrees of talent, some famous, some not. I have found that few have respect for other singers. But Don has earned the respect of his peers. Years ago I performed with the legendary Chet Atkins, genius of the guitar, and one who recognizes true musical talent. In every one of his performances, Chet would play a haunting version of 'Vincent.' He told me that Don McLean is a song-writing genius and a 'singer's singer.'

I feel blessed that Don has chosen to take me on his musical journey for the past twenty years, first in the recording studio, then traveling together. I've seen him perform in all kinds of settings, from great concert halls to festivals in the fields. He loves to sing. Even when he's not feeling well, he'll power through, and the audience never knows that he wasn't feeling well before the show. He's not one to take all the glory for himself, either. He shares the stage with four other gifted musicians, and he features each of them for their own talents during every performance. His music and performance give him an energy that few performers possess. We also share in this energy, and we all come off the stage with great exuberance.

Many in today's entertainment industry view music as a job. But Don has showed us that it can be a life, that it has a life of its own within us. It takes over a true musician's being, if he is true to himself and to his music. Thanks, Don, for showing us the way.

Ralph Childs began appearing with McLean and Migliore in 1986, playing bass guitar. Childs first worked with McLean on the *For The Memories* album. Like Tony, he had attended the Eastman School of Music, but he had majored in the tuba. He received a prestigious Fulbright Scholarship to the Royal Conservatory of Music in Manchester, England, but, because of Vietnam, he ended up being drafted to play the tuba in the West Point Army Band, where he met up with Tony again.

Childs describes his work with McLean like this:

> Don McLean saved my musical life. Although I've known Don since 1986 when I started playing bass on his records, he rescued me from musical obscurity in 1997 by hiring me to play bass and sing backup, live, in concert. He could have gotten anybody he wanted to work with him, but he chose me. He has a depth of awareness that allows him to see things in people that even they may not know about. Maybe it's this highly tuned sensitivity that comes pouring out in his music, or maybe it's just another aspect of his genius. Whatever the reason, I'm eternally grateful he saw something in me that made him take me on and keep me for these past nine years.
>
> Don occasionally gives me a glimpse of what it takes to go from good to great. One of the things he said that made a huge impression on me was when I was going to my first gig with him in Canada. I don't remember the context, but he said that he had

never done anything in his life just to please someone else. I found this so profound that I asked him to repeat it. It hit me that the idea of remaining true to yourself was a key, not only to a person's success, but especially to their longevity. The longer I know Don, the more I appreciate and respect his brilliance.

One of the most beautiful and profound musical moments in my whole life happened in Australia in 2004. Don called me out on the stage without the rest of the band, to accompany him as a duo. He does this from time to time to give the show variety and to showcase the talent of his musicians. I was prepared to go into some Josh White blues or a bluegrass instrumental, when he took me totally off-guard by launching into 'Vincent.' Because it was just the two of us, it afforded me the opportunity to play more melodically and expressively. Tony Migliore usually adds the flavoring with the oboe and string sounds on his keyboard, but this time I stretched out and found myself in the throes of musical ecstasy. It was an exhilarating, creative moment. I'll never forget that moment, and I will always be grateful to Don for giving it to me.

Don loves music and musicians and performing in front of a loud, boisterous crowd. I hope I get at least another nine years of playing with this American icon."

For two or three years, McLean frequently changed the make up of his band, working sometimes with Platania, sometimes with Migliore, and sometimes with Migliore and Childs. They were all friends, and no one thought someone else was stepping on his toes. Eventually Don settled on Tony and Ralph. They continued this way until the end of the 1990s, when the band was expanded to include Jerry Kroon on drums and Pat Severs on guitar. Pat's brother, Mike Severs, sometimes takes his place, and, on occasion, the band is expanded further by the addition of guitarist, Kerry Marx, who regularly tours with Bob Dylan.

Jerry Kroon says of working with Don:

> Don is one of the finest singers I have known. His voice is truly his instrument of communication. Long after most singers from the 1970s have lost the spark and passion for singing and, frankly, the ability to sing, Don has taken his singing to a higher level.
>
> His song-writing is amazing. He paints pictures with his lyrics and his voice.
>
> And he is to be admired for his brilliant career moves. He did his career the way he wanted and the only way it would work for him. It was how he wanted to be thought of as an artist. He is an artist whose music will never die.

Don and Patrisha became parents on February 4th, 1990, when Jackie Lee McLean was born. For a while it looked as if Jackie Lee would be born on February 3rd, the day Buddy Holly died. Her name was chosen with another important figure from Don's past in mind: his friend and mentor, Lee Hays. "That was the most exciting, most wonderful experience in my entire life. Getting married had been fraught with anxiety, not knowing what was going to happen, whether it would work this time. But the birth of a child, a healthy child, is nothing but pure joy." Two years later, Don and Patrisha had a son, born on August 30, 1992, at the Pen Bay Hospital in Rockport, Maine. Don made a point of naming him Wyatt McLean, because he did not want to repeat the confusion that had come from having the same name as his father and grandfather.

In 1990, McLean moved his family to a 200 acre estate named Lakeview, in Camden, Maine. Lakeview remains the McLean's residence today, and its expansive grounds are populated by dogs, cats, horses, coyotes, mountain lions, bears and turkeys. It provides the McLean family with rustic elegance.

At Lakeview, 1990

McLean has loved to maintain and decorate his home since his first home in Cold Spring, New York, in 1968. He has collected antique furniture for over 30 years, and often sells items at a profit. He also collects antique watches. He loves to be surrounded by beautiful objects. He wants everything neat and tasteful. He hates plastic, which he considers "instant trash," and he will not have fluorescent lighting in the house. Patrisha is busy with her career as a children's portrait photographer and with her extensive rose gardens, so she and Don do not clash over taste.

Despite his sometimes conflicting public statements about the matter, McLean is no techno-phobe. His home is not caught in a 19th century time warp. The only item of modern technology that is not found in the McLean home is a PC with an Internet connection. From time to time, McLean surfs the Internet from a hotel or airport terminal. Otherwise there are plenty of people who can obtain information from the Web for him. He prefers to have his children watch a movie with him than spend hours sitting at a computer. He wants them to be able to follow through with a full story. Wyatt and Jackie are more likely to be found watching *Some Like it Hot* than *American Pie: The Wedding*.

Don's hobbies have changed little since childhood. His main hobby is his music. At home he loves to play the guitar and sing for family and friends, just as he did as a little boy in New Rochelle. His love of riding horses, which he developed at his home in Garrison, New York, in the early 1970s, is as strong as ever. He stables three Appaloosa horses on his estate and takes care of them himself. He has had the oldest horse, "Cupid's Arrow," for twenty years. Cupid nearly killed him, so McLean decided he would never be an "honest" horse as the cowboys say, but he keeps him because he is so damned smart. He opens his own stall door, he turns on water when he needs it, and he likes to have the lights on when it gets dark.

"Silver" is the white horse McLean is riding on the cover of his Western CD. Silver is fourteen and is the best trained horse. Don can do anything with him, because he is so willing. The third horse, named "Chief," is the half brother of Silver. He is seventeen "hands" (very tall) and would look perfect with an Indian chief in full feather regalia riding him. Chief is also fourteen years old, and is a work in progress. He was a nervous wreck when McLean got him, but he is actually a gentle, frightened giant. He reminds McLean of the Tin Man in the Wizard of Oz.

Along with his love of horses, McLean has a passion for all things Western. He has a vast collection of Western movies, cowboy boots (about 40 pairs), Western belts and silver.

And then there was Thor, the McLean's most beloved dog. He was a very gentle Shiatsu that McLean bought for his wife soon after they were married. Thor was so gentle that when Jackie was a baby, they often played together on the floor. Don and Patrisha never had to worry that Thor would nip. Thor's passing, at fourteen, was the most painful experience the McLean kids have had. According to Don, "Thor was a person in a dog suit."

Between the children's escapades and McLean adventures at home and on the road, there is never a dull moment. The McLeans believe in getting out of the house and into nature. The horses require daily care and sometimes doctoring, so the McLeans don't hang around the house too much.

Don on "Chief" at Lakeview

In 1991, EMI re-issued the "American Pie" single in the UK on CD, together with "Vincent" and "Crying." The CD had a cover photograph of a youthful Don, taken ten years earlier by David Gahr. Much to everyone's surprise, the single picked up airplay and entered the Top 50 as McLean began a nationwide tour of Britain. From nowhere, interest in McLean and his song began all over again. BBC Radio 1 produced a one hour special about Don McLean, hosted by Nicky Campbell, a popular DJ. As the song climbed the charts, Don was invited to perform "American Pie" on the *Top of the Pops*. He was accompanied by the Jamie Marshall Band for the fantastic Halloween night performance. That performance turned the clock back and helped propel the single into the Top 10, twenty years after its first release in 1971. McLean said, "When I first played *Top of the Pops*, the girls had their hair parted in the middle and wore rimless glasses. In 1991, I was preceded by a girl whose black hair was twisted into a massive G-clef on top of her head. The fashion was attention-getting, but the melodies are gone."

On tour, UK 1991

Every show of the 1991 UK tour was a sell-out. In terms of excitement, it felt like 1972 all over again. McLean was in demand from the media, but he turned down many invitations, choosing to ration his time. He received lots of publicity during one interview, when he said that the assassination of John Lennon may have involved the FBI. The story made headline news and caused a lot of controversy. McLean said, "It just slipped out," but he stands by his claim. The controversy assisted "American Pie's" second climb up the charts. The single and the tour received little record company promotion, so the news story helped many Don McLean fans discover that their hero was touring the country and had another hit record on the market. The Manchester show was recorded and is available on the video release, *Don McLean: The Voice, The Music, The Concert.*

During the 1991 tour there was talk of a musical named *Till Tomorrow,* based on McLean's songs. It was being staged at the Liverpool Playhouse, with a West End run planned for a later date. McLean and his UK promoter, Jef Hanlon, and Michael Rudman, the artistic director of the Chichester Festival Theatre worked on the project. They held a production workshop at the Chichester Theatre in London during December of 1990. The project was the subject of a Camargo Fellowship. The Camargo Foundation maintains a study center in Cassis, France, for the benefit of fellows who wish to pursue projects in the humanities and social sciences related to French culture, as well as creative projects by visual artists, photographers, video artists, filmmakers, media artists, composers, and writers. The creative projects do not need to have a specific French connection, but much of the *Till Tomorrow* story was set in southern France.

The story involved a 1960s rock musician who falls in love with a young woman during a whirlwind tour of the United States. They part, and, without the musician's knowledge, the woman gives birth to his son. During the height of his success, the musician fakes his own on-stage suicide, because of his disgust with all the trappings of commercial musical success. The second part of the story takes place twenty years later, when the woman has become a formidable magazine journalist. She travels to Europe with her adult son to cover the fall of the Berlin Wall. Her son is unaware of his father's identity, and ironically performs the musician's ballads in an innocent tribute to the bygone era of rock. There are rumors that the musician is alive and painting canvases under an assumed identity in a seaport town in southern France. Mother and son decide to check out these reports. They find the musician cavorting with a young French singer in a cabaret in Marseilles. The old lovers recognize one another, and, after a difficult confrontation, they reconcile. Their son falls in love with the young French singer.

The musical floundered due to lack of financing. Hanlon and Rudman had hoped that McLean would inject the necessary capital, but McLean could not accept the licensing arrangements for his songs. When negotiations reached an impasse, the idea faded.

EMI Records capitalized on the successful re-issue of the "American Pie" single by releasing a twenty-track compilation called the *Best of Don McLean*. It charted and went on to achieve gold record status. However, EMI did not issue a follow-up single. David Hughes was in charge at EMI Records, and he was not interested. He wouldn't even consider something simple like "Vincent" or "Crying." Don came close to screaming at him over the phone and calling him every name under the sun. McLean was extremely frustrated, because that has been the story of his relationship with record companies since 1971.

But the joy of having a family inspired Don to write more songs. By the end of 1990 he had recorded *Headroom*, an album full of new McLean songs. Sessions were held April 24th through the 26th. Dave Burgess had followed up the Capitol Records deal with a contract with Curb Records.

This four-record deal included *Headroom* in 1990, *Don McLean Christmas* in 1991, *Don McLean Classics* in 1992, and *The River of Love* in 1995. McLean recorded all the albums in Nashville with musical arrangements by Tony Migliore. Dave Burgess produced the first three albums.

In the *Headroom* album McLean returned to songs which provide a commentary on America and the world. The song "1967" is about Vietnam, just as "The Grave" had been on *American Pie,* twenty years earlier. "You Who Love the Truth" is reminiscent of "Vincent," while "Have You Seen Me" puts a human face on the problems in the Middle East. "Headroom" is an updated version of "Prime Time," and it became a hit single in Australia. A video was made to accompany the song, and it won a prize at the Houston Film Festival.

While *Headroom* was an album of new songs, *Don McLean Classics* was significant because it featured new studio recordings of "American Pie," "Vincent," and "And I Love You So." McLean wanted to have studio versions of these songs that were independent of EMI Records. EMI owned master sound recordings of the original versions, and, although McLean enjoyed a lot of control over their use, he was anxious to have something to offer other record companies with no strings attached. The album's cover features a photograph of a bust of McLean by award winning sculptor Zenos Frudakis, commissioned several years earlier.

In 1992, EMI America released a 42 track compilation called *Favorites and Rarities.* This CD included songs that were previously unreleased or extremely rare, including the BBC version of "Everyday," which was a

British hit for McLean in 1973. A concert version of "Mountains of Mourne," recorded at the Albert Hall in London, features McLean singing the wrong words and quickly correcting himself. Studio recordings that were excluded from the *Tapestry* and *American Pie* albums include songs like "Milkman's Matinee," "That's Alright," and "Aftermath." Some of the songs are so good they make a listener wonder why they weren't included on the original albums. An example is the excellent recording of Tim Hardin's "Black Sheep Boy," recorded for *Playin' Favorites,* but ending up on the cutting room floor in 1973.

EMI had scheduled an appearance for McLean on the Today Show to promote *Favorites and Rarities.* He spoke with a staffer for the show, and was asked, "Don't you get sick of singing that song all the time?" He responded, "Is this one of the questions I'll be asked on the show?" "Of course," she replied. To this McLean responded, "Now listen very closely. Take the Today Show and shove it up your ass!" He left town with EMI and the Today Show screaming.

His relationship with Dave Burgess ended in 1993, when he still had one record to make for Curb Records. "I have to give Burgess a great deal of credit for a lot of things he did for me." McLean has managed his own affairs since then.

The final album of the Curb Records deal, *The River of Love,* was the first record McLean produced himself, and it reflected his life as a family man. In the liner notes, Don said: "*The River of Love* is an album about my life today, and I place it high on my list of writing and recording experiences." Songs like 'You're My Little Darlin',' 'This Little Girl (Daddy-O),' and 'Little Cowboy,' were written with my children in mind. One of my favorite recordings on this album is titled 'If I Hadn't Met You,' and it was written for my wife, Pat."

If I Hadn't Met You

If I hadn't met you
I never would have done this thing
Never would have worn this ring
I wouldn't have this love and all the things
That being with your lover brings

If I hadn't met you
I never would have found my nitch
Never would have zapped that glitch
I wouldn't have this life to brag about
Cause I'd be drinkin' by myself no doubt

Or talkin' superficial barroom jive
While tryin' to keep romance alive
But I'd be fallin' flat on aimless chat
And wonderin' just where my life was at

If I hadn't met you
Depression would be all but sure
The doctor wouldn't find a cure
And there would be no hints of tiny little fingerprints

But the clock would tick
And the bell would chime
I'd play the trick that I still had time
But I'd be alone
When my time was through
If I hadn't
If I hadn't
Met you

Chet Atkins played the guitar on "You're My Little Darlin'." McLean has always admired Chet and is proud that Chet kept "Vincent" as a staple on his play list.

"Chet loved that song. I had heard he always played 'Vincent' in his shows. I could never learn his arrangement though; I can't learn anything! I just do what I know how to do. One day we were both on the television show *Nashville Now*, and he and I did the song together, along with the Jordanaires. Those were the guys who built Nashville! And I thought to myself, 'What am I doing here?' That experience always amazed me.

"The first Atkins record I had was his Christmas record. I got it in high school, and I have listened to it every Christmas since. One of the most beautiful things that ever happened to me was when Chet called Tony Migliore – my musical director who also worked with Chet – and left a message on his answering machine saying that he was listening to *my* Christmas album (*Don McLean Christmas*, 1991,) and wanted to say, 'Don is one of the best singers and interpreters of music in the world.' Imagine that, coming from a man who interpreted one of my songs ("Vincent") in a most amazing way. Tony saved the message and sent me a copy of it.

"Chet was such a straight-ahead, brilliant person. No airs. He was all about music. And he had such a wonderful sense of harmony; his changes were always so surprising and so beautiful. He was a lot like Segovia in a way. Of course, Segovia played what was written on the page, while Chet thought it up."

With Chet Atkins at his home in Nashville following his overdub on You're
My Little Darlin', 1995

In addition to his Curb Records deal, every album McLean had released in his career was becoming available on CD. In 1994, BGO Records released *Tapestry*, *Don McLean*, *Playin' Favorites*, *Homeless Brother* and *Solo*. The BGO CDs featured original photographs, art work and detailed liner notes. Thanks to the Internet, these releases, by an English company, are available worldwide. These sound better than the UA records due to expert re-mastering.

In the US, McLean signed a deal with Hip-o Records to re-issue *Prime Time*, *Believers*, *Chain Lightning*, *Greatest Hits Live* (the *Dominion* album) and *For the Memories Volumes 1 and 2* on CD. In addition, Hip-o Records issued a second volume of Christmas songs called *Don McLean's Christmas Dreams*.

McLean's two Christmas albums included "White Christmas," "Santa Claus is Coming to Town," and "Oh, Little Town of Bethlehem." Both albums were re-issued as a single CD collection in 2004. His older songs were still in demand, and record companies licensed his material to release numerous compilations in the mid 1990s.

He toured Australia in 1992, and did not go back until 1998. He toured the UK in 1993, and did not go back until 1997. The Dutch market for Don McLean concerts had evaporated, although Dutch record companies were busy releasing compilation CDs. The strong US dollar made McLean's fee seem expensive in the UK, Holland and Australia, so, for a while, there was a lull. He received invitations from South Africa and South Korea, but he was not willing to travel so far from his young family. For a while, in the mid-1990s, he toyed with the idea of retirement. And then in 1994 Don did a very special concert. He describes it like this:

> "On February 3rd 1994, I agreed to appear at the Surf Ballroom in Clear Lake, Iowa. I didn't know they did a lot of surfing in Iowa, but I did know this was the last stop for Buddy Holly. It had been exactly 35 years since Buddy's plane crashed in a desolate corn field near this surreal venue left over from the Big Band era of the 1930s and refurbished for post-war Big Bands in the late '40s. In 1948 a fire broke out in the ballroom, and after the ballroom was rebuilt, rock tours stopped there in the '50s. It was scheduled for demolition in the decades that followed, but nobody could be bothered. Now it is a shrine to Buddy Holly, Richy Valens, and the Big Bopper. It is a temple to the day the music died.
>
> The Surf Ballroom looks like a brick planetarium with a central dome. It is located off of a Midwestern highway that cuts through

endless fields and an occasional sleepy farm town and then passes miles and miles of corn fields, endless fields of dreams. Just outside Clear Lake and heading west, you make a left hand turn onto a side street that passes motels and bars that have not changed since February 3, 1959. Architectural appointments on some of these establishments mirror the era of cars with big fins. Soon you find yourself by the shore of a lake, in the middle of flat farmland, in the dead of the frozen Iowa winter. Inside the ballroom, the tables and booths have a tropical motif. The sides of the booths are painted with palm trees, yellow suns, and smiling, bathing-suited vacationers in the sand. You can almost feel an ocean breeze, except the breezes are sub-zero and come off oceans of grain outside the front door. They are the winds of death. The hall leading to the bar is papered with dusty, framed, sepia photos of the big bands that stopped there. There's a picture of the Clooney sisters. I'll bet few people realize that Rosemary Clooney began her career as part of a sisters act when she was a kid.

The guy who drove Buddy to the airport is here. Richie Valens' nephew is here. Peggy Sue is here. Donna is here. And so is Tommy Allsop, who played with Bob Moore on my *Chain Lightening* and *Believers* albums. We're old friends.

Tommy Allsop played in Buddy's band and was with him on the last tour. He hasn't seen the ballroom for 35 years. Niki Sullivan shows up with his children. He left the Crickets after the first album. As a teenager growing up in New Rochelle, I always wondered what happened to him. And of course Buddy's widow, Maria Elena, is here.

The Fireballs play their guitar rock. They look like four guys impersonating the dying Howard Hughes, with shoulder length white hair. They do not have much fire left, and yet there are several thousand people here.

There is no place near Clear Lake, Iowa. Des Moines is about 200 miles to the south. Minneapolis is about 150 miles to the north. Eastern and western cities are even farther away. Everything else is just corn fields.

I'm part of all of this now. I carry ghosts with me wherever I go: van Gogh, Andrew McCrew, Jim Croce, Roy Orbison, Josh White, Lee Hays, Buddy Holly, and the rest. You don't tour places like Clear Lake unless you have to, and never in the wintertime. But these performers come here once a year now, and by being here I feel I have come full circle. I sing my show and thousands sing along to the chorus of 'American Pie.' They're all there with me on stage. Afterwards, I go to the dressing room and write the words to the opening stanza of 'American Pie' on the wall and sign my name."

Tommy Allsup, Maria Elena Holly, Nicki Sullivan (original Cricket), Don and Donna (a la Ritchie Valens), Surf Ballroom 1996

Chapter 13: Garth Brooks and Madonna...Another Planet

From 1994 to 1997, McLean spent much of his time at home, riding horses and enjoying life as a family man. Patrisha describes their life together:

> "Even though we have a very big house, we often find ourselves in the same room. Traveling on the road, we've slept in the back of Don's Saab when there was only four hours between the end of a show and an early morning flight. And we've slept in more than one castle and a lot of kingly suites.
>
> Over the time I've known Don, he has turned down offers from high-level power brokers that I thought would be terrific career boosters. But Don does not want to be owned or controlled. He has turned down large amounts of money for performances that didn't fit the picture he has of himself. And he works hard. I've seen many big deals come to pass that I know Don put a lot of work into. He is not an egotist, but he does believe in himself, and I think that is a crucial quality that has made him a star.
>
> Don does not want freebies. I can't get him to upgrade a plane ticket with his million-plus frequent flier miles. He'd rather just pay extra when he occasionally decides to fly first class. He doesn't want the fancy lunch he's been invited to by the owner of the hip Napa Valley winery where he will be singing. He doesn't want to meet and greet with Madonna at the New York premier of 'The Next Best Thing,' or Garth Brooks' private jet to fly him to their concert. And, just as he doesn't want what is not his, he doesn't want anyone taking what is not theirs — this includes former managers, agents, and publishing companies. When we are at a restaurant, if Don orders an appetizer that I want to try, I order my own, because he won't try my food, and he would rather I not try his. I think this comes from being raised as an only child.

Don doesn't need a limo picking him up at the airport, only good directions. On the road he chooses a good motel over a Ritz Carlton that takes longer to get to. He will happily take a nap on a ratty couch in a dressing room. And he does not travel with an entourage, preferring to carry his own carry-on bag and his guitar, to make sure that he has them. The difference between Don and what he calls 'logo-loco' celebrities is that Don enjoys luxury, but does not need it. He equates needing luxury with being vulnerable, dependent, and weak.

Nobody can relax like Don when he is at home, has no project in sight, and no show for at least ten days. But in 'road mode' he is a whirlwind of efficient activity, and nothing stands in his way. I have gone to bed in Maine in January when Don is scheduled to fly out the next morning, with a blizzard blowing outside, a winter advisory on the TV, and I am certain there is no way planes will be leaving the Portland airport. But, invariably, I wake up at 3 am to the familiar sound of Don getting ready and heading out in the frigid, snowy dark to the airport, with a plow attached to the front of his truck and shovels and an ax in the back.

Like the westerns Don loves, there's a lot of black and white in him and not a lot of gray. He's like Holden Caulfield, because he hates phonies and can't stand to see someone in a position of power stepping on a little guy. Don is always gracious when a fan approaches him for an autograph or to relate a story. He says it took courage for that person to come up to him. He loves children, even crying babies on planes make him smile.

One of Don's favorite quotes is from Tennessee Williams' play, 'Cat on a Hot Tin Roof.' It goes: 'I've always had too much space around me to be infected by the ideas of other people.' He is the only truly independent thinker I have ever known."

McLean kept busy managing the careers of his songs, as every album he'd made found its way back onto the market in CD format and numerous Don McLean compilations were released. For the first time, he was earning more from album sales than from his concert work. He received frequent requests to license "American Pie" or "Vincent" for a compilation album, TV show, or film. Oliver Stone featured "American Pie" in his hit movie, *Born on the 4th July*. Julio Iglesias received a platinum record for his album, *Starry Night*, from which Don received a great deal of publicity. And dance music DJ Just Luis produced a techno-music version of "American Pie" that became a smash hit single in Europe. It became the most played song in clubs around Europe's popular summer resorts such as Ibiza and Faliraki, and it rose to No.34 on the singles chart in the UK.

A major star recording a Don McLean song would boost his career, but it had been many years since a star like Perry Como or Elvis had recorded a McLean song.

Suddenly, without warning, a major piece appeared in the Sunday *New York Times* in February, 1997, foreshadowing the re-emergence of Don McLean and "American Pie." It was entitled "American Pie: 25 Years Ago, America Listened."

> "Twenty-five years ago this week, Don McLean's 'American Pie' ended a four week run as the No. 1 song in the country. It was McLean's first and biggest hit, it galloped on for eight and a half minutes, and it sold more than a million copies.
>
> Those are the facts, but the legacy of 'American Pie' is much greater and more lasting. 'American Pie' took over the airwaves and the consciousness in a way that few records had done before or since. Whenever it was played, everyone seemed to listen. Like much '70s singer-songwriter rock, this behemoth was an earnest slice of unplugged folk-pop with a sing-along chorus. But its

allure wasn't merely attributable to a musical hook. Here was a pop phenomenon that grabbed the public's attention not so much with chords as with words.

...In mourning the end of rock's Brylcreem era and its first counterculture, 'American Pie' set the tone for the remainder of the '70s: it implied that the best of rock and the best of times were over. By mythologizing an era that had just ended, it also presaged the instant nostalgia of '90s pop culture, and it was the first song to ask if rock was dead — a question that continues to be mulled, most recently with the suicide of Kurt Cobain.

For McLean, the impact of 'American Pie' was so overwhelming that for a while he refused to play the song in concert. On the stark black-and-white cover of his next album, he is seen hunched over, staring grimly; its songs bemoaning his fame, making him the Eddie Vedder of his day... McLean's other lasting contribution is inspiring the songwriters Norman Gimbel and Charles Fox to write 'Killing Me Softly with His Song' (popularized by Roberta Flack and again last year by the Fugees) about McLean's live performances. Given the current talk about the death of grunge and hardcore rap, perhaps the time is right for a faithful, yet updated remake of 'American Pie'..."

Then, out of the blue, an extraordinary request arrived over the McLean fax machine.

On a morning in April, 1997, the McLeans started the day in the usual way. Don was downstairs preparing coffee, while Patrisha checked the fax machine for messages that had arrived overnight. Suddenly Don heard a scream from upstairs. "I thought somebody had died. I called up the stairs and asked Patrisha what the matter was, and she said, 'Garth Brooks wants to sing with you in Central Park!'" Garth had left his phone number and had offered to send his private plane to collect McLean, so they could meet.

Since the late 1980s, when he was a relatively unknown country singer, Garth Brooks had been performing "American Pie" in all his shows. As his career developed, the venue size increased proportionately, until Garth was performing to more than 60,000 people, night after night, and making a point of including "American Pie." As Garth's fame grew, Dave Burgess advised Don that they should contact Garth about working together. McLean dismissed this idea, saying, "If he wants to contact me, some day he will."

Now Garth had contacted Don and was proposing that they sing "American Pie" together as part of Garth's huge free concert being planned to take place in Central Park in New York City, on August 7th, 1997. McLean was flattered and quickly accepted the invitation. He made it clear that he was happy for Garth to change his mind at any time about his participation. In return, Brooks said, "If you change your mind then I will understand." Don said, "I'll be there."

> "My first reaction when I got off the phone was to become a nervous wreck. I get very nervous about anything that's really big. I'm not a person who craves the limelight. I do not enjoy anything with huge amounts of publicity, and this was going to bigger than anything I'd done before. The biggest live show ever!"

In this case, McLean would be there in a supporting role. Had he been asked to be the star of the show, then the concert would not have occurred. He had starred in his own mammoth concert in Hyde Park in London, 22 years earlier, and he had no intention of repeating the experience. Though he loved singing and playing for people, he could not stand the associated pressure and publicity. Since the concert was a few months away, McLean had plenty of time to dwell on the magnitude of the event. However, after much deliberation, he decided that this was something he had to do.

The night before the show he stayed at the Lotos Club in New York. McLean had been a member of this exclusive club for many years, and he preferred to stay on familiar turf, instead of accepting the luxurious hotel suite arranged by Garth Brooks' team. At breakfast on the day of the show he was racked with anxiety. He told Patrisha, "If these people have an attitude, if they seem to be thinking: 'Who are you? What you doing here?' Then I'm gone."

McLean arrived at Central Park at 10 o'clock in the morning. By this time, the stage had been assembled and scaffolding to hold giant video screens was in place all around the park, so that everyone in the anticipated audience of 500,000 would get a good view. The sheer scale amazed him. He has done some pretty big shows, but this was enormous. The stage was the size of a football field. McLean noticed that the stage floor was constructed of aluminum grating with holes one or two inches wide. He realized that if he wore cowboy boots he could get a heel caught in one of the holes. So he had to plan for that. He didn't want to fall on his face on live television.

Backstage, people went about their business in the small town of trailers accommodating the musicians and stars, and the huge logistical operation that supported Garth's touring circus. The scene was like a Hollywood film set. Security was extremely high. All access to Central Park had been closed off, except for one single entrance.

It was a different world from McLean's concerts. He usually turned up for a sound check three or four hours prior to a show, at which point the necessary equipment might or might not be in place. The final setup modifications often happened during the first song of the show with McLean telling the engineer to "turn up the sound on the monitor." For this show, however, nothing was left to chance — this was another planet.

At midday, McLean went on stage for his personal sound check. The engineer offered him a face microphone, like the one Garth would be using. Don explained that he didn't use such things, and that he had brought his own microphone. This was no problem. The engineers were happy to work with him; there was no back talk. Every person he encountered was happy, courteous and completely capable of whatever it was he was doing. They made him feel like he was a member of the family. He told Patrisha that this showed Garth was genuine. Attitude always comes from the top down. If the guy at the top is a jerk, then everyone under him is a jerk.

As McLean left the stage, he saw Garth Brooks alighting from his limousine. Garth ran over to him and gave him a bear hug, nearly knocking him off his feet. He had no idea Garth was such a power house. He thanked Garth for inviting him to take part in the concert, and Garth thanked Don for doing him this big favor. They went into

McLean's trailer, and Garth asked if he would do something for him. "Would you sing 'Empty Chairs' for me?" Don said okay and sang the song. Garth told him that he had always loved that song, but McLean wondered whether Brooks was checking to see if he could still sing.

In any event, that was the end of their rehearsal. Brooks didn't want to sing "American Pie" prior to the show. He wanted to work out what to do live, on stage. He said, "Perhaps we could trade verses." For a show that was so well organized, down to the finest detail, this relaxed attitude surprised Don. He was terrified that he would forget the lyrics to "American Pie," so he wrote the words of the first verse on a piece of paper and taped it to the top of his guitar.

With Garth Brooks, 1997, after historic Central Park concert

As show time approached, Joel Dorn joined McLean in his trailer. Don had recently re-established contact with his old friend and had invited him along. A series of opening acts started, and Patrisha stood outside watching. As McLean and Dorn talked, there was a knock on the door, and in walked Jock McLean, Don's cousin. They had grown up together in Larchmont Woods, but had not seen much of each other recently. Jock had worked in the music business for many years, first for Columbia Records, then for James Taylor and MTV, and now as a top executive at Show Time Television. They had a lot of catching up to do.

Engrossed in conversation, time flew by. Garth Brooks had been on stage for some time. Suddenly, McLean heard Brooks begin to sing "American Pie." He got up and ran to the stage, no one had told him he was on. Fortunately, the show had paused, because one of the stage lights had blown and was on fire. When the fire ended, Garth Brooks gave Don McLean the most glowing introduction he had ever heard. Don walked out on stage and the crowd of a million people went completely crazy.

Brooks had sung the first part of "American Pie," and, without any instructions, McLean said, "Let's sing it again," hoping for an indication as to how the routine would proceed. He glanced over at Garth who seemed to be in a trance. So Don continued singing. Television footage showed Brooks with an intense stare fixed on Don. After the show, Joel Dorn quipped, "If there had only been food for one, Garth would have gotten it."

CNN reported: "Brooks was joined on stage by two surprise guest stars, Billy Joel and Don McLean, who brought down the house with an acoustic rendition of 'American Pie.'" A film clip of McLean and Brooks singing "American Pie'" was shown around the world. Don McLean was back on top.

Joel Dorn described the concert this way:

> "I'm not good at counting the house, but there must have been at least a million people in the park that night. It was a pickpocket's dream come true. And HBO, which was capturing the event for posterity, had enough cameras and sound trucks to make Cecil B. DeMille a happy man. There were more people backstage than there are in most audiences. But the best thing about that night, for me, was that it felt like the old *Homeless Brother* days. We were hanging out, and the million watt spotlight Don deserves was shining on him for all the right reasons.
>
> Don has done quite well for himself, and he's done it on his own terms. He tours and records where he wants, when he wants, how he wants. But the rush of recognition and appreciation that night was for who he is and what he's done. It's something any artist would like to feel at least once in his life. It was a reaffirmation that came at just the right time."

After the show, Brooks invited McLean back to his hotel opposite the Metropolitan Museum of Art. Expecting to be offered a celebratory drink, Don was politely informed by Garth's manager that Garth did not drink alcohol. McLean got a beer and met Garth's family. Once again, McLean was impressed by Garth's intensity. There was no wild, after-show party that night. In fact, Brooks boarded his jet and returned home.

As far as McLean was concerned, his appearance with Garth Brooks in Central Park marked his third comeback. The biggest star in America, at the high point of his career, had said, "Don McLean is my idol." Everyone who saw the show thought, "Yes, I like that song, and I like Don McLean, too."

After "American Pie" made McLean famous, it was such a big phenomenon, that everyone thought he couldn't follow it. His first comeback happened when "Vincent" was released and became No.1 all over the world. Again, people said, "He can't follow that."

McLean's second comeback was "Crying." The era of the singer-songwriter had died in 1975. Disco was in full swing, and we've been dancing ever since. Artists who had been big stars, like Harry Chapin, were desperately looking for record deals. They weren't getting air play on the radio. "Crying" put Don back on top and showed he was adaptable.

Then if it hadn't been for a brief renewal of interest in 1996, following the Fugees' hit version of "Killing Me Softly With His Song," Don McLean could easily have been forgotten by the American public. But his career displays a remarkably cyclical nature, and the ten-minute concert appearance with Garth Brooks served as his third comeback.

In 1998 Weird Al Yankovic, a well known American parodist produced his own "Star Wars" version of "American Pie," called "The Saga Begins." His amusing version of "American Pie" created additional publicity for McLean. When the recording came out McLean said, "Al is the best there is at what he does, whatever that is. In addition, my kids love his videos, so I am honored that he thought of me and did such a great job."

And then, that same year, McLean heard that Madonna wanted to include "American Pie" in her film, *The Next Best Thing*. The film's producers applied for a license to use the song, and McLean was happy to agree. At first, his original recording was going to be used. However, the project was put on hold, as the production company changed two or three times, and in the end the movie included a version recorded by Madonna herself, as well as the original McLean recording. McLean was delighted and issued the following press statement, quoted in *Time* magazine:

> Madonna is a colossus in the music industry, and she is going to be considered an important historical figure, as well. She is a fine singer, a fine songwriter, and a fine record producer. She has the power to guarantee success to any song she chooses to record. It is a gift for her to have recorded "American Pie." I have heard her version and I think it is sensual and mystical. She has chosen autobiographical verses that reflect her career and personal history. I hope it will cause people to ask, "What's happening to music in America?" I have received many gifts from God, but this is the first time I have received a gift from a goddess.

Madonna's version of "American Pie" was not released as a single in the US, but it became a hit single in the US, anyway. It made the Top 30 on airplay alone. The song was issued in the UK, and, based on actual record sales, entered the singles chart at No.1 in March, 2000, making McLean the first songwriter to have No.1 singles in two different centuries.

In an interview in the *New York Daily News*, Madonna said she recorded her version at the urging of co-star Rupert Everett. "I thought, 'Who am I to do a cover of a pop classic?' But I was working in the studio on other music, and I said, 'OK, let's just try it.' And it worked."

Madonna's cover was savaged by many fans and critics. Some wondered why McLean allowed his song to be used this way. In any case, McLean had no problem with a major recording star taking an active interest in his music.

However, critic Ann Powers wrote a lengthy review of Madonna's "American Pie" for the *New York Times,* published on March 19, 2000. In it she was critical of McLean's song:

> "American Pie" is one of the great monuments of musical cheese, a song everyone scorns but few can resist. Since its overwhelming success in 1972, its eight minutes of tangled allusions to the icons of the turbulent 1960s, offered by Mr McLean in a collegiate folkie's warble, have come to represent the nadir of songwriterly self-seriousness.

Don wrote her in return:

> Dear Ann:
>
> Thank you for your article. At this stage in my life almost all publicity is good publicity. However, if I were to express my true feelings using your writing style I would have to say: You are disliked by everyone but truly well-loved; although you are unattractive you're quite pretty and although you're a terrible writer you do have a way with words.

To quote the great comedian Jack E. Leonard: "Some day you'll find yourself, and I know you'll be disappointed. It's a pleasure saying good bye to you."

Sincerely,
Don McLean

McLean quickly forgot his annoyance over Powers' criticism of Madonna's recording when his royalty check appeared. He received a one-time payment for licensing the use of the song in the film, plus 100% of the writer-publisher's royalties for the broadcast of the song, not only in the movie, but whenever it was publicly broadcast on radio, on television, or on the Internet. In fact McLean earned more from this release than he had from his original hit in 1971.

Once again, Don McLean was hot. Interest from the media was renewed, and a new wave of Don McLean fans emerged. Jef Hanlon hastily booked a short tour of England, and McLean performed to a sell out crowd at the Hammersmith Apollo Theater in London, on June 27th. A new generation of fans danced in the aisles to his unmatchable version of "American Pie."

EMI capitalized on McLean's popularity by re-issuing the 1991 *Best of Don McLean*, under the title *American Pie: The Greatest Hits of Don McLean*. During the first week of its release, it entered the album chart at No.27, giving Don his first Top 30 album in the UK in twenty years. Meanwhile, momentum from the Madonna hit caused the original *American Pie* album to appear on some industry charts, making the "Amazon Top 10."

In 1998, McLean was asked to contribute an article on "taste" to the *Wall Street Journal*. He wrote:

> "America is so hardwired and networked that it is in constant communication. Nothing artistic can get started in the once dark corners of Tupelo or Hibbing. There are no dark corners left in America. Every square inch is spoken for and spoken to, and as a result the American public is psyched out and homogenous. We've been simplified. Today self-esteem is more important than Shakespeare. Slogans and information manipulation have been substituted for ideas. As technology moves us forward technologically, it moves us backward culturally.
>
> All this leaves a funny feeling in the collective gut that something is missing. William James said that Americans are pragmatists. We do what works. I think now we do what feels good. Only, it's not working."

In 1999, the Martin Guitar Company honored Don McLean and "American Pie" with the introduction of the D-40 DM Don McLean Limited Edition Signature Model Martin guitar. The D-40 DM is a 14-fret Dreadnought with a solid Engelmann spruce top, and its sound-hole is inlaid with an abalone pearl rosette. The ebony fingerboard is a truly unique feature. It is inlaid with the trademark Martin hexagon pattern and each hexagon contains routed lettering filled with crimson, spelling out the significant names from "American Pie:" "King," "Queen," "Jester," "Father," "Son," "Holy Ghost," "Jack Flash," "American Pie," and Don McLean's signature. The D-40 DM edition was limited to 71 instruments to commemorate the year "American Pie" was released. McLean has played Martin guitars throughout his career and owns over forty Martin guitars. He said that if he were given a choice between winning a

Grammy and being chosen for a Limited Edition Signature Model Martin guitar, he'd take the Martin, any day.

After the introduction of the D-40 DM Limited Edition guitar, Dick Boak, a top executive at the Martin Guitar Company and the head of the Limited Edition guitar program, wrote to Don: "More than any other musician, your passion for Martin guitars shines through like a Maine lighthouse beacon. I have always enjoyed our conversations and connections. I know you and I share a great pride in having created a fabulous signature guitar. Thumbs up to you."

Don McLean and his current touring band.
(From left to right: Tony Migliore, Jerry Kroon, Don, Pat Severs and Ralph Childs)

Pat Severs, who plays guitar in McLean's band, wrote this about guitars and Don McLean:

"I swore I'd never tour with anyone ever again. No more airports, hotels, bad food, late nights, early mornings. The only guitar playing I wanted to do was in the recording studios of Nashville, Tennessee. The work is interesting, fun, and you get to sleep in your own bed every night. The I got the call — Don McLean was planning to tour with a full band for the first time in years, and would I be interested in playing guitar with the band on a few of the dates? "THE Don McLean," I asked? "'American Pie,' 'Vincent,"'Castles in the Air,'and all-the-other-great-songs-Don McLean?" Well, I've gotta do this one. Besides, I thought, it's only a few dates. Well, here I am, going into my seventh year, traveling around the world, playing guitar with Don McLean.

The Guitar — it always comes back to the Guitar. Over the years, we've had hundreds of conversations about books, movies, music, even religion and politics. Some things we agree on, some things we don't, but the one thing we always agree on is the guitar. We've spent hours talking about guitars, looking at pictures and old catalogs, driving the other guys in the band crazy. They're only hunks of wood, what's the big deal? Well, you either get it, or you don't, and when it comes to the guitar, Don McLean gets it. After years of studio work, I was used to working with singers who held the guitar as a stage prop, while some studio cat did the real playing! One show with Don, and I knew this was not going to be the case. This guy can play.

Don's style and approach to the guitar certainly deserve attention. His finger style picking is unique in that he uses all five fingers on his right hand for picking and all five fingers on his left hand for fretting, so his sound is almost is more like a grand piano than a guitar. Then, sometimes, when playing the blues in the style of the great Josh White, you'd swear his guitar had become a full horn section, hitting you right in the gut. And then there's Don's rhythm guitar — that piston driving, churning undercurrent of sound that drives the back beat right up your... well, you get the idea.

Guitars are a lot more than hunks of wood to Don McLean. They are living, breathing creatures with voices that give life to his songs, and wings that take those songs all over the world. The great guitars made by C. F. Martin Company of Nazareth, Pennsylvania, have always been Don's favorites, and one of his proudest achievements was seeing his design for the D-40 DM

Don McLean Signature Martin Guitar become a reality. And what a guitar it is! I always knew it sounded great, but one day after visiting some guitar shops, as we often do, and playing some very rare and expensive vintage Martins, we returned to the hotel, and Don took his new signature model out of the case, strummed one big G chord, and smiled. The new guitar blew the others out of the water!

And now, after many nights of great music on stages all over the world, I'm proud to be working on a new project with Don. My brother, Mike, and I are co-producing, with Don, an album of all new Don McLean songs called *Addicted to Black*. And just like those Martin guitars, Don's songs and song-writing get better with the passing of time. Don has said this will be his last album of self-penned songs. I hope that isn't so, but if it is, rest assured, there's enough great music on this one to keep us happy for a long time.

It has been my pleasure, indeed my honor, to work with Don professionally, and to get to know him personally. Over the years, I've seen the many interesting sides of Don McLean — the guy who can go it alone, traveling the world, playing to thousands with just his guitar; and the guy who loves rockin' with the band, hustling to airports, crowding into vans and cars, rolling with the punches and still loving it. And of course, there's Don McLean, husband to Patrisha, father to Jackie and Wyatt, the guy who would be happy never to leave their retreat in Maine. I think that is the Don McLean I like best."

Recent years have seen a rash of new Don McLean albums. Since 1993 McLean has issued new albums through his own label, Don McLean Records. So far, he has released three studio albums: *Don McLean Sings Marty Robbins*, *You've Got to Share*, and *The Western Album*. He also released one live album: *Starry, Starry Night*.

The live album is actually a recording of his first American television special, commissioned and broadcast by PBS. The PBS show was recorded at the Paramount Theater in Austin, Texas, in November, 1999, and featured two special guests: Nanci Griffith and Garth Brooks. Garth was repaying the favor that Don had done him two years earlier, and McLean repaid Brooks by asking him to sing "Empty Chairs" live on stage without a rehearsal. Brooks did well. And, together, the three stars provided a memorable rendition of "American Pie."

Rehearsing with Garth Brooks for Don's Starry Night PBS television special

A video recording of the show, including Garth Brooks' appearance was offered to viewers who made a financial pledge to PBS television. The video and DVD later released in record stores omitted Garth's performance, due to record company complications. The DVD also features clips from McLean's three music videos: *Till Tomorrow; The Music of Don McLean*; and *Don McLean: The Music, The Voice, The Concert.*

The *Starry, Starry Night* project had been in the pipeline since the Central Park concert in 1997, but the people McLean was working with just couldn't get it together. In the end, Terry Lacona saved the project. Lacona had interviewed Don for the radio in 1968, when he was the Hudson River Troubadour. He also booked McLean for the *Austin City Limits* program in the 1980s. Lacona had become a senior executive at PBS television and had the weight to carry the project through to completion. It is strange that it took so long for American television to broadcast a Don McLean special, when such programs had been successful in other countries. The show was a fund raising success for PBS and is frequently rebroadcast.

McLean's career had become more than writing and performing songs; it was more than touring and having hit records; Don McLean had become an American icon. He had 150 songs available on CD, but he was an icon because of one or two songs. Today, he is more famous in the US than ever. He has been called an American poet laureate. He is hailed as a national treasure.

Madonna had said, "To me, "American Pie" is a real millennium song." And on New Year's Eve, 1999, McLean was invited by President Clinton and the First Lady to attend the Founders' Dinner at the White House and perform at the Millennium Concert in front of the Lincoln Memorial in Washington, D. C. The guest list for the dinner included cabinet members, White House aides, senators, congressmen, business leaders, Hollywood stars, Hollywood directors, musicians, composers, opera stars, authors, playwrights, dancers, and media professionals: some of the most famous and influential Americans of the second half of the 20th century.

The guest list included:

Daniel Abraham, SlimFast Foods Company chairman, and Ewa Abraham.

David Al-Ameel, ATLAN Group chairman, and Martha Al-Ameel.

Edward Albee, playwright, and Jonathan Thomas, sculptor.

Madeline Albright, Secretary of State, and Ricardo Del'Orto, Barter Technologies Corporation chairman.

Muhammad Ali, former heavyweight champion, and Yolanda Ali.

Robert Altman, Zenimax Media Inc. chairman, and Linda Carter, actress.

Bruce Babbitt, Secretary of the Interior, and Harriet Babbitt, United States Agency for International Development deputy administrator.

Elizabeth Frawley Bagley, advisor to the Secretary of State, and Smith Bagley, Arca Foundation president.

Robert Barnett, Williams and Connolly senior partner, and Rita Braver, CBS News.

Leonard Barrack and Lynne Barrack.

Kathleen Battle, opera singer, and Dean Mitchell.

Samuel Berger, National Security Advisor to the President, and Susan Berger.

Senator John Breaux, Democrat from Louisiana, and Lois Breaux.

John Brophy, Lockheed Martin president, and Louise Brophy.

Dave Brubeck, musician and composer, and Iola Brubeck.

Sid Caesar, entertainer, and Florence Caesar.

Benny Carter, composer and musician, and Hilma Carter.

Vinton Cerf, MCI WorldCom senior vice president, and Sigrid Cerf.

Rashad Chaudray, Raani Corporation chairman and CEO, and Samia Chaudray.

Vance Coffman, Lockheed Martin chairman and CEO, and Arlene Coffman.

Lodwrick Cook, Global Crossing co-chairman, and Carole Cook.

Andrew Cuomo, Secretary of Housing and Urban Development, and Kerry Cuomo.

William Daley, Secretary of Commerce.

Senator Tom Daschle, D-S D, and Linda Daschle, Baker, Donelson, Bearman and Caldwell counsel.

Robert De Niro, actor.

Ruby Dee, actress, and Ossie Davis, actor and author.

Thomas Demetrio, Corboy & Demetrio attorney, and Eve Marie Reilly, Cook County State's Attorney.

Murli Deora, Bombay Congress president, and Hema Deora, artist.

Representative John Dingell, D-MI, and Deborah Dingell, G M Foundation president.

E. J. Dionne, The Washington Post, and Mary Boyle.

Senator Christopher Dodd, D-CT, and Jackie Clegg, Export-Import Bank vice ch.

Rita Dove, professor of English, University of Virginia, and Fred Viebahn.

Ronald Dozoretz, ValueOptions chairman and CEO, and Beth Dozoretz.

Todd Eberle, Todd Eberle Photography, and Richard Pandiscio.

Maria Echaveste, Deputy Chief of Staff, and Professor Christopher Edley.

Mark Ein, Venturehouse Group CEO, and Marion Ein-Lewin, National Academy of Science.

Sahir Erozan, Overseas Partners president.

Huda Farouki, Financial Instrument and Investment Corp. CEO, and Samia Farouki.

Renee Fleming, opera singer, and Rachelle Fleming.

John Fogerty, musician, and Julie Fogerty.

John Hope Franklin, James Duke Professor of History, Duke University.

Mary Mel French, U. S. Chief of Protocol.

Representative Martin Frost, D- TX, and Kathryn Frost.

John Gardner, AT&T vice pres., and Nancy Rawlings, International Monetary Fund.

Murray Gell-Mann, co-chair of the Science Board, and Talia Shire.

Neil Gershenfeld, MIT Media Lab professor, and Laura Brewer.

John Glenn, former U. S. Senator, and Annie Glenn.

Daniel Glickman, Secretary of Agriculture, and Rhoda Glickman, Housing and Urban Development Deputy Chief of Staff.

Michael Graves, architect, and Lynn Min, Shibao International Corporation president.

Alan Greenspan, Federal Reserve Board chairman, and Andrea Mitchell, NBC News.

Brian Greenspun, Las Vegas Sun Newspaper president, and Myra Greenspun.

Janice Griffin, Griffin and Associates Inc. president.

Vinod Gupta, infoUSA Inc. chairman and CEO, and Laurel Gottesman.

Carl Gutierrez, governaor of Guam, and Geraldine Gutierrez.

Julie Harris, actress, and Jennifer Crier Johnston, actress.

Laurence Harris, Teligent Inc. senior vice president, and Susan Harris.

John Hendricks, Discovery Communications Inc. CEO, and Maureen Hendricks.

Bono, singer, and Ali Hewson.

Alexis Herman, Secretary of Labor, and Charles Franklin.

Robert Isabell, owner of Robert Isabell Inc., and James Reginato, W Magazine features director.

Reverend Jesse Jackson, Rainbow PUSH Coalition president, and Jacqueline Lavinia.

Quincy Jones, America's Millennium Gala executive producer, and Lisette Derouaux.

Vernon Jordan, attorney, and Ann Jordan.

Robert Kahn, Corp. for National Research Initiatives president, and Patrice Lyons.

Said Karmi, George Washington University prof. of surgery, and Mary Jane Karmi.

Walter Kaye, former civilian aide to the Secretary of the Army, and Selma Kaye.

Ellsworth Kelly, artist, and Jack Shear, artist.

Senator Edward Kennedy, D-MA, and Victoria Reggie Kennedy.

Kamran Khan, Raani Corporation senior vice president, and Hamida Khan, physician.

Peter Kovler, Marjorie Kovler Fund director, and Judy Kovler, psychotherapist.

Raymond Kurzweil, Kurzweil Technologies Inc. chairman, and Sonya Kurzweil. Robert Langlois, Motorola Inc. director of international relations, and Julia Langlois.

Patricia Lazak, financial assistant to Agnes Gund, and James Lazak.

Senator Patrick Leahy, D- VT, and Alicia Leahy.

Jonathan Ledecky, Washington Capitals Hockey Team co-owner, and Marina McClelland, Marriott International manager.

James Levin, JHL Enterprises chairman and CEO, and Kristy Swanson.

Carl Lewis, Olympian and actor, and Carol Lewis, television broadcaster.

Ann Lewis, Counselor to the President, and Mike Sponder, Office of Naval Research.

Maya Lin, artist and architect, and Daniel Wolf, Warm Spirit Inc. chairman.

Mark Lindsay, Director of White House Mgmt. and Admin., and Carla Lindsay.

Bruce Lindsey, Deputy Counsel to the President, and Cheryl Mills.

Joseph Lockhart, White House Press Secretary, and Mary Lockhart.

Sophia Loren, actress, and Carlo Ponti, producer.

William Maloni, Fannie Mae senior vice president, and Heidi Maloni.

Robert Maurer and Barbara Maurer.

Terence McAuliffe, American Heritage Homes chairman, and Dorothy McAuliffe.

Paul McCarthy, American Millennium director, and Marsha Berry, Director of Communications for the First Lady.

Ellen McCullouch-Lovell, Advisor to the First Lady, and Christopher Lovell.

Bobby McFerrin, opera singer, and Debra McFerrin.

Judith McHale, Discovery Communications Inc. CEO, and Michael O'Halloran.

Don McLean, singer and songwriter, and Patrisha McLean.

Arthur Mitchell, Dance Theater of Harlem president and Ambassador for the Arts, Virginia Johnson, Dance Theater of Harlem former prima ballerina.

Leslie Moonves, CBS Television president and CEO. and Nancy Moonves.

Mary Tyler Moore, Juvenile Diabetes Foundation chairman, and Robert Levine, Progressive Policy Institute Health Priorities Project chairman.

Jack Nicholson, actor, and Lara Flynn Boyle, actress.

Beth Nolan, Counselor to the President, and Dimitri Nionakis.

Jessye Norman, soprano, and George Norman, Bell South.

Dennis O'Connor, Smithsonian Institution provost, and Anne O'Connor.

Edward James Olmos, actor, and Bodie James Olmos, actor and film maker.

Michael Oreskes, New York Times Washington bureau chief, and Jill Abramson, New York Times Washington editor.

Dean Ornish, Preventive Medicine Research Institute president, and Molly Ornish.

Representative Donald Payne, D- NJ, and Denise Banks, Department of Agriculture. .

Itzhak Perlman, violinist, and Toby Perlman, Perlman Music Program director, and Ariella Perlman.

Robert Pinsky, U.S. Poet Laureate, and Ellen Pinsky.

John Podesta, Chief of Staff to the President, and Mary Podesta.

Sunil Puri, First Rockford Group chairman, and Jenine Cannell-Puri.

Robert Rauschenberg, artist, and Darryl Pottorf, artist.

Bruce Reed, Assistant to the President for Domestic Policy, and Bonnie Lepard.

Janet Reno, U. S. Attorney General.

Steven Ricchetti, Deputy Chief of Staff, and Amy Blanchard.

William Richardson, Secretary of Energy, and Barbara Richardson.

Richard Riley, Secretary of Education, and Anne Riley.

Dennis Rivera, Health and Human Service Employees' Union, and Maria Alvarez.

Maxwell Roach, composer and musician, and Connie Crothers, pianist.

Senator Charles Robb, D-VA, and Lynda Robb, Reading Is Fundamental chairman.

Liz Robbins, Liz Robbins Associates.

Wayne Rogers, Synergics Energy Development Inc. CEO, and Valerie Rogers.

Allen Salmasi, NextWave Telecom Inc. chairman, CEO, and Nicole Salmasi.

Michael Saylor, MicroStrategy Inc. CEO, and Phyllis Saylor.

Arthur Schlesinger, author and historian, and Alexandra Schlesinger.

Bernard Schwartz, Loral Space and Communications Ltd. CEO, and Irene Schwartz.

Martin Scorsese, film director, and Helen Scorsese.

Niranjan Shah, Globetrotters Engineering Corporation chairman, and Pratima Shah.

Walter Shorenstein, Shorenstein Companies chairman, and Clotilde Alvarez.

Robert Shrum, Shrum, Devine, Donilon chairman, and Mary Louise Oates, author.

Arnold Simon, ARIS Industries CEO, and Debra Simon.

Neil Simon, playwright, and Elaine Simon.

Rodney Slater, Secretary of Transportation, and Cassandra Slater.

Will Smith, actor, and Jada Smith, actress.

Senator Gordon Smith, D- OR, and Sharon Smith.

Jean Kennedy Smith, former Ambassador to Ireland.

Harold Snyder and Tamar Hirschl.

Gene Sperling, Asst. to the President for Economic Policy, and Susanne Weinrauch.

Robert Stanton, National Parks Service director, and Janet Stanton.

David Steiner, Steiner Equities Group, Sylvia Steiner.

George Stevens, film maker, and Elizabeth Stevens.

Michael Stevens, America's Millennium producer.

Maria Tallchief, prima ballerina.

Elizabeth Taylor, actress, and Firooz Zahedi, photographer.

Julie Taymor, director, and Elliot Goldenthal, composer.

Howard Tullman, Tunes.com Inc. chairman and CEO. and Judith Tullman.

Melanne Verveer, Assistant to the President and Chief of Staff to the First Lady.

Philip Verveer, Willkie Farr & Gallagher partner.

Edward Villella, Miami City Ballet artistic director, and Linda Villella.

James Watson, Cold Spring Harbor Laboratory president, and Elizabeth Watson.

Mark Weiner, Financial Innovations president, and Susan Weiner.

Togo West, Secretary of Veterans Affairs, and Gail West, Armstrong Worldwide director of government relations.

John Williams, composer and conductor, and Michael Gorfaine.

Anthony Williams, Mayor of the District of Columbia, and Diane Williams.

August Wilson, playwright, and Constanza Romero.

Mary Wilson, author and member of the Supremes, and Linda Green, event planner.

Joseph Wilson, National Council for the Traditional Arts executive director, and Kathryn James, Oasis Program director.

James Wolfensohn, World Bank president, and Elaine Wolfensohn.

Avis Young, Tommy Hilfiger USA vice president, and Leroy Young.

Pinchas Zukerman, musician, and Amanda Forsyth, National Arts Center Orchestra principal cellist.

Don with Muhammad Ali, White House, December 31ˢᵗ 1999

Don was honored to be included in this group of illustrious American icons of the twentieth century, and Patrisha was in her element. But McLean began to worry about the concert planned for later that evening. He saw that a time problem was developing which could affect his performance. The process of transporting guests who were to perform in the concert from the White House to the Lincoln Memorial was not running smoothly. The dinner and concert had been organized by different people, and, at times, it showed. McLean spoke to one of the Marine guards about his concern, and the Marine commandeered a vehicle and whisked him off to the Lincoln Memorial. Other artists were not so fortunate. Bobby McFerrin didn't make it in time to perform. But in spite of the disorganization, the concert was thrilling. In the cold, dark night, over 300,000 people stood around the Reflecting Pool as some of the greatest performers at the turn of the century greeted the New Year in the shadow of Abraham Lincoln. At the stroke of midnight, lights outlined the Washington Monument at the other end of the Mall, a large "2000" appeared at the top of the Washington Monument, and fireworks lit the night sky.

The Millennium Gala Concert at the Lincoln Memorial heralded the start of a new century. Millions of people around the world watched the Millennium Concert, live on CNN. One of the correspondents reported that "Clinton was ebullient as he joined Don McLean to sing 'American Pie.'"

In 2000, McLean was invited to comment about the future of newspapers for a feature in the *New York Times*, and he warned with characteristic bluntness:

> "The real challenge to newspapers is not electronic advancement or the desire of dot com philistines to remake the entire intellectual landscape with their gizmos and ugly language (dot org?), but the likes of Rupert Murdoch and the continual downward intellectual direction that everything his kind of 'media' represents."

In recent years, McLean's songs have received various awards and commendations. In 2001, the Recording Industry Association of America and the National Endowment for the Arts compiled a list of the 365 "Songs of the Century." "American Pie" was voted No.5 in a poll of musicians, critics, industry professionals, elected officials and amateur music fans.

The top five were:

"Over the Rainbow," recorded by Judy Garland

"White Christmas," recorded by Bing Crosby

"This Land Is Your Land," written and recorded by Woody Guthrie

"Respect," recorded by Aretha Franklin

"American Pie," written and recorded by Don McLean

In 2001, Iona College invited McLean back to receive an honorary doctorate, 33 years after he graduated. The program for the commencement of the Class of 2001 said that McLean's music provided "solace as well as insight in our search for meaning and purpose. His more than 40 albums strike universal themes of loneliness and loss, love and longing, reality and illusion, death and rebirth. With a repertoire that incorporates the diverse styles of folk, rock, pop, and bluegrass, this legendary artist has woven a collection distinctive in content, as well as composition, a tapestry celebrated by two generations for its sensitivity and lyricism and, above all, for the honesty of its voice... For leading a life of integrity, guided by a determined refusal to compromise the nature and caliber of his art, for using the language of song as a weapon against isolation and indifference, and for leaving a lasting musical legacy that lifts the spirit and surely does touch the soul, Iona College hereby confers on Don McLean the degree of Doctor of Human Letters." From that moment on, he was Dr. Don McLean. The academic honor would have made his father proud.

A year later, in 2002, "American Pie" was inaugurated into the Grammy Hall of Fame, and BMI confirmed that the song had received over three million airplays. In the same year, BMI accredited "Castles in the Air," "Vincent" and "And I Love You So" with over two million airplays each.

In 2003, George Michael had something far more serious in mind when he chose to record McLean's song, "The Grave" as a protest against the war in Iraq. Originally written as a haunting commentary on the darkness of war (Vietnam being the focus) the lyrics are both beautiful and shocking. Michael's version was not released as a single or on an album, but the video produced for MTV received wide airplay. Michael performed the song live on *Top of the Pops* in England. Few Don McLean fans would have predicted that George Michael would record a McLean song. A performance on *Top of the Pops* appeared just as unlikely.

The Grave

> The grave that they dug him had flowers
> Gathered from the hillsides in bright summer colors
> And the brown earth bleached white
> At the edge of his gravestone
> He's gone...

When the wars of our nation did beckon
A man, barely twenty, did answer the calling
Proud of the trust
That he placed in our nation
He's gone...

But eternity knows him
And it knows what we've done

And the rain fell like pearls
On the leaves of the flowers
Leaving brown, muddy clay
Where the earth had been dry

And deep in the trench
He waited for hours
As he held to his rifle
And prayed not to die

But the silence of night
Was shattered by fire
As the guns and grenades
Blasted sharp through the air

One after another
His comrades were slaughtered
In the morgue of marines
Alone, standing there

He crouched ever lower
Ever lower, with fear
"They can't let me die
They can't let me die here!
I'll cover myself
I know I'm not brave!"

"The earth!
The earth!
The earth is my grave."

The grave that they dug him had flowers

Gathered from the hillsides in bright summer colors
And the brown earth bleached white
At the edge of his gravestone
He's gone...

McLean approved of Michael's efforts. He said, "I am proud of George Michael for standing up for life and sanity. I am delighted that he chose a song of mine to express these feelings. We must remember that the Wizard is really a cowardly old man hiding behind a curtain with a loud microphone. It takes courage and a song to pull the curtain open and expose him. Good Luck George."

Don's comments were published around the world in every major newspaper and on every major news organization's website. At the time, it was a risky thing to be saying, particularly in America, and McLean lost a few friends as a result.

George Michael and Madonna were not the only high profile artists to show interest in McLean's music. American rap artist Tupac Shakur said that "Vincent" was one of his favorite songs. He told the *Los Angeles Times*: "That's how I want to make my songs feel." A year later he was killed in a drive-by shooting.

Martin D40-DM UK tour 2003

Since the lull of the mid-1990s, Don's international touring was back on track. Tours of Britain (1997), Australia (1998), and Ireland (1998) were followed by further visits to Northern Ireland and Ireland in 2001, Britain in 2003, and Australia, Hong Kong, the UK and Ireland in 2004. In fact, in the summer of 2004, McLean embarked on his first world tour in over a decade.

He still loves to travel, and in spite of terror threats directed at Americans, he continues to tour with abandon, while other stars have curtailed their traveling. Wherever he goes, he always travels economy class. He has performed in dozens of countries throughout his career, from Norway to the Philippines, but his favorite places outside of the US are still Britain, Ireland, Australia, and Holland. He knows these countries as well as his own. His favorite city to visit is Amsterdam, because in his youth he loved the freedom and the women. "It is a wonderful place, a magical place, with a distinct vibration."

McLean's love of Britain comes from his interest in art and architecture. One of his favorite stores is located opposite the British Museum in London. It's a small film and book store specializing in movie material. McLean has shopped there on every visit to Britain since 1972. The same man has owned and operated the store for all those years, and he has no idea who Don McLean is. He is the same age as Don, and McLean has watched him grow old, as he himself has aged. Like Prince Charles, McLean considers the Lloyds Building in London to be an ugly and un-British atrocity.

When McLean is in Britain, he likes to eat a full English breakfast of kippers, black pudding, sausage, bacon, beans, fried bread, mushrooms, tomato and anything else that is piled on his plate. He loves it all. In fact, the "all day" breakfast buffet was so good at the Holiday Inn in Glasgow, that he cut short a show by 20 minutes, so he could get back before the buffet closed at 10:30 pm.

In 2003, in the United States, Capitol Records released *The Legendary Songs of Don McLean*, a 20-track greatest hits compilation, which received widespread television advertising. Scheduled to be a three-month ad campaign, it went on for more than two years. In August 2003, Capitol followed that release with a re-issue of the *American Pie* album, featuring bonus tracks "Mother Nature" and "Aftermath," recorded during the original studio sessions in 1971, but not on the original album. This release was well publicized, and McLean appeared on nationwide television and radio, including the Regis and Kelly show on CBS television. "American Pie" was also featured in a television advertisement for Chevrolet with Prince, the Beach Boys, and Elton John. This campaign ran for more than one year, on television and in print.

Also in 2003, McLean took his family to Nashville and recorded *You've Got to Share* with his children. The album of songs for children was recorded live, and Don, Jackie, and Wyatt did all the singing. With Don on lead guitar, Bobby All on guitar, Hank Singer on the mandolin and fiddle, Mike Kropp on the banjo, Ralph Childs on electric bass, Jim Ferguson on string bass, and Tony Migliore playing beautiful piano; the album brings a homemade harmony to the folk songs and rock 'n' roll that Don and his children love to sing around the kitchen table. Jackie wrote and arranged the title song. She and Wyatt occasionally join their father in concert for one or two songs.

With the kids recording You've Got to Share at the Chelsea studios, Nashville

Also that year, American singer Josh Groban included his version of "Vincent" on the *Josh Groban in Concert* CD and DVD. The DVD topped the Billboard chart, and the CD sold over five million copies. Producer David Foster phoned Don to get his reaction to Josh Groban's version. McLean told him that it was very good, but the strings were loud. He said, "I like Josh's singing, and he did a beautiful job with the song."

Foster, apparently, did not like any criticism, but promised to send Don a gold record. "I never got the gold record, as punishment, I guess."

In the summer of 2003, CBS Television filmed an extended feature on Don McLean, his family, and his music for CBS Sunday Morning. For several weeks TV crews followed McLean, interviewed fans, and wandered the trails and rose gardens of Lakeview, his estate in Maine. CBS Sunday Morning has ten million viewers and is a flagship of the CBS news department. The segment aired on July 4th, 2003. It was a huge success and has since been rebroadcast. Don McLean and his music have become symbolic of America, and were a logical subject for an American Independence Day broadcast.

Then on November 22, 2003, the 40th anniversary of President Kennedy's assassination and the 40th anniversary of the day he decided to follow his dream of a career in music, Don McLean received notification in the mail that he had been elected to the National Academy of Popular Music Songwriters' Hall of Fame.

In 1969 Johnny Mercer started the Songwriters' Hall of Fame to honor America's great songwriters. Over the years more than 500 have been inducted into the Songwriters' Hall of Fame, including George Gershwin, Richard Rodgers, Oscar Hammerstein, Paul Simon, and Bob Dylan. The 35th annual gala event of June 10th, 2004, at the Marriott Marquis in New York, filled the Grand Ballroom with stars and major executives of the music industry. Bill Cosby and Cedric, the Entertainer, were there. So were Dionne Warwick, Roberta Flack, Stevie Wonder, Michael

McDonald of the Doobie Brothers, and songwriters Charles Fox, Neil Sedaka, and Hal David. Garth Brooks and his wife flew in from Nashville and sat at the table with Don and Patrisha, Wyatt and Jackie, and Don's good friend and lawyer, Alan Shulman.

Garth Brooks introduced his friend and inspiration with these words:

> "Don McLean brought his own style of tender heart to folk music, and just like the man himself, his work is very deep and very compassionate. His pop anthem, 'American Pie,' is a true cultural phenomenon, a phenomenon that people are still trying to decode, now, more than 30 years after its release. Don's other great songs include: 'And I Love You So,' 'If We Try,' 'Wonderful Baby,' 'Winterwood,'and my personal favorite, a song called 'Empty Chairs,' which kills me as a fan and as a writer. Ladies and gentlemen, a great songwriter and a great friend — Mr. Don McLean.

Don stood and said a few words, and then he sang that sad, thrilling introduction to "American Pie." And when he got to the chorus, a sea of stars and music industry executives rose and sang: "So, bye, bye Miss American Pie..."

With Garth Brooks at the Songwriters' Hall of Fame, 2004

With Stevie Wonder and Michael McDonald at the Hall of Fame

Chapter 14: A Long, Long Time Ago...Don McLean on American Pie

I know that I will always be remembered for this song. It was not just a hit record. It was an immediate phenomenon in the truest sense of the word.

As a young man it was very exciting to be shot out of my own cannon. I had created the vehicle which took me from poverty and obscurity to instant world fame. But after a while the critics turned to taunt me with: "He can't follow it." The artistic and commercial success of "Vincent," which followed, was more important, more difficult, and more necessary than anyone can realize.

Two important and unique hit records were better than twenty forgettable hits. If you count "Castles in the Air," "Crying," and "And I Love You So," I have had five enduring hit records. They represent the best writing and singing I could hope for. It took a long time for the name Don McLean to become as famous as the name "American Pie," but they have both lasted, and today they are both known the world over.

If fame had been my only goal, and if I had known how long it would take, I would have quit show business. But that was not my goal. I learned one very important lesson from Pete Seeger. I learned that grass roots work is just as important as commercial success, and the two go together. I loved the work, and that was always enough for me. When I made the children's album with my kids, I enjoyed it as much, or more, than making the *American Pie* album. The love of singing, performing, writing, and recording has made me very happy. It makes me feel ageless. I could not live without the music. I love the success I've had and the impact my music has had on other artists. I'm proud of the happiness I have been able to give to people in a world where other professions bring trouble to folks. But it is the totality of the work that brings me deep satisfaction. I don't wait around for another hit record or CD, like an addict. The little things and the big things together have made my career perfect for me.

I believe that adversity builds character. After the popularity of "American Pie" began to subside in the seventies, I realized I was in a real fight to build my career and keep working. I never stopped performing, whether I was singing at Carnegie Hall or doing a benefit from the back of a truck. It was all part of what I knew I had to do to build my career. I knew that no record companies, no promoters, and no major investors were going to spend major dollars on Don McLean. I would have to build my career by hand, and I believed that I had to do certain things to accomplish this.

First I had to control all my publishing rights and recordings. Second I had to tour constantly, even peripatetically (on foot) as the Hudson River Troubadour, to keep my name out there and to learn my craft with constant practice in front of audiences. Third, I had to make sure that every recording I ever made was still available. Major record companies usually delete albums as soon as they quit selling. But today, if someone remembers a song I sang years ago, that song is out there, available, and it will be in the future. I knew that the key to having the career I wanted was to have an album career, not a singles career.

I did not fall into the trap of feeling like a failure because I was not having hits. I realized that the work was the key, and that I had plenty of tools to allow me to pursue the work, even without the support of a record company. That's how I began the process of beating show business.

In order to beat this business, one must control the sources of income one has created, and not allow those sources to be in the hands of others. Nothing happens to a Don McLean recording, song, or trademark without my permission. This has allowed me to build on what I have created. It is what has allowed many great things to happen since my appearance with Garth Brooks in Central Park in 1997. When many people are involved with how a song or master will be used, it often does not get used. People use little power plays to turn off deals. Because of the many things that have happened in recent years, my name is known as it never was in the past, and I am constantly amazed at the places my music is played. It is like seeing a garden grow into a forest. I am thankful that, unlike Jim Croce and Harry Chapin, I have been given the gift of time to see this happen and to share it with my beautiful family.

In 2005 Joel Dorn and I produced *Rearview Mirror*, a retrospective of career highlights on CD and DVD. I had not worked with Joel since we made *Homeless Brother* together in 1974. For *Rearview Mirror* we used a lot of archival material, and I had to get a lot of material archived. I had over

100 video tapes in various formats that had to go to Nashville in a truck. Some of the formats are becoming obsolete, and they had to be copied before they were lost. After I appeared on Immus in the Morning in October of 2005, *Rearview Mirror* rose to No.17 on Amazon.com.

Recently, the tribute to the late George Best, the UK football star, featuring the song "Vincent," was No.4 on the UK singles charts. It sparked a renewed interest in all my albums over there. And now, I am working on an album of all my original songs. It will be called *Addicted to Black*.

Here for the first time are the lyrics to one song on that forthcoming album:

The Three of Us

See the picture that I'm holding
a picture of us three
Standing in the summertime
At Quogue down by the sea
We stood there just a minute
Quogue is an Indian name
There were no cars back then
There were no cars back then
When the Indians came.
We never traveled anywhere
We never did a thing
Compared to them, I guess you'd say
I'm some kind of travel king
We lived near Mamaroneck
That's an Indian name
There were no houses there
There were no houses there
When the Indians came

When the Indians came there were no private schools
No traffic cops, no highway rules
When the Indians came they left a name
The word alone
Can outlast stone
The Indians lie in holy ground
A place my parents now have found

They're buried on a hill of stone
Rocks of ages stand alone
Their names are carved for all to see
And no one knows their names but me
I remember in that picture
my life had just begun
Now the three of us are fading
In an Indian sun

Philosophy separates man from animals. Every man is a philosopher. We each develop our own personal philosophy to explain the mystery of life as we experience it. With that in mind, perhaps the proximity of death is a large part of my personal philosophy. It is reflected in many of my songs and, in some reverse effect, has allowed me to be extremely happy with the life I have been given.

THE END

The Three of Us

Appendix I: Behind the Scenes with Don McLean: A Fan's View by Ron Buck

It's not often you get the chance to meet up with your all-time musical hero. It's even more unlikely that you'll get the chance to spend more than five minutes with him when you do, especially when he is actually in "work mode."

Me, I've always been a bit of a jammy so-and-so, but back in May I somehow managed to exceed even my own greatest achievements/expectations in the "dream-come-true" department. Here are all the gory details, and if it makes any of you out there jealous as hell, well, I'll understand! Seriously, I wish you could all have been with me, but I hope this will suffice for now.

The Background

As some of you know, I was fortunate enough to be asked by Alan Howard back at the beginning of the year, to put together a set of questions for him to use as the basis for interviewing Don in more detail, than ever before, about his guitars and his guitar playing.

Don appeared to enjoy this guitar Q&A exercise a lot, firstly because not a lot of people ask him about this aspect of his work, and secondly because he simply loves talking about guitars and guitar-players. This was reiterated by Alan Howard when he relayed to me that Don was interested in saying "Hello and thanks" in person, during the May, 2003, UK tour. Don wanted to thank me? The more I thought about that, the more bizarre it seemed! But also VERY exciting!

But, as I was about to find out, it was a truly indicative measure and insight into the man that he had no problem giving praise where it might just be due and offering further positive encouragement to someone who shares his passion for great music and his desire to "spread the gospel" according to Don McLean. After all, his is Dr. Don McLean these days!

First Introductions

It turned out that the first opportunity to hook up with Alan Howard (and consequently Don) was at The Chicago Rock Café in Northampton. Alan felt that because of the somewhat informal nature of this venue, that getting alongside Don during the sound-check would be a lot easier for both of us, than in one of the more formal, large theatre venues also featured on the Tour, where things were likely to be run more to the clock.

Late afternoon (around 5:30 pm) he was proved right, as Don's tour bus (a large, black VIP coach with blacked-out windows) pulled up at the front of the building, and an entourage of people departed from it, the last to emerge being our man himself, bespectacled and wearing a light-colored raincoat, looking more like a bank manager, I must say, than an international superstar!

The first thing I noticed about Don was his fast-paced, business-like demeanor, as he shot straight through the foyer leading into the performance area, acknowledging and beckoning Alan to follow, Alan in turn giving me the "nod" to do likewise.

Inside, the performance area was already a hive of activity, with the sound (PA) system and stage already set up and the sound crew headed by Chris Dunne busy fiddling with various bits of equipment. Don hardly needed any time to whip his coat off, sit on a chair, unzip his already roadie-delivered guitar out of its case-cover (his guitar travels in a case inside another case!), and quickly crank up his guitar strings to "concert pitch." He always detunes his guitars whilst they travel, to take tension off their necks.

Alan and I watched as Don expertly got his trusty Martin D-40DM perfectly in tune in a matter of seconds, like "a man possessed." At this point he looked over at Alan and me and made a beckoning gesture to join him! Alan was straight over there, but I held back a little, not being sure that it was indeed both of us he wanted to talk with at this stage. After acknowledging Alan's arrival, Don repeated the gesture, this time with that big toothy grin of his, and I knew without any doubt that he really wanted to meet me after all!

"Have a seat Ron," he said, pointing at a spare chair directly next to him. "Thanks for the guitar questions. They were really great questions. It was real fun giving answers to them."

Despite feeling a bit tongue-tied, I told Don it was great to have him back in the UK once again, and I had a million other questions that I wanted to ask him about all sorts of stuff, while he was over here, and that I was really looking forwards to the concert later that night.

"I'd love to chat right now, Ron, but I have simply GOT to save my voice for tonight. But, we will catch up for a proper chat soon, that's a promise!"

At that point, one of the sound-crew shouted across to Don that they were "Ready when you are." Alan and I jumped back off the stage to let Don get on. (We were also excited as we knew we were about to hear Don start his sound-checking!) Don rose to his feet, plugged in his Ripcord guitar cable, and that fantastic acoustic guitar tone of his cracked out through the speaker-stacks on either side of the stage, as he looked around to see if everyone else was ready to join in. No count-in (Nashville cats don't need one!), just one E major chord to get the right pitch and Don was into "Tulsa Time," short-lived, however, as Don's vocal mic screamed with feedback about three bars in. Whoa!

Now, one thing you can always say about Don, above everything else, is he is a perfectionist! He only wants things to be ABSOLUTELY, TOTALLY PERFECT, not for his sake, but for the sake of his audience, because he REALLY cares about us. (And, I mean, REALLY cares.) If anything (or anyone) isn't 100% right there with him, he blows like a small (no make that large) volcano!

The sound guys got a blinding look the first time the mic howled. The second time it happened, they got some VERY strong advice from Don. The third time, it was "Strike!" as Don unplugged his guitar, put it back in the case, and, over his shoulder, grabbed his coat, and (as Elvis fans would say), left the building!

If actions do indeed speak louder than words, then the sound crew had been told to get things sorted for later! This was a new side of Don I hadn't seen before, but Alan Howard found it very amusing, and reassured me all was okay. The way Don had left, I was wondering if he would come back to play the concert at all!

Fascinating Insight Number One — as already stated, Don is NEVER less than a total perfectionist when it comes to his music, and, even more importantly, his audience. If he has something he wants to say to us, if he has a special chord or bass line he wants us to hear freshly, if he's doing something special with his vocal phrasing, being "nearly right" is completely wrong, as far as Don is concerned! There is no compromise when it comes to Don's music. He is the consummate professional in that respect; and everyone around him, be they musicians, roadies, or sound-crew, must work to meet his exacting standards and strive to exceed them wherever possible!

EVERY time Don performs, whether it is the sound-check or that night's concert proper, Don will be attempting (like his wife and children's lives depended upon it) to perform any song better than he (or anyone else) has EVER performed it. He can never just "go through the motions." (Which would probably blow all of us away anyhow!)

Nope, he wanted to sing "Tulsa Time" the best he had ever sung it, right there and then at the Northampton sound-check. And when the sound crew inadvertently stopped him from doing so, he left them in no doubt whatsoever that by the concert proper that evening, they would want to do "Tulsa Time" better than they had ever done it in their lives too! (In defense of the sound crew, this was not an easy venue to run sound for, it being basically a nightclub with few high-tech facilities. Did anyone who was there notice that the lighting sequences were not always entirely appropriate?)

I've noticed, on other occasions, that Don leaves anyone, who is not a positive influence and conducive to things being right, little doubt that he is "surplus to requirements!" This is not so much an "artistic temperament" as Don setting such high standards that everyone else's game has to rise to meet them. (As a postscript, on the last night of the tour, the sound crew confided in me that working with Don, although very demanding, had taught them more in a relatively short space of time, than working with anyone else, and was something they would not have missed for anything! They all hoped it wouldn't be the only time.)

I also concluded that Don was having some health problems with his voice, and his anxiety and patience levels were affected adversely by this fact. He worries about that voice, not surprisingly.

Now, "it's an ill wind that blows no good," as they say; and Don's "instant" sound-check routine meant that the rest of his musicians hung around a bit longer than usual after his early departure, making sure their sound was right too! Seizing the opportunity, I offered to buy some beers, and eventually got into a long and interesting conversation with Kerry Marx, mostly about equipment (as guitar players always do when they first get together), but I had my eye on a stack of papers that Kerry had with him.

I knew that Kerry was the latest edition to Don's group, and, as such, was still getting familiar with Don's extensive repertoire. (Tony Migliore later told me that Don knew at least 1000 songs from memory!) The stack of paper was in fact "Nashville Charts," the musical short-hand used by everyone in Nashville to quickly learn new songs.

The evening concert at "The Hard Rock" was absolute magic. Alan Howard reckons it was the best night of the tour, and he should know, he went to most of it!

Don popped a "Feedback Buster" rubber plug into his guitar sound-hole, and hey presto, the sound was bang-on-the-button all night long! Don's voice held up too, assisted by an unusual mid-concert exit while the band played on with the blues, and a pocketful of cough-sweets, which he skillfully unwrapped and popped into his mouth, from time-to-time, with lightening speed and dexterity.

The Second Meeting – Let's Talk Guitar with Don McLean

My next encounter with Don was at De Montfort Hall, Leicester. Having now seen both sides of Don's personality, I was a little apprehensive that someone might have upset him before my requested arrival at the stage door around 5:30 pm.

My anxious and late arrival was not helped when the stage doorman turned out to be a real "Jobsworth" and refused me entry despite my confident approach. "I'm here to meet up officially with Don McLean's team." Quizzical look and response, "Got any ID?" Well no actually, I didn't. No one told me I needed any! Had I not been held up on the M1, I probably would have met up with Alan Howard outside first and been inside by now! The big black tour bus was already parked, but there were no sound-check noises emanating from inside, so I guessed the gang hadn't been there long either – what to do next?

In a stroke of genius I called Alan Howard's mobile phone, and he laughed when he answered it from inside the building, and I told him about the Jobsworth. Apparently, he had challenged even Don! Alan came and let me in through the stage door (much to the chagrin of a number of fans, Don memorabilia in hand, waiting to see if Don exited AFTER the sound check – one even tried to get in with me!) Alan reassured me that Don was in a great mood today and very relaxed upstairs. "His voice has fully recovered, too," Alan said perkily.

At the top of the stairs, we turned left into a kind of waiting room with a few chairs. I guessed it to be one of those sparse "Green Rooms" you find in theaters all over the UK. (Those of you who ever go backstage will know that there seems to be an inverse law that operates in theaters that states: the more palatial the theater is out front, the more decadent it is backstage! The De Montfort Hall, at the risk of being sued by them, was no exception. Cheap furniture, and decorated like your old school sickroom).

I recognized a few faces just before I entered the room, Alan's wife, Diane, and Mike, another friend of Alan's. I figured we were all waiting for Janet (the McLean tour manager) to summon us officially to the theater to watch the sound-check from a distance.

You can imagine my surprise when after entering the room and saying, "Hi," to everyone, the open door was swung shut behind me by none other than the man himself, guitar already in one hand and an electronic tuner in the other. His Calton flight case was opened on a table behind the door and various garments (I recognized the black tunic-type shirt with various embroidery) hung on a makeshift pole (told you it was sparse in there!) Then reality dawned on me — I WAS IN DON'S ACTUAL DRESSING ROOM!

AH : "Ron's here."
DM: "Hi Ron."
RB: "Hi Don."
DM: "Nice to see you again, grab a seat." He gestures towards the one next to his.

Don apologized that he could not speak to me for long at Northampton because he had to save his voice. Back in the States he didn't do so many shows "back-to-back" these days, and so this UK tour was tough at times, even for him! Plus he was doing more "vigorous" stuff with his voice these days, always pushing harder, further.

I nodded, like a wise vocal-coach, not really having a clue what singing for two hours at a time for days on end must be like! Still, it was nice that he remembered me and cared enough to say "Sorry." I was of course pinching myself all the time by now.

Don then chatted openly with Alan, wondering how long he could keep on touring outside of the States as he approached his next birthday, when he will be 58 years old! "I still feel like I'm up for it all right, but I've started having to "work out" again," he said, somewhat disappointedly. (He obviously doesn't enjoy it!)

He asked Alan if he "worked-out" too. (Alan appears to be a natural "ectomorphic type" from what I've seen of him — eats like a horse, never puts on an ounce!) Alan said he didn't. I then said to Don that "Tony Bennett is still traveling the world, and sounding better than ever to boot," trying to reassure Don that he should definitely not think about not coming to England again. It must have worked, as a tour was later announced for 2004!

I think Don's comment was half-prompted by his voice problems back at Northampton more than anything, but it is also worth remembering that Don's UK tour schedule was a lot more rigorous than what he generally does over in the States, i.e. he has a few day rest between shows for his voice to recuperate.

The conversation then switched to houses, with Don enquiring how Alan's was doing. (Alan was having a new kitchen fitted, which he must have told Don about.) Don observed that, "Once you buy a house, you never have any money again." We all nodded in agreement. It was nice to know that even a superstar's house keeps costing him money too! All this "chit-chat" was great. By this time I had several bruises appearing from all the pinching I had been giving myself!

Guitar on lap, Don thanked me for my guitar questions again and said some of them really took him down "Memory Lane," which he really enjoyed. He then went on to address each one further, from memory, as he tuned his guitar with the electronic tuner on his lap (A Korg model, if I recall correctly.) This meant he must have either carried them in his head or looked them over just prior to our meeting again, since not a single one was overlooked. Very impressive!

Don's D-40DM Guitar – Don first talked to me about his own guitar

Guitar Action — Don showed me his high "Like a Bluegrass Player's" guitar set-up. The further the distance the strings are from the fret-board, the louder they sound, but the harder they are to press-down at the bridge-end. A low "action" at the nut (peg end) makes them easier to play.

Medium Gauge Strings — Don pointed to a number of fresh packets of medium gauge LaBella strings on the dressing room table. He explained that these days he considers himself primarily a rhythm guitarist, but that he always favors medium gauge for their full sound. He has built up his hands over many years to be able to do all his stuff on them and that high action.

All the time Don was chatting, he was strumming away at immediately recognizable passages and riffs from his own songs. I was, of course, transfixed!

Only Guitar — Don pointed to his open Calton case on the side and reminded me that he only took one guitar on the road these days. He then talked about the materials the D-40DM was made from, especially the Engelmann spruce top, which he found so much better than Sitka spruce, particularly for his rhythm playing. One thing I noticed about Don's guitar was just how immaculate it was. Most pro's guitars get pretty beat up over time, especially when touring with the frequency that Don does, but there was not a single mark on it! This made sense, when I remembered that Don generally seemed to arrive and depart always carrying his own guitar, instead of roadies doing it for him. He obviously really loves that guitar!

The Bridge — Don had me inspect the bridge of his guitar to see if I could detect where it had been removed and replaced by one of his own design by his personal repairman, Ron Pinkham, of Woodsound Studios in Maine. I couldn't see anything, but I noticed how tall the bridge was and how wide the saddle strip was. Don had a lot of early Martins whose bridges split on him, because of his high set-up and medium gauge strings, so he now beefs up the guitars in that region to avoid that problem plus early neck resets. When a steel-strung guitar gets to being

20-30 years old, the pull stress exerted by the strings being about 11 stones tends to "fold" the guitar up in the middle. For it to continue to be playable, it needs to have the neck taken off and reworked.

Machine Heads — Don showed me the gold finished metal machines heads (tuning pegs) on his own stage guitar. "I got the design for the D-40DM wrong there!" he said, referring to the fact that the production model has plastic, mother-of-pearl buttons. They're pretty, but less robust. Don worries about the tuning pegs being easily damaged and having to tune with a pair of pliers!

Don's Guitar Style – Next Don talked about his actual playing

Playing "Clean" — Don explained that he is always striving to make every note in-between his vocals notes count. He illustrated this with "If We Try," playing the opening phrase: "When I see you on the street, I loose my concentration," — bass notes, open E (6th) and open A (5th) emphasized. Same in "Crying:" — "Crying — bass note E open (6th) — ov-er you."

Let me say, that Don's guitar sound is not wimpy! He lays into the bass strings hard and near the bridge for maximum effect! His actual flat picking technique is interesting in that he frequently gets under the bass string, rather than picking across it, which emphases it loudness further still. Now we are starting to see how he gets that clear strong sound in his flat-picking!

Using The Left Hand Thumb — When I first had Alan ask him the question back in January, Don stated that he didn't use his left hand thumb much to fret notes. But he has since thought about it and realized he did it quite a bit! Examples followed: "1967," and once again "Crying." "But nearly always only in the first position (fret)," he added. Don felt pleased that he could actually use his left hand thumb to fret both the 6th and 5th strings in the Fm6 chord in "Crying!"

Some of the chords that Don uses in "Crying" are not the same as those shown in the Don McLean Songbook, which claims to have authentic guitar transcriptions, especially the ending ones which are very nice indeed!

Finger Style — Don emphasized that he uses his thumb plus his first, second, and third fingers when finger picking. He rests the fourth, "pinky," finger on the surface of the scratch-plate for stability and as a "depth-gauge." But he occasionally even employs that for picking, especially when playing Josh White material. Also, Don said he sometimes uses a combination of plectrum plus fingers (a la Glen Campbell) more than people realize, even whilst playing rhythm guitar. He holds the plectrum between his thumb and first finger and uses his second, third and pinky on the 3rd, 2nd, and 1st strings, respectively. He also commented: "Strangely enough, I also play more with just my bare fingers on the right hand. And I record that way." (i.e. no finger picks or plectrum.) Don's hands are not particularly large, and his fingers are quite short, but they are very strong and stocky with good muscular development.

Don's Plectrum — Don has a pile of Don McLean "signature" picks made especially for him by Northern Kingdom Music in Camden, Maine. These come in three colors: black, white and tortoise-shell. They are large and triangular and medium gauge (thickness).

Don does some picking

All the time Don was chatting, he was noodling away on his guitar. All the stuff he was doing was catching my ear, because they were actual Don songs, and I was keen to see what he did with his fingers. One notable example was the solo section from "The Grave" which he played beautifully for us (with bear fingers!), and boy was it clean and LOUD! Now, a top-quality acoustic guitar is loud, and the Martin D-40DM is as good a guitar as money can buy, but there is no doubt Don means it when he plays anything. This was quite a revelation to see "up close and personal." And THAT VOICE really is a gift from God. Even while Don is chatting, it seems to fill the room, but whenever he sings a little, it is so loud and clear it seems to be full of certain frequencies that just resonate everywhere. This was fascinating too, because you are always curious to know if a star's voice really is that good without a microphone, reverb, and compression, etc. Well, Don's is! I think that the mic also loves the frequencies his voice contains; it just has all these overtones running through it that amplify well. You can't learn to produce those in your voice – you just get them with your genes. By this time, I'm severely bruised up one arm!

I told Don how great the guitar sounded when he played "The Grave," and how I loved the flat picking solo, "Under The Double Eagle," that he did with Ralph Childs at Northampton; and how good he was at "cross picking" (using the plectrum to "pattern pick" a difficult technique to master.) Don was very modest about his abilities on the guitar: "There are a bunch of people who play a lot more guitar than I ever will," he said sadly. But he went on to state, "But what I do play is real clean. — I've spent a lifetime perfecting that."

It was one of those "throwaway Don lines" that got me thinking for many weeks after he made it, as do many of Don's "asides," musical and otherwise. This is the thing I have found about Don, whenever I hear him talk – there are little "pearls of wisdom" that show he is a really deep thinker, and, as I said before, HE REALLY CARES. This is no revelation, considering who Don is, but it never fails to impress me!

Now, I, like most of you, have a number of Don songs for which I haven't been able to work out the guitar part exactly. I have a constant "list" in my head. I was about to get specific about my list with Don, when he SUDDENLY passed his guitar over to me and said: "See what YOU think of this."

Ron does some picking!

Now, I'm a grown man, I've been through many "life-changing" experiences as most middle-aged blokes, and I'm happy to play the guitar in front of anyone these days. But at this point, I couldn't have got as large an "adrenaline rush" if I'd bungeed after first doing a free-fall parachute jump in the middle of the night! I gotta tell you guys, to be sitting in Don McLean's dressing room, a couple of hours before he's due on stage to play in front of 2000+ people, and to find yourself with Don's ACTUAL guitar on YOUR lap and Don passing his own plectrum over to you with the comment "See what YOU think of this" is something your intestines don't recover from for some days. (In my case about three.)

Both my left and right hands now seemed to have developed a severe nervous twitch, and my left leg and right eye were well on there way too! All eyes in the room were on me, Don's included. Now at this point you wonder what Don might be expecting. Here's what I did next (brain temporarily short-circuited of course).

Played the introduction to "Empty Chairs"
Played the first verse and ending to "And I Love You So"

Fortunately, Don's guitar appeared to have a built-in self-recognition system that meant I didn't stall or fumble, despite the fact that I was gripping the neck like a vice just to stay on its fingerboard. I looked at Don throughout, and he could obviously see the terror written on my face, as he nodded with approval. As the last phrase of "And I Love You So" rung out and filled the little room, he smiled that big beamy smile of his. "Good." he commented.

Now I went from one extreme to the other, as I started thinking of all the flashy Chet Atkins or Tommy Emmanuel licks I could impress him with, and how I might just become the third guitar player in Don's band! Hell, he already had two electric players; he needed another guy on acoustic. — Why not me! Perhaps I could show him my singing too? Before I had the chance to really blow it, Don retrieved his guitar from me and showed me how he fingered the ending to "And I Love You So," very differently from my version

"Same notes, different sound" said Don.

Who was I to argue? After all, he wrote it!!!! But once again, this was Don really caring that I got it properly "nailed" and was not just playing it. Was he rehearsing me for my debut appearance with him later in the evening, I dreamed? (Well, I am a Pisces after all.)

The next couple of minutes were as great as they were unreal, as Don and I "chatted guitars" like a couple of regular guys in a dressing room a few hours before playing to 2000+ people. Kerry Marx knocked on the door at this point and took a great photo. (Thanks Kerry!).

Don's own guitar is a truly fabulous instrument. I've played almost every brand of top-line guitar over the years, but the loudness and depth of sound of this one was just stunning. — It was like having a Steinway piano on your lap!

The neck was quite wide (I'd say 1 and 3/4 inches), just lovely for finger-picking. The high bridge action just disappeared on the first half of the neck, and it was a dream to play bare chords, anywhere. The strings were a bit heavy for me, being used to lights, but I have now started using mediums on my own Dreadnought. No doubt the sound and the intonation are worth the extra work of building up the strength in my hands and the calluses on my fingers, which only takes a few weeks of regular playing. Do give them a try. I'm also trying to track down some LaBella brand strings, but these are not so thick on the ground in the UK, it seems.

Kerry arrived to tell Don that they needed to do a sound-check soon, and Don, quick as a flash goes into "work mode." I now know it is time to leave, and I can see that Alan Howard is like-minded, as he rises from his seat to go.

"Got to change these strings," says Don, as we all bid him farewell for the time being, and I thank him for his generosity and the guitar lesson. Once again, he thanks me for the guitar questions and for coming to the concert early to meet with him. "The pleasure was all mine," I tell him, and I could not have meant that more in my whole life.

Don shut the dressing room door, and we stood in the corridor outside, watching Don's musicians, Kerry, Tony, Ralph, Jerry, and Pat wandering the corridor with their various instruments and accessories, getting ready to set up for yet another sound-check. Kerry seems genuinely pleased to see me again, after meeting me for the first time at Northampton, and tells me he will be happy to let me have a copy of his personal "charts" as soon as he has "cleared it" with Don. This is proving to be a very memorable afternoon for me!

The backstage area at De Montfort Hall has a large corridor running its entire length across the back of the stage itself, and Kerry is keen to show me where he and the "boys" are camped, should I want to come visit them. This I immediately interpret as an invitation to do so at some stage, after the sound-check maybe. "Do you like Pizza?" asks Kerry. Boy, I'm really starting to feel I might get on stage with the band. (But, don't hold your breath, folks).

Eating seems to be a ritual thing with the band before shows, and they have Janet send out for a "take-away" at every venue. "The Chinese food in England is superior to what we get in the States," comments Tony Migliore, with his usual preciseness. "Yeah, the one we had last night was awesome," added Kerry. These boys are "real pros," no sign of nerves here, before the show! It's also good to know our UK Chinese take-aways are as good as any that America can offer!

Five minutes later, Don emerges from his dressing room, guitar in hand. (Did he really change strings that quickly?) There is a hive of activity, as Don rushes around like a man possessed. His energy level is infectious, as the whole place seems to turn into Piccadilly Circus at rush-hour. I think of his earlier remonstrations about "getting too old to tour anymore," and wish I had Don's energy and constitution, myself, now! However he's "working out" these days, it's a routine that is obviously successful!

I know Don won't mind me saying this (I hope), but for a guy who's heading towards 60 his demeanor is a bit scary. With a constitution like an ox and a mind like a razor blade, the pace at which he works, once his guitar is over his shoulders, is really quite impressive! As Kerry Marx said to me later, "What the heck was Don like in his twenties, thirties, and forties?"

When you think about Don's ability to circumvent the globe for 30+ years, much of the time traveling solo, you start to appreciate what an extraordinary human being he is, not just creatively, but also his pure tenacity, energy and focus are staggering!

Sound-check Time!

Don starts the sound-check with "Tulsa Time" again. No squealing mics this time. Don has a big cheesy grin, too. He's happy. Lot's of voice in the monitors. (Don likes that!) And the hall is a big one Don has played many, many times — a comfort zone for sure.

Now something interesting happens, as Don takes the band through a number of his "lesser" (I use the term loosely) known songs, stopping them at certain points and asking that they "change this slightly," or "leave that out, completely, tonight." Even some of the chords appear to be getting changed! Kerry's scribbling this down on his charts like his life depends on it. (It probably does!) "Perfect Love," in particular, gets a good working over. "Slow the middle section down like this," Don tells the band and demonstrates as they all watch him insert some nifty passing chords. "Have you seen me?" ends the sound-check, again, a little "re-worked" by Don. I guess because of the vocal range, it checks out that Don's voice is doing nicely for the upcoming show. No vocal problems tonight, the golden tonsils have had a well-deserved rest the previous night and have benefited!

I realize that I am witnessing something quite amazing taking place. Here is Don McLean, the world-class artist, playing with musicians who have been on the road and in the studio with him continually, many for years, top flight musicians from Nashville, the cream of session players, taking instruction from their "boss," an hour before show-time, on songs they have played before. Don is "customizing" his potential play-list to suit the actual venue! Don's incredible ears are telling him that some of these lesser-known songs will work well here tonight; this theatre and sound-system can handle them! Don, the perfectionist, strikes again! Another fascinating insight into just how much Don "cares" about the show being ABSOLUTELY, TOTALLY PERFECT for everyone, and a little different from usual, perhaps?

The sound-check goes on for some time in this fashion. I watch it all "from the wings" this time, which is a terrific experience for me and a real insight into how the "pros" work. It goes without saying that ALL the guys in the band are staggeringly quick to pick up and act on anything Don suggests they do. I imagine it must be a similar scene in the recording studio in Nashville with these guys. Their "ears" are just amazing. By the end of the sound-check, the atmosphere amongst Don and the band is very "upbeat" and jovial. "It's gonna be a good one tonight," says Don to the entire band.

Kerry tells Don, "Your singing sucks!" Don waves a finger at Kerry with no comment before disappearing back into his dressing room and shutting the door. It's been a good sound-check, and Don is relaxed and dying to get on with the show, which means, of course, that everyone else can relax too! It's going to be a good night

"Hey Dude, check this out!" Kerry beckons me to his dressing room in the back corridor, where he already has his laptop computer running, surrounded by several half-empty boxes of pizza. Kerry has been keeping up with the tour via the UK Tour Page. He is an avid "surfer" whilst on tour, and not just on Alan's site. There is lots of email, to and from "the folks back home." I comment that for musicians on the road halfway around the world email must be a great thing to have. "We're getting a bit homesick now," adds Pat, who is having a lot of work done on his house, which he looks forward to seeing completed when he gets back. There ensues about half an hour of chat with all the band members, mostly about things musical. Those "charts" were explained to me in greater detail.

I realize that we are only an hour away from the concert itself, so I feel like it is only right to leave everyone to get ready without my further interruptions. I bid the band farewell, and as I'm leaving Kerry suggests: "Hey, why not watch the concert from backstage in the wings?" I figure that is an offer I cannot refuse, but I also know that I need to get official clearance to do that! I ask Janet, the tour manager, to fix it for me. She knocks on Don's dressing room, and, after a muffled conversation behind the half-opened door, comes back with the verdict: "No problem."

Just when it couldn't get any better, I thought.

Just time now to go to the "front-of-house" and grab a beer or two and a quick bite to eat. I exit through the stage door, reminding Jobsworth that I will be back before the show starts and "not to forget a face like mine." He comments, sardonically, that he never would. And, with a push of the door-bar, I am out into a beautiful May evening, walking around the side of the building to the main entrance to meet up with Alan Howard and his gang, who all left a bit earlier.

The downstairs reception is now humming with people in excited anticipation, busy buying last-minute tickets and talking of Chevys and Levees and Starry Starry Nights, all ages, all types. It is a marked contrast to the peaceful, calm atmosphere I just left back-stage, and the whole experience is quite surreal for me, I can tell you.

Five minutes later I am sitting drinking cold beer and munching sandwiches with Alan and the gang and wanting to tell everyone else at the bar, "Hey, I played Don's guitar!" But modesty and the realization that no-one would probably believe me dull my enthusiasm. I'm joining in the great conversation, but my mind is fixed on the clock above the bar, as I know I must get backstage again, several minutes before the 8:00 pm curtain-up, to get the full "backstage experience." Panic sets in, as I think of the possibility of Jobsworth leaving his post and me stranded again in the corridor, or a swap of shifts producing a new Jobsworth who won't let me back in at all!

By 7:50 pm I find myself at the stage door again. The original Jobsworth is still there and plays a jokey game of "Do I know you?" with me. — It is not well received at this juncture! I get to the top of the stairs outside the dressing room area, and there are a lot more people around the place now, stagehands, theatre staff and Janet, the tour manager, a bit more stressed than I have seen her so far. Kerry and the band appear at about 7:55 pm "dressed for the stage" this time and gather around Janet like she has the clue to a treasure hunt. A little tannoy system cracks out "Five minute call." I'm keeping well out of the way. The guys are a little nervous now, and I'm wondering if I really should be here, at all.

"Excuse me," says a stagehand, beckoning me away from the wall I am leaning against. The "wall" turns out to be a huge, steel fire door on sliders, which the stagehand proceeds to push open, revealing the actual performance area about ten feet away. Through the crack in the stage curtains, I can see the whole auditorium, filled with a capacity crowd, and hear that gentle "buzz" of people about to get the show they have all . been waiting for.

Tony and Kerry decide they will enter the stage from the other side and quickly trot off down the back corridor to the other stage wing. Janet is on a phone attached to the wall at the side of the stage. She is deep in conversation. Is something wrong? "We have clearance!" she says excitedly. (Stage-speak for "the theater is now full, and there are no stragglers anywhere in the rest of the building.") Pat is standing next to me, nervously tuning his guitar just one more time, via an electronic tuner. It's 7:59 now. Don's dressing room door opens, and Don emerges with that black tunic shirt hanging over his jeans, guitar over his shoulders, and glugging an already half-empty bottle of water. Don nods at Janet; Janet nods at Don.

Showtime!

Seconds later the lights in the main theatre and the stage area go down, and weak "foot-lights" appear at the front of the stage, just enough to allow the band to see where they are heading without falling over. Pat unplugs his electronic tuner, slipping it in his back pocket. "Here we go!" he says to me, excitedly.

The band wanders onto the stage, and there is a faint flicker of applause as the members of the audience closest to the stage get some benefit from the footlights and notice the shadowy figures crouching around, plugging in various instruments, and switching on bits of equipment on "stand-by." Just Don, Janet, and I are left standing in the wings, as the main house speakers announce: "LADIES AND GENTLEMEN, PLEASE WELCOME AMERICA'S LEGENDARY SINGER-SONGWRITER, DON MCLEAN!"

Lights come up on stage to reveal the band in their full glory all set and ready now. A "follow-spot" appears at Don's on-stage mic. A curious thing then happens. Janet whips out a flashlight and shines it directly in front of Don in the still dark stage-area between the wings and the lit stage area.

Don takes another gulp of water, looks me in the eye and raises an eyebrow, as if to say, "Here we go!" and casually saunters towards his own mic on stage. As soon as he enters the stage area, the crowd erupts. Wow! Is that loud!

"AWLRIGHTTTT!" screams Don, as he plugs in his guitar, and within seconds, the band and Don are in perfect unison with "Maybe Baby." At the end, the audience goes wild! Don was right; it is "going to be a good one!"

Watching a Don McLean concert from the wings is a COMPLETLEY different experience from being in the audience. There is a lot of banter on stage between songs, whilst the audience is applauding. Mostly, the guys are winding each other up, and Don always gives as good as he gets! The atmosphere on stage is one of everyone having a great time, and this transmits itself to the audience. Don keeps it all fun out there!

There Is Never a "Set-list" (or so it seems) — Don either shouts out what's coming up next, or sometimes he just plays an opening chord or phrase and the band "jumps on it." They have played together for so long, and the band is made up of such great musicians, that they all play totally intuitively. Don talks about a similar empathy in recording studio sessions.

The Arrangements Are "Loose" — these guys play so well together that they can all "improvise" their parts mid-song to keep things fresh for them every night. They have "set points" where they have to hit a certain note or chord at a certain place in time, but in between they seem to have a very "free-hand." Don's total confidence in them means they are encouraged to be creative. Kerry and Pat, in particular, go out on a limb and "trade quotes," i.e. they play riffs and phrases at each other together, like a guitar "shoot-out." At Leicester it was Beatles riffs all night!

Don Keeps Everyone On Their Toes! — At Leicester, for example, Don made a snap decision to start the second half completely solo. The entire band were lined up and ready to go on in the wings, and Don suddenly blurted: "You guys hang back and let me have it on my own for a while."

I think the audience was so enthusiastic in the first half that Don wanted to give them something special, i.e. on his own again with "Mountains O' Mourne," "And I Love You So," "The Grave," (After practicing it in the dressing room!) and "Where Were You Baby." His voice was totally healthy, the audience was totally on-board, and it must be a most special feeling for Don to sit there on his own, holding 2000+ people spellbound.

Sitting in the wings at this point was absolutely fantastic, as I could see the faces of the audience, many with their eyes closed and floating off to some special place in their mind, as Don's beautiful, clear voice made the hairs on everyone's neck stand to attention, as only he can do. Like I said earlier, it's a gift from God, to Don, and then on to us. It was a big kick to see, "up-close," how Don was getting really pumped-up by the whole interaction. He absolutely loves it when the audience is right behind him, a fact attested to by Kerry's aside comment to me in the wings: "Are we ever going to get back on tonight?"

It was indeed a long "solo spot," but Don shared the good vibes, first with Ralph Childs on "Where Were You Baby," and finally with Kerry, as they played a duet on "It Had To Be You," in which Don introduced him as Paul Simon. (Kerry had a baseball cap and did indeed look like the man himself!) Don warned Kerry onstage that he was going to "Show you some jazz chords he'd never used before." Kerry's musicianship and ears are so good that he just "busked" this one through with Don and confided in me later that he'd never heard Don do it before, let alone rehearsed it with him! These Nashville guys are just amazing musicians.

During the interval Don is always led off by Janet lighting the way with her flashlight, and he heads straight for the privacy of his dressing room. He gives it EVERYTHING when he is on stage and is really drained by the time he comes off — you can see it in his face. I think he must take a cat-nap and a shower during the interval, because when he emerges again for the next half he is full of beans! For a "good old boy," his energy levels are truly, truly amazing.

The Band is a contrast to Don — they retire to their dressing room to finish off their half-eaten pizzas, Kerry does some more "surfing," and the rest of the guys swap notes on how the first half went. They are most genuinely interested in how it felt for me to be watching them from the "side-lines," and they are concerned about the sound quality I was getting: "On stage you only here the amps and the monitor mix, which is less than half the story," Kerry tells me as he munches pizza. He adds, "You should go out front for the second half, to see how it sounds out there."

It is a sobering thought to realize that the people on stage, giving us all that pleasurable sound, can't ever enjoy it as much as we do in the audience, but this is undoubtedly true, as I acted on Kerry's advice and took a seat in the auditorium halfway through the second half, and noticed the contrast in sound!

I stay to watch Don's solo spot from the wings, before heading out to the auditorium proper. I am stunned by his artistry, as is the audience. On my way out from backstage, I pass the stage-door Jobsworth once again, while Don is on stage singing "Crying." Jobsworth is overcome: "Wow, I wish I was up front, myself," he confides. "We don't get many people who can sing like that these days, do we?" It never ceases to amaze me how Don is still "collecting converts" 30+ years on!

I watch the concert conclude from up in the circle of the theatre. "American Pie" has them "dancing in the aisles," and "This Little Light" gets everyone singing at the top of their voices, inhibitions gone now. It is a CLASSIC Don McLean concert tonight. And, Kerry was right; the sound "out-front" is awesome.

The End of a Wonderful Night

The concert finally finishes and we decide to go back-stage after the show. We discover from Jobsworth that Don has had such a great time that he wants to "Meet the folks" and has hung around inside the theatre to do so, and all the staff must wait too! Before we get a chance to go back inside the building, the band emerges through the Stage Door looking tired but very happy. "Wow, what a great audience," exclaims Tony. "Come and get a beer, Dudes," invites Kerry, as the side of the black tour bus opens to reveal a stash of cooled bottled beers already chilled! We (the band plus Alan's gang) all stand alongside the tour bus talking about the concert, the state of British pizzas compared to Chinese take-aways, and the lack of channels on British television in hotel rooms. Tony Migliore exclaims his disbelief at the UK Eurovision entry singing a quarter octave flat the previous evening. (Apparently the Eurovision Song Contest was compulsive viewing for Don and the band.) Alan is optimistic that I may get invited back to the hotel for a "night-cap" with Don and the band, and soon Kerry even suggests it! (Kerry has more energy than any human deserves and is obviously still running on adrenaline at this point!) A few pictures are taken, and more chat ensues, when, we realize that Don has not yet emerged! He has spent a good three-quarters of an hour signing autographs for the fans. Kerry comments, "He's amazing, when he came off-stage he was TOTALLY wiped out!"

It is another example of how Don REALLY cares about his audiences. They had given their all that night and he wants to show it means

EVERYTHING to him by meeting them. He knows what it REALLY means to them to do so.

Eventually Janet appears, and we know Don can't be far behind. He emerges, wearing those horn-rimmed glasses of his, transformed once again into a "bank manager with a guitar case." The bus driver takes the guitar and reverently places it in the hold of the tour bus, next to the cold beers!

"We gotta go!" says Don, jumping straight on the bus and smiling at us "car-park boozers." Once again, Don had gone into "hyperactivity mode."

It is a strange feeling of both pleasure and disappointment. I realize I have had one of the greatest experiences of my life, and it dawns on me how privileged I have been to share Don's (as well as the band's) private space for so long and so closely. It was more than I could ever have hoped for. I thank Alan for setting it up, and I tell him I can't believe it all really happened.

Appendix II: Concert Review by Alan Young: De Montfort Hall, Leicester, England, May 25th 2003.

I first saw Don McLean back in 1978. He came on stage with only his guitar and banjo. Since then, as most of us know, his musical backing has changed several times. From the rock 'n' roll orchestra he had on his 1980 tour, to being accompanied by John Platania on electric guitar, I always felt that the backing was not quite right, almost, but not quite - until I heard his band at the De Montford Hall. Quite simply, this is a group of extremely accomplished and versatile musicians. From the hard edges of "Have You Seen Me," to the soft embellishments of "Winterwood," they tailor their playing to suit the style and mood of the song. I might upset a few people when I say this, but take "American Pie" for example. Sure, it sounds fine with just the guitar, but I think it sounds even better with the drums, the electric guitar, and especially with the piano. I concede that Paul Griffin did a fantastic job on the original version, but I think that Tony Migliore surpasses that. After hearing his piano playing, I'm convinced that there must be at least three people playing the keyboard! How many fingers does that man have?

What you always get when you see Don McLean is variety: so many different types of songs, but all with a common denominator. They all have chords and a melody. Remember them? Chords and melodies are very hard to find in a lot of today's music. Don McLean's vocal performance at Leicester was near faultless, with "Crying" deserving special mention. This must be a very difficult song to sing, but he hit every high note with unerring accuracy. Another highlight was "And I

Love You So." It sounded sincere and heartfelt, no mean achievement considering the number of times he must have sung this song.

When Don McLean tours, I always try to see him at least twice, because every night his set is different. At Leicester, I counted at least 10 songs that he hadn't done at Tunbridge Wells: "Chain Lightning," "Perfect Love," "The Grave," and a beautiful duet with Kerry Marx on electric guitar of "It Had To Be You" were amongst them. Which other performer anywhere in the world can guarantee that?

Nowadays, much to my liking, Don McLean does the whole show. He'll play for an hour or so, take a break, and then it is anyone's guess. At Leicester, he finally came off stage at 10:40 pm, and that was after the third encore. For me, what can make an excellent Don McLean performance into a memorable one is the audience. A receptive and appreciative audience can inspire him, and, in my opinion, so they should. He earns our applause and admiration by putting everything into his performance. He even makes the audience part of the concert experience, as he did in Leicester by getting them to sing "Love Oh Love" with him.

When the show was finally over, I consoled myself with the thought that my wife and I have already bought tickets to go and see him in Ireland with The Beach Boys. It's a long way to go, but I'm sure it will be worth it. Who knows? He might even sing our favorite song: "To Have and To Hold."

Appendix III: Concert Review by Bill Nisbet: Olympia Theatre, Dublin, Ireland, August 8th 2004.

Veterans of Don McLean concerts (and there are legions of them, thank goodness) will tell you that, over the years, they have had to maintain a watchful vigil, by whatever means, to ensure that The Man did not flash through the country on a whistlestop tour without their knowledge. Communication has, at times, been rather limited, and on more than one occasion I have only just heard in the nick of time of an imminent performance. Despite these difficulties I have racked up well into double digits in attendances (and every one a gem). No such problem exists now, thanks to the brilliant efforts of Alan Howard on the web site, and to him I express my gratitude.

Don McLean in concert is a rare feast, an unforgettable, totally unique experience. It is only now, two weeks after his triumph in Dublin that I commit my thoughts and recollections to record. Years ago, when I was but a lad, there was a famous chocolate bar, made by Fry, called 5 Boys Chocolate. The wrapper showed 5 photographs of a small boy's face, each sequentially displaying the emotions he was going through as he anticipated and finally realized his 5 Boys Chocolate experience. The emotions were: Desperation, Expectation, Pacification, Acclamation, and finally Realization. Maybe it is the small boy in me, but, as I think back over my Don McLean concert experience in Dublin, my range of emotions has been uncannily similar to those depicted in the chocolate advert!

The web site announcement in March of a Dublin concert in August brought the usual rush of excitement and an instant determination to be there. The prospect of a weekend in the Fair City, topped off by Don McLean, was heady wine indeed, and I was desperate to get a plane seat booked and a good concert seat secured. "Now steady up," I told myself, "don't jump in with both feet. Have some patience. There will be UK concerts announced, you'll see." Hmm, aah, well I'll just check the ticket situation anyway. Not on sale yet, so I'll have to wait. Expectantly I view the web site daily for news of UK concerts. Nothing forthcoming... Desperation level is rising. Then the web site tells us that Dublin tickets are now on sale. Straight on the phone to Ticketmaster with a request for the best seat they can give me. "You're in luck," said the young man, "I have that right here: 6 rows from the front in the Stalls and right on the centre aisle, best seat in the house." I snapped it up, gulped a little at the price, 54.5 euros, and clean forgot about that Irish blarney for which they are famed the world over. (As I found out on the night, it was no blarney. He was spot on.) With a few deft strokes of the mouse, I had my flight booked and was well into the Pacification mode. We are getting somewhere now!

My inner thoughts now come to the top, and I am deeply saddened that my dear darling wife Ray, who died a year ago, will not be with me on this trip. We saw so many Don concerts together over the years, and I take comfort knowing that she will be with me in spirit.

I announce the news to Ross, my son, on his arrival home from work, and to my surprise, got the impression he would like to go. What a power of attraction Don McLean must have when he can leap the lofty barriers of time and bridge the musical gap between father and son! In a flash I have a seat for Ross, only 3 seats apart from me and his plane ticket booked and Pacification is assured.

What's this? Castlewellan then Glasgow concerts! My first choice would have been Glasgow in my native Scotland, where they are proud of Don McLean and regard him as one of their own. And rightly so, Don told me himself when I had a lengthy one on one with him in Glasgow, some years ago, that he is a Scot and proud of it. After much investigation I had to give up on my quest to see all 3 concerts, and it is Dublin here we come.

Expectation levels are high, as Ross and I leave East Midlands Airport and arrive in Dublin at 5:10 pm, the flight schedule having been changed from 2:10 pm. We are a bit short of time, so hail a taxi to speed our journey to our hotel in the City Centre. Consternation, a major hurling match has just ended at Croke Park, and the roads are choc-a-bloc with supporters, resplendent in blue and white and black and gold shirts. There were loads of police (Garda) around, many on horseback, among the supporters who were mingling freely with their opposite numbers, unfortunately for our progress, in the middle of the road. The taxi driver seemed unperturbed, particularly as the meter was ticking away very well, say's he, over 40 thousand at the game today, these blue fellers are not laughing, they lost 3-1 today. I asked if there would be trouble with all the police present. "Not at all," says he, "they are only here to direct the traffic. There will be no trouble at all." The only trouble was they stayed in the middle of the road which was choked all the way to the City Centre. Hats off to the Dublin fans - it was good to see that sportsmanship still prevails somewhere.

We managed to check-in and got out of the hotel by 6:20 pm. Thankfully, it was only a few minutes from the Olympia Theatre, and we set out to try and find a restaurant. Amazingly, every building seemed to be either a pub or a restaurant - all kinds of international cuisine was on offer, and the choice was staggering. Dublin has made a big leap forward and seems to be thriving. Now we have to pick somewhere not too busy. The doors open at 7:15 pm and time is going on. We look at a few, and Ross grasps the nettle. There is a Cantonese 50 metres from the Olympia, and he strongly suggests we go in there. What a good decision it turned out to be.

The name of the Restaurant was FANS, and it was nearly empty. How appropriate that name seemed when we sat down and found ourselves sitting next to Tony Migliore, Ralph Childs, and Pat Severs! They were enjoying a pre-concert meal and were probably a little mystified when I looked over and said, "If you have time for a meal, I guess so do we." At this point, I could just feel that everything was falling into place. After the musicians had finished their main course, and I had had my first, I went over and said hello. They were most welcoming and told me all about the Castlewellan and Glasgow concerts. We reminisced for a while about concerts over the years. They asked if I looked at the web site, and clearly they do, which is most encouraging. They assured me they would be perfectly happy for me to mention our shared restaurant experience if

I got round to writing a review. Their admiration and respect for Don McLean really stood out. Tony said that Don was in great voice and really enjoying the trip. Before they left, they each waved over and wished us well. Not only brilliant musicians, but great guys as well. Many thanks.

The Olympia Theatre was pretty much as I expected - a survivor from the great days of old time music halls, when ladies and gentlemen dressed in their finery and went in style to the theatre. Intimate and dimly lit, the splendid opulence of the theatre was at its best. The magnificent ornamental rococo plaster work was predominantly red and white and exhibited a richness in depth swirling over the ceiling and the balconies. Tiers of boxes, similarly decorated, added to the opulent picture. Don later said, "This is like performing inside a Faberge Egg." A most apt description.

Over the years, many of the world's great artists have plied their craft on this stage, and, in the tradition of the theatre, their ghosts are said to be there still, to inspire and bring out the best in all who tread the famous boards. I had the distinct feeling that this setting would prove eminently suitable for Don McLean to produce a vintage performance. This theatre is located directly opposite Dublin Castle, alas Dublin has no king. But tonight, perhaps the people would find one.

The Dubliner sitting next to me confided that he had seen Don McLean in Dublin in the 1970's, but not since, and he was unsure of what to expect. I said he might be pleasantly surprised.

"The Legendary Don McLeen!" said the announcer, and I winced, but that was instantly forgotten as Don swept straight into "Maybe Baby," and we had confirmation that the voice was indeed great, in fact it was glorious. As he soared and powered through that first number the full McLean impact came back, like an old friend, to forcibly remind us of what we have been missing and what we have traveled all these miles to rediscover and celebrate. The huge ovation that followed has placed us in that acclamation mode.

A quick change of mood brought out "When You're Down and Out" then the uniquely Don McLean "La, La, Love You." The voice is really good, and Don turns round to the band and launches into "Crying." I was not expecting it so early, and the lyrics, which are so intensely meaningful to me now, were never more stark. I was grateful for the darkness of the auditorium. Don McLean, you were really "Killing Me Softly With Your Song." A great "Tulsa Time" maintained the momentum, before a thoughtful Don sang a piece adapted from a poem by Shakespeare, "It was a Lover and His Lass." A Don song called "Promise To Remember" was well appreciated, and Don said he would get round to the "Favorites," as he was a "good boy." He seemed to dig deep into the thousands of songs he told us he knew and sang, unaccompanied, acappella "I Have Been a Good Boy." Whether it had any connection with the lyrics of "Promise To Remember," we can only speculate, but there seems to be a lot of Don in his songs.

"And I Love You So" and "Crossroads," brilliantly sung, both hit the spot before Don told Pat to bring out the Dobro, and he did a Dylan number followed by a Western song called "Timber Trails," in which Don yodelled, and seemed to be really enjoying himself. He put his voice to the test with the very challenging "My Saddle Pal and I," and it was superb. Great accompaniment from Pat on the Dobro! The Irish songs "Over The Mountain" and "The Mountains of Mourne" brought a huge ovation to bring a magnificent first half to a close.

I spoke to Ross at the interval and he was most impressed, describing the first set as a highly eclectic mix. I wish I had said that, as it seemed to sum up what we had just watched. Although not all the "Favorites" were included, I was delighted as I want to hear what Don feels like singing, and anyway I can play the favorites all day, every day, at home if I choose. Ross thought, as I did, that Pat's guitar sound level was set below Don's and needed adjustment.

By chance we bumped into someone whose face I recognised from the web site. He confirmed he was Bill Hamilton, and we enjoyed an interval drink together and arranged to meet up for lunch on Monday.

My Irish neighbor said he was having a ball before the start of the second set, and it was clear that that applied to everyone there, including Don and his brilliant musicians. "Jerusalem" gave us a great start. Clearly Don has his mind focussed on world events these days. This theme was reinforced later with "Masters Of War." "Have You Seen Me" continued on that same track, but it is also a wonderful showpiece for the band, Pat's guitar having been given proper emphasis in the mix now. Ralph, on bass, is just perfect, so tight and right, he makes it look so easy. Tony, of course, continually demonstrates his mastery of music and is always a joy to listen to. A more understated set from Jerry on drums this time, but he is a very professional drummer, up there with the best. "Brand New World" again set the mood, and the performance of this song was so professional that anyone listening had to be seriously impressed. The live performance is far ahead of the CD track. A Don solo, straight from the heart, "You're My Little Darlin'," was delightful, and, as he was in a Western mood tonight, I thought we may get "Little Cowboy," but no, it was back to the main theme and "Masters of War," a great Dylan song, but Don sings it better and tonight with feeling. He means it alright. He has previously played his own great banjo lick to this song, and that was highly effective. So much so that when the talented Michael Johnathon recorded the song, he got Don to teach him the lick Another call for the banjo, Don, now you are into a Western phase. Come on, give us a treat. We got a great "Vincent" to continued and well deserved acclamation, then a brilliant "Castles In The Air." The voice has never been better, the maturity is complete, and the master craftsman is enjoying this as much as we are.

With the audience in the palm of his hand, Don sits and re-tunes his Martin, and it is into "Winterwood," a masterpiece, followed swiftly by an effortless and great Buddy Holly medley, ending with "Peggy Sue Got Married." To an old Buddy fanatic like me, this is pure magic, and it was another reminder of the respect Don has for him.

Somewhere along the line I have missed "Superman's Ghost" and possibly a few more, but this was such a great night I could not keep tally with them all.

As he rose to launch "American Pie," I took the liberty of taking another photo and hoped it would be worthy of the occasion. "American Pie" is an event, and the effect it has on audiences everywhere is astonishing. There they were, all in one place, a generation lost in.......yes, the magic of the one and only Don McLean. The rafters were raised, the joint was jumping, and I am sure I saw the ghosts of artists past, rockin' in the aisles. Hands were sore with clapping, and throats were bruised from cheering, as we yelled for more. After well over 2 hours, we were asking a lot, but Don, you told us earlier you would not be back for a long time, and you would do it all tooooooniiiiight (you know how he makes that emphasis.) And back he came, the King in Waiting, and treated us to "Run, Diana, Run," which I was hearing properly for the first time. Yes, you are a deep man, Don McLean, and deep in your breast there lies a treasure chest. We watch and listen in awe. The final song is "Someone To Watch Over Me," and fans all over the world will echo that sentiment. Let Someone watch over him for a very long time.

And so we made our way out of that great old theatre, and, as I listened to my Irish friend say he was shocked that Don was even better now than in the '70s, and heard the acclamation from all around, I crowned Don McLean the King of Dublin Castle. Long may he reign.

I watched Don take a dignified leave of the theatre and watched as he took time to sign many autographs. The crowd there was very orderly and seemed to be respectful of the man. Then a small and very excited Irish lady, brandishing an autograph, thrust her face towards mine and yelled, "That man is ****** BRILLIANT!" Now that summed it up. Ross and I carried out our post-concert review in several Dublin bars, and yes, we concluded, very easily, that Don did perform the oracle and had bridged our musical gaps. No mean feat, by anybody's standards.

Realisation. Looking back in appraisal is something we savor, and thereafter we recall the various elements of our total experience all our lives. This has been a wonderful experience, the best Don McLean concert I have ever attended, and an experience I would dearly wish to repeat at the earliest opportunity. To what lengths would I go to fulfill this aim? Well, I think the words of Robert Burns as written to his friend James Smith sum up my feelings, and hopefully yours too:

For me, I swear by sun an' moon,
An' ev'ry star that blinks aboon (above)
Ye've cost me twenty pair o' shoon (shoes)
Just gaun to see (going)
you ;
An' ev'ry ither pair that's done,
Mair taen I'm wi' you (more taken)

Appendix IV: Album Discography

Tapestry (1970, 1971)
Castles In The Air
General Store
Magdalene Lane
Tapestry
Respectable
Orphans Of Wealth
Three Flights Up
And I Love You So
Bad Girl
Circus Song
No Reason For Your Dreams

MEDIARTS 41-4, Released April 1970 [LP]
MEDIARTS M 84, Released April 1970 [8T]
UNITED ARTISTS UAS-5522, Reissued August 1971 [LP]
UNITED ARTISTS U-8280, Reissued August 1971 [8T]
UNITED ARTISTS UAS-29350 (UK), Reissued 1971 [LP]
PICKWICK SPC-3702, Reissued 1979 [LP]
LIBERTY LN-10157, Reissued January 1982 [LP]
BEAT GOES ON (BGO) 2779 232 2 [CD]
EMI E2-53928, Reissued 1996 [CD]

American Pie (1971)
American Pie
Till Tomorrow
Vincent (Starry Starry Night)
Crossroads
Winterwood
Empty Chairs
Everybody Loves Me Baby
Sister Fatima
The Grave
Babylon (Arranged McLean & Hays)

UNITED ARTISTS UAS-5535, Released October 1971 [LP]
UNITED ARTISTS U-8299, Released October 1971 [8T]

LIBERTY LN-10037, Reissued October 1980 [LP]
EMI MANHATTAN CDP 7 46555 2, Reissued 1987 [CD]
ULTRADISC MFSL UDCD 728, Reissued July 1998 [CD]

Don McLean (1972)
Dreidel
Bronco Bill's Lament
Oh My What A Shame
If We Try
The More You Pay (The More It's Worth)
Narcisissima
Falling Through Time
On The Amazon (Grey-Newman-Ellis)
Birthday Song
The Pride Parade

UNITED ARTISTS UAS-5651, Released November 1972 [LP]
UNITED ARTISTS K-0461, Released November 1972 [CS]
UNITED ARTISTS U-8461, Released November 1972 [8T]
UNITED ARTISTS (FESTIVAL) UAL-34676 (AUS), Released 1972
[LP]
BEAT GOES ON (BGO) 2779 246 2 [CD]

Playin' Favorites (1973)
Sitting On Top Of The World (Carter-Jacobs)
Living With The Blues (McGhee)
Mountains O'Mourne (French-Collisson)
Fool's Paradise (Linsley-Petty)
Love O'Love (Trad.)
Bill Cheatham-Old Joe Clark (Trad.)
Everyday (Hardy-Petty)
Ancient History (Stanton-Walker)
Over The Mountains (Trad.)
Lovesick Blues (Mills-Friend)
Muleskinner Blues (Vaughn-Rodgers)
Happy Trails (Evans)

UNITED ARTISTS UA-LA161-F, Released October 1973 [LP]
UNITED ARTISTS UA-EA161-6, Released October 1973 [8T]
UNITED ARTISTS (FESTIVAL) L35000 (AUS), Released 1973 [LP]
BEAT GOES ON (BGO) 2779 21 2 [CD]

Homeless Brother (1974)
Winter Has Me In Its Grip
La La Love You
Homeless Brother
Sunshine Life For Me (Sail Away Raymond) (Harrison)
The Legend Of Andrew McCrew
Wonderful Baby
Great Big Man
Tangled (Like A Spider In Her Hair)
You Have Lived
Crying In The Chapel (Glenn)
Did You Know

UNITED ARTISTS UA-LA315-G, Released August 1974 [LP]
UNITED ARTISTS UA-EA315-G, Released August 1974 [8T]
LIBERTY LN-10211, Reissued September 1983 [LP]
BEAT GOES ON (BGO) BGOCD247 Reissued 1994 [CD]

Solo (1976)
Magdalene Lane
Masters Of War (Dylan)
Wonderful Baby
Where Were You Baby (White)
Empty Chairs
Geordie's Lost His Penker (Trad.)
Babylon (Adapt. from Psalm 137)
And I Love You So
Mactavish Is Dead (Trad.)
Cripple Creek-Muleskinner Blues (Trad.) (Vaughn-Rodgers)
Great Big Man
Bronco Bill's Lament
Happy Trails (Evans)
Circus Song
Birthday Song
On The Amazon (Grey-Newman-Ellis)
American Pie
Over The Waterfall-Arkansas Traveler (Trad.)
Homeless Brother
Castles In The Air/Three Flights Up
Lovesick Blues (Mills-Friend)

Winter Has Me In Its Grip
The Legend Of Andrew McCrew
Dreidel (Starry Starry Night)
Vincent
Till Tomorrow

UNITED ARTISTS UA-LA652-H2, Released August 1976 [LP]
UNITED ARTISTS UA-EA652-J2, Released August 1976 [8T]
UNITED ARTISTS (FESTIVAL) L70067 (AUS), Released 1976 [LP]
BEAT GOES ON (BGO) 2779 300 2 [CD]

Prime Time (1977)
Prime Time
The Statue
Jump
Redwing (Trad.)
The Wrong Thing To Do
The Pattern Is Broken
When Love Begins
Color TV Blues
Building My Body
Down The Road-Sally Ann (Trad.)
When A Good Thing Goes Bad
South Of The Border (Kennedy-Carr)

ARISTA 4149, Released October 1977 INTERFUSION (FESTIVAL)
L36446 (AUS), Released 1977 [LP]
HIP-O HIPD-40055, Reissued September 1997 [CD]*
*With Bonus Track: If You Can Dream

Chain Lightning (1978, 1981)
Words and Music
It's Just The Sun
Crying (Orbison-Melson)
Lotta Lovin' (Bedwell)
Chain Lightning
Your Cheating Heart (Williams)
Wonderful Night
It Doesn't Matter Anymore (Anka)
Since I Don't Have You (Beaumont-Vogel-Verscharen-Taylor-Lester)

Genesis (In The Beginning)
It's A Beautiful Life

EMI INTERNATIONAL INS-3025 (UK), Released December 1978 [LP]
INTERFUSION (FESTIVAL) L36758 (AUS), Released 1979 [LP]
MILLENIUM BXL1-7756, Released January 1981 [LP]
HIP-O HIPD-40061, Reissued July 1997 [CD]*
*With Bonus Track: If You Could Read My Mind (Lightfoot)

Very Best of Don McLean (1980)
American Pie
Vincent (Starry Starry Night)
Castles In The Air
Dreidel
Winterwood
Everyday (Hardy-Petty)
Building My Body
And I Love You So
Mountains O'Mourne (French-Collisson)
Fool's Paradise (Linsley-Petty)
Wonderful Baby
La La Love You
Prime Time
Jump
Crying (Orbison-Melson)

EMI Records. UK, Holland, Australia, Worldwide (not US)

Believers (1981)
Castles In The Air (1981 version)
Isn't It Strange
Left For Dead On The Road Of Love
Believers
Sea Man
I Tune The World Out
Love Hurts (Bryant)
Jerusalem
Love Letters (Heyman-Young)
Crazy Eyes
Sea Cruise (Smith)

MILLENIUM BXL1-7762, Released October 1981 [LP]
INTERFUSION (FESTIVAL) L37705 (AUS), Released 1981 [LP]
HIP-O HIPD-40060, Reissued August 1997 [CD]*
*With Bonus Track: Dream Lover (Darin)

Dominion (1983)
It's Just the Sun
Wonderful Baby
Building My Body
The Very Thought Of You (Noble)
Fool's Paradise (Linsley-Petty)
Baby I Don't Care (You're So Square) (Lieber-Stoller)
You Have Lived
The Statue
Prime Time
American Pie
Left For Dead on the Road of Love
Believers
Sea Man
It's A Beautiful Life
Chain Lightning
Crazy Eyes
La La Love You
Dream Lover (Darin)
Crying (Orbison-Melson)
Vincent (Starry Starry Night)

EMI DOM 82 (UK), Released 1982 [LP]
GOLD CASTLE D2-71332, Released 1990 [CD]
HIP-O HIPD2-40033, Reissued March 1997 [CD] as "Greatest Hits LIVE"

For the Memories (1986)
Wonderful World (Cooke-Adler-Alpert)
I Can't Help It (If I'm Still In Love With You) (Williams)
Maybe Baby (Petty-Hardin)
Lonely As The Night
He's Got You (Cochran)
A White Sport Coat (And A Pink Carnation) (Robbins)
Don't (Stoller-Lieber)

Crazy (Nelson)
Travelin' Man (Fuller)
Slow And Easy
You Don't Know Me (Walker-Arnold)
Sittin' In The Balcony (Loudermilk)

Festival Records (Australia)
MUSIC FOR PLEASURE MFP5836(UK), Released 1986 [LP]

Greatest Hits Then & Now (1987)
He's Got You (Cochran)
American Pie
To Have and To Hold
Castles In The Air (1981 version)
But She Loves Me (Fuller)
Superman's Ghost
Vincent (Starry Starry Night)
And I Love You So
Crying (Orbison-Melson)
Don't Burn The Bridge

EMI AMERICA ST-17255, Released May 1987
EMI AMERICA 26 1359 1 (EUR), Released 1987 [LP]
EMI AMERICA 26 1359 4 (EUR), Released 1987 [CS]
EMI AMERICA 7 46586 2 (EUR), Released 1987 [CD]

Love Tracks (1988)
Love In My Heart (Brewer)
Eventually (Sharp)
Dust For Blood
Going For The Gold (Browder/Ryles)
What Will The World Be Like
The Touch Of Her Hand (Swofford)
You Can't Blame The Train (Sharp)
It's Not Your Fault
Everyday Is A Miracle
Blues Train

CAPITOL C1-48080, Released August 1988 [LP]
CAPITOL CDP-7-48080-2, Released August 1988 [CD]

For the Memories Vols I & II (1989)
Maybe Baby (Petty-Hardin)
A White Sport Coat (And A Pink Carnation) (Robbins)
Don't (Stoller-Lieber)
Travelin' Man (Fuller)
Sittin' In The Balcony (Loudermilk)
I Can't Help It (If I'm Still In Love With You) (Williams)
Crazy (Nelson)
You Don't Know Me (Walker-Arnold)
If I Only Had A Match (Morris-Johnston-Meyer)
But Beautiful (Burke-Van Heusen)
Over The Weekend (Brooks-McCarthy, Jr)
Someone To Watch Over Me (Gershwin-Gershwin)
Somebody Loves Me (Gershin-De Sylva-MacDonald)
Count Your Blessings (Berlin)
It Had To Be You (Kahn-Jones)
Not A Moment Too Soon (Grand)
Change Partners (Berlin)
Nobody Knows You When You're Down And Out (Cox)
Stardust (Carmichael-Parish)
Wonderful World (Cooke-Adler-Alpert)

GOLD CASTLE D2-71330, Released 1989 [CD]
GOLD CASTLE D4-71330, Released 1989 [CS]
HIP-O HIPD-40054, Reissued April 1997 [CD]*

*WITH bonus track: Somewhere Over The Rainbow-Brother Can You
Spare A Dime AND without He's Got You.

Don McLean Christmas (1991)
Winter Wonderland (Smith-Bernard)
Oh Little Town Of Bethlehem
Santa Claus Is Comin' To Town (Gillespie-Coots)
I'll Be Home For Christmas-Have Yourself A Merry Little Christmas
Burgundian Carol (Brand)
White Christmas (Berlin)
God Rest Ye Merry Gentlemen
Pretty Paper (Nelson)
'Twas The Night Before Christmas
Go Tell It On The Mountain

CURB D2-77512, Released August 1991 [CD]

Headroom (1991)
Headroom
Fashion Victim
1967
Infinity
One In A Row
You Who Love The Truth
Lady In Waiting
Have You Seen Me
Siamese Twins (Joined At The Heart)
A Brand New World

CURB D2-77427, Released October 1991 [CD]

Don McLean Classics (1992)
Since I Don't Have You (Beaumont-Vogel-Verscharen-Taylor-Lester)
It's A Beautiful Life
Vincent (Starry Starry Night) (new recording)
Jerusalem
American Pie
Crying (Orbison-Melson)
Castles In The Air (1981 version)
American Pie (new recording)
And I Love You So (new recording)

CURB D2-77547, Released 1992 [CD]

Favorites & Rarities (1992)
Castles In The Air (Mediarts version)
And I Love You So
American Pie
Vincent (Starry Starry Night)
Babylon (Adapt. from Psalm 137)
Empty Chairs
Dreidel
If We Try
Fool's Paradise (Linsley-Petty)
Sitting On Top Of The World (Carter-Jacobs)

La La Love You
Wonderful Baby
Crying In The Chapel (Glenn)
Magdalene Lane (live)
Crying (Orbison-Melson)
Since I Don't Have You (Beaumont-Vogel-Verscharen-Taylor-Lester)
Castles In The Air (1981 version)
He's Got You (Cochran)
Superman's Ghost
You Can't Blame The Train (Sharp)

Good Old Wagon (Smith-Balcomb)
Milkman's Matinee
Aftermath
Mother Nature
Everyday (Hardy-Petty) (BBC Version)
That's All Right (Crudcup)
Profiteering Blues (Bibo-Wilson)
Hit Parade Of Love (Martin)
The Carnival Has Ended (Fagan)
I'm Blue, I'm Lonesome (Smith-Monroe-Williams)
Nature Boy (Ahbez)
Black Sheep Boy (Hardin)
Mountains O'Mourne (French-Collisson)
And Her Mother Came Too (LIVE) (Novello-Titheradge)
Yonkers Girl (LIVE) (Sky)
Turkey In The Straw (Trad.)
Dubuque (Trad.)
Sally Ann-Muleskinner Blues-Old Joe Clark (Trad.)
If We Try (Version 2)
Perfect Love
Little Child
Gotta Make You Mine

EMI 0777-7-98603-2 6, Released 1992 [CD]

River of Love (1995)
The River Of Love
You're My Little Darlin'
If I Hadn't Met You
Better Still

You Got A Way About You, Baby
Angry Words
This Little Girl (Daddy-O)
Planet Noise
From A Beautiful Star
Little Cowboy
My Love Was True

CURB D2-77791, Released 1995 [CD]

Don McLean Christmas Dreams (1997)

The Christmas Song (Chestnuts Roasting On An Open Fire) (Torme-Wells)
Oh Holy Night (Trad.)
I Heard The Bells On Christmas Day (Longfellow)
Blue Christmas (Hayes-Johnson)
Christmas Waltz (Cahn-Styne)
Let It Snow (Cahn-Styne)
Toyland (Herbert-McDonough)
The Last Month Of The Year (Trad.-McLean)
It Came Upon A Midnight Clear (Trad.-McLean)
Silent Night (Trad.)

HIP-O HIPD-40074, Released October 1997 [CD]

Don McLean Sings Marty Robbins (2001)

Singin' The Blues (M. Endsley)
Kaw Liga (Hank Williams/Fred Rose)
Among My Souvenirs (E. Leslie/H. Nichols)
Don't Worry (Marty Robbins)
Ribbon of Darkness (Gordon Lightfoot)
The Story of My Life (Hal David/Bert Bacharach)
El Paso (Marty Robbins)
I Can't Quit (Marty Robbins)
Love Me (Jeanne Pruett)
Devil Woman (Marty Robbins)
Time Goes By (Marty Robbins)
You Gave Me a Mountain (Marty Robbins)

Don McLean Records

Starry Starry Night (2001)
Everyday (Hardy-Petty)
La La Love You
Homeless Brother
If We Try
Winterwood
Crossroads
Castles In The Air
Tulsa Time (Flowers) / Deep in the Heart of Texas (Flowers)
Castles In The Air (Retake)
Angry Words
My Love Was True
Singin' The Blues (M. Endsley)
You Gave Me a Mountain (Marty Robbins)
Crying
And I Love You So (duet with Nanci Griffith)
Raining in my Heart (B. Bryant) (duet with Nanci Griffith)
Jerusalem
You're My Little Darlin'
American Pie
Superman's Ghost
Fashion Victim
Headroom / Dreidel
It was a very good year (Ervin M. Drake)
Vincent (Starry Starry Night)

Don McLean Records

Legendary Songs of Don McLean (2003)
Words and Music
American Pie
Since I Don't Have You (Beaumont-Vogel-Verscharen-Taylor-Lester)
Maybe Baby (Petty-Hardin)
Crying (Orbison-Melson)
Castles In The Air (1981 version)
If I Only Had A Match (Morris-Johnston-Meyer)
Your Cheating Heart (Williams)
And I Love You So
Vincent (Starry Starry Night)
Winterwood

If We Try
Everyday (Hardy-Petty)
Wonderful Baby
Crossroads
Jerusalem
Dreidel
Headroom
Have You Seen Me
Just to Hold My Hand (Robey)
Empty Chairs

EMI CAPITOL RECORDS

You've Got to Share (2003)
Little Rooster
Be Kind to your Parents (Rome)
You've got to Share (McLean, Jackie Lee)
This Old Man
Windy Old Weather
I'm an Old Cowhand (Mercer)
The Eagle
You have no right (solo Jackie McLean)
Luby Lu
The Cat came Back
The Horse Named Bill
Pick it up (Guthrie)
Hush Little Baby
Blackberry Blossom
Birdies Three (Keeves)
Where Have All The Flowers Gone (Solo Wyatt McLean) (Seeger)
Going to the Chapel/Goodnight Sweetheart (Hudson/Carter)

Don McLean Records

The Western Album (2003)
Timber Trail (Spencer)
Ridin' Down on the Canyon (Autry/ Burnett)
Pat O' Mine (Nolam)
I Ride an Old Paint
I've Got Spurs (That Jingle) (Lilly/Loesser)
The Trail to Mexico

Blue Prairie (Nolan/Spencer)
The Wild West is Where I Wanna Be (Lehrer)
Tulsa Time (Flowers) / Deep in the Heart of Texas (Flowers)
Lyndon has a Bear Hug on Dallas
(Take me back to my) Boots and Saddles (Samuels/Whitcup/Powell)
Song of the Bandit (Nolan)
Philidalphea Lawyer (Guthrie)
I'm an Old Cowhand (Mercer)
Sioux Indians
My Saddle and I (Rogers)

Don McLean Records

American Pie: Original Recording Remastered (2003)
American Pie
Till Tomorrow
Vincent (Starry Starry Night)
Crossroads
Winterwood
Empty Chairs
Everybody Loves Me Baby
Sister Fatima
The Grave
Babylon (Arranged McLean & Hays)
Aftermath
Mother Nature

Christmastime! (2004)
Winter Wonderland (Smith-Bernard)
Oh Little Town Of Bethlehem
Blue Christmas (Hayes-Johnson)
Christmas Waltz (Cahn-Styne)
Santa Claus Is Comin' To Town (Gillespie-Coots)
Toyland (Herbert-McDonough)
Rudolph the Red Nosed Reindeer (Marks)
I'll Be Home For Christmas-Have Yourself A Merry Little Christmas
The Christmas Song (Torme-Wells)
White Christmas (Berlin)
Let It Snow! Let It Snow! Let It Snow! (Cahn-Styne)
Silent Night (Trad.)
Oh Holy Night (Trad.)

I Heard The Bells On Christmas Day (Longfellow)
Go Tell It On The Mountain
God Rest Ye Merry Gentlemen (Trad.)
The Last Month Of The Year (Trad.-McLean)
The Burgundian Carol (Brand)
Little Child
It Came Upon A Midnight Clear (Trad.-McLean)
Pretty Paper (Nelson)
The Night Before Christmas (Moore)

Don McLean Records

Rearview Mirror (2005)
If You Could Read My Mind (Lightfoot)
Vincent (Starry, Starry Night)
Wonderful Baby
Love Me Tender (Matson & Presley)
(It Was) A Very Good Year (Drake)
El Paso (Robbins)
My Saddle Pals and I (Rogers)
And I Love You So
Crying (Orbison & Melson)
Empty Chairs
Homeless Brother
TB Blues (Rodgers)
Magdalene Lane
Infinity
Prime Time
American Pie
Run, Diana Run
You've Got To Share (McLean, Jackie Lee)

Rearview Mirror also includes a DVD.

HYENA

Appendix V: Singles Discography

Castles in the Air/And I Love You So
   Mediarts 1969

American Pie/American Pie (continued)
   United Artists 1971

Vincent/Castles in the Air
   United Artists 1972

Dreidel/Bronco Bill's Lament
   United Artists 1972

If We Try/The More You Pay (The More It's Worth)
   United Artists 1972

Fools Paradise/Happy Trails
   United Artists 1973

Mountains of Mourne/Bill Cheatham-Old Joe Clark
   United Artists 1973

Everyday (non LP, live from BBC)/ The More You Pay (The More It's Worth)
   United Artists (UK) 1973

Sitting On Top of the Word/Muleskinner Blues
   United Artists 1973

Wonderful Baby/Birthday Song
   United Artists 1974

Prime Time/When a Good Thing Goes Bad
   Arista 1977

It Doesn't Matter Anymore/If We Try (non LP)
   Arista 1978

Crying/Genesis (In the Beginning)
  Millennium 1981

Lloras (Crying in Spanish)/Genesis
  EMI (Spain) 1981

Since I Don't Have You/Your Cheating Heart
  Millennium 1981

It's Just the Sun/Chain Lightning
  Millennium 1981

Yo Soy Tu Eres (It's Just the Sun in Spanish)/Chain Lightning
  EMI (Spain) 1981

Castles in the Air (new version)/Crazy Eyes
  Millennium 1981

Jerusalem/Left for Dead on the Road of Love
  Millennium 1981

Jerusalem (film version)
  Columbia (Israel) 1981

L'Affair D'Amour/Jerusalem
  Interfusion (Australia) 1984

He's Got You
  Capitol 1986

Superman's Ghost
  Capitol 1987

Eventually
  Capitol 1988

Love in my Heart
  Capitol 1989

Maybe Baby
  Interfusion (Australia) 1989

American Pie/Vincent
        EMI 1991

Farewell
        Right Records 2006

Appendix VI: Videos, DVD, Sessions

Video

The Music of Don McLean (1980)
The Voice The Music The Concert (1993)
Starry Starry Night (2000)

DVD

Starry Starry Night (2000)
Rearview Mirror (2005) (also includes CD)

Albums – as a featured artist

Clearwater – Clearwater (1974)
Clearwater – Clearwater (1977)

Sessions

I Like it this Way by Lisa Kindred (Vanguard 1977)
Greatest Hits by The Clancy Brothers with Lou Killen (Vanguard 1965)
Banks of Marble by Pete Seeger (Folkways 1974)
On the Track by Leon Redbone (Warner Bros. 1975)
Double Time by Leon Redbone (Warner Bros. 1977)

Index

Printed in Great Britain
by Amazon.co.uk, Ltd.,
Marston Gate.